Student's Guide
to the BIBLE

Student's Guide
to the BIBLE

Stephen M. Miller

BARBOUR
PUBLISHING

CONTENTS

INTRODUCTION

With a daughter in college and a son in high school, I have a clue about how busy students are these days.

My daughter, Rebecca, attends a Christian college just a couple of miles from our front door. But I feel lucky whenever I see her long enough to carry on a conversation.

Oh, she'll dart in and out a few times a week. Drop off her laundry. Raid the pantry at Mom's Quick Stop Shop, as we've come to call it. Pick up a fist of printer paper at Pop's Office Supply.

But sometimes she'll come home to study for an important test, when she wants a quiet and utterly boring environment, conducive to study. We get to talk then, when she takes study breaks. And sometimes she actually comes back for a home-cooked meal, or for Chinese ordered in. We talk then, too.

Otherwise, Rebecca is ever fluttering like a butterfly—lighting here and there as though stamping out fires with her tiny feet and then quickly flying off. College women, I've concluded, are perhaps the closest thing in God's creation to perpetual motion. They rush to classes. Bang out their homework, pounding the keyboard with the rhythm of a jackhammer. Cram for tests, one after the other. Flirt with the basketball team—all three strings. And then they head off to work an evening job, only to return to the dorm for a midnight shift of studies, snacks, and chatter—until they drop unconscious into bed.

High school boys like my son, Bradley, are just as busy, but their pace seems more erratic. Nagged out of bed, they trudge downstairs late—but not too late to read highlights on the sports page while shoveling breakfast into their face. Then they zoom off to school, hoping they're flying under radar—and occasionally discovering they're not.

If they're fortunate enough to attend a school that fills its classrooms with teachers who care about kids, the students are busy thinking and working all day—perhaps catching a quick nap in a class taught by the zombie who got mistaken for a teacher.

Going to school is a full-time job, 8 a.m. to 3 p.m. in our district—with plenty of evening commitments. Tennis practice and matches, as I write this introduction. Practice stretches until 5 or 6 p.m. Then there's the after-school job, which we managed to steer both of our kids away from until their final semester of high school. (We kept telling them they already had a job.) We tried to limit their work to 10 hours a week, mostly on the weekends, though it has been a constant battle. They and their bosses want more hours.

Then there's homework from teachers, busywork from zombies, jazz band concerts, plays, swim meets to support fellow students, guys who want to play video games on networked computers, and a girl who calls for long talks. About the girl, I've discovered that a father can harvest a pause by telling her, "My son's not here, but you can talk to me for a couple of hours."

IT'S ON THE TEST

Reading a book is not a high priority for students—unless they'll be tested on it. Even then, they prefer used books, already highlighted with the main points.

Well, here's the news.

Life is a test.

There's one book more than any other that prepares us for that test. It's the Bible, which is actually a library of 66 books.

Consider the *Student's Guide to the Bible* a collection of all the highlighted parts of the Bible—the good parts that'll be on the test.

What does the Bible say about sexual abstinence, anger, forgiveness, and success? Believe me, it's all on life's test.

You'll find these topics and others just as important in one of this book's two main sections: "Where to Find It in the Bible." This is an A to Z list of topics that young people tell me they wonder about—along with key Bible passages about those topics.

"Sixty-Six Books—the Short Course" is the second main feature. It condenses every book of the Bible into about a single printed page, not counting the pictures we added. This is a visual age.

Why bother with a Bible intro section like this? There's pre-med and pre-law. Now there's pre-Bible. This section of the *Student's Guide to the Bible* helps prepare you for studying the Bible. You get a quick overview of each Bible book, including a concise summary, followed by the five W's (who, what, when, where, and why it was written), the most famous quote, the biggest scene, and the biggest idea.

You'll find other fast-paced features in the book, too.

- Fifty heroes and jerks in the Bible
- Who wrote the Bible
- Half a dozen easy-reading Bibles—comparing student-friendly translations
- Two best ways to read the Bible
- An index search engine to help you find anything you want in the book, with just a few flips of the page

STUDENTS GUIDING THE STUDENT GUIDE

I didn't create this book based on some imagined ideas about what students want. I met with groups of students—in high school and college.

They surprised me with their suggestions. I wouldn't have guessed that students would want something as boring as an index in a book like this. But they said a good index helps them quickly find what they're looking for.

I was surprised, too, at many of the topics they wanted. Even students in a Christian college wanted to know what's wrong with a guy and a girl living together and sharing the rent—as long as they don't have sex. So I added "living together" as one of the topics in "Where to Find It in the Bible." It's cross-referenced to "Temptation."

A WORD OF THANKS

I've never written a book by myself. I've always had partners helping me. And I'd like to thank a few of the folks who helped me with this book.

My wife and kids. Linda, my wife, is my frontline proofreader and my most constructive critic. Rebecca and Bradley orchestrated the focus groups to help me decide what to put in this book and how to write it. Bradley took some of the pictures in this book. He was patient enough to work with me on the photography when we visited a string of museums in the United States and Europe. He also helped me make the final picture recommendations for the book designer.

Focus group members. *High school:* Cooper Arnold, Eryn Campbell, Reuben Dermyer, Bradley Miller, and Kevin Simpson. *College:* Kourtney Seaman, Melissa Johnson, Rebecca Miller, Suzie Carlson, Jennifer Boender, Laurie Wilson, Lisa Freeburg. Thanks, guys and gals. Your advice was well worth the pizzas it cost me, and the heartburn that followed.

Rick Edwards. Rick is a longtime friend of mine and an associate pastor in the Kansas City area. He started losing his hair about the time he started working with junior high and high school students. Probably no connection. But I wonder. Before pastoring, he worked for a dozen years as a youth curriculum editor at his denominational headquarters. Rick helped me identify topics to cover in this book.

Steve Laube. He's my agent. But I think of him as more of a partner. That's because he does more than sell my work. He's my most trusted professional advisor. I make decisions about what book ideas to tackle only after consulting with him. And when he offers advice about how to improve something I've written, I follow the advice. My momma didn't raise no dummy.

Virginia Miller. And speaking of Momma, here she is. I don't think I've ever mentioned her on my list of partners, but she has been cheering me on and praying for me longer than anyone on the planet. (Dad's off the planet now.) I guess I thought of her this time because she and I were classmates in college. When I enrolled at Kent State University, so did she—though she still had four other kids at home at the time. Don't ask me who got better grades. It's just plain embarrassing. Mom went on to become a schoolteacher.

Paul K. Muckley. A gentle-spirited Barbour editor, Paul somehow talked his boss into giving me money to write five books. This book is number four. Number five is due in bookstores in a few months.

Catherine Thompson. She finished some amazing design work on my book *The Complete Guide to the Bible* and jumped right into this project—with equally impressive results.

George Knight, Kelly Williams, Connie Troyer, and **Annie Tipton,** who all contributed in various ways to the editorial processes.

God bless them, every one.

And God bless you as you read this book and, more importantly, as you read his Book.

P.S. ONE REQUEST

If you discover any mistakes in the book—we're only human—please let us know. We can correct them in the next printing. Same thing for ideas you have for improving the book—such as adding certain topics or Bible verses to "Where to Find It in the Bible." You can contact the publisher. Or you can reach me through my Web site: www.stephenmillerbooks.com. Thanks.

BIBLE EVENTS

BC

Before 4000 God creates the world

Before 2500 Flood kills most of humanity

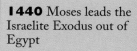

2100 Abraham moves from what is now Iraq to Israel

1440 Moses leads the Israelite Exodus out of Egypt

1275 Alternate date for the Exodus of Moses, say many scholars

1050 Saul becomes first king of Israel

1000 King David declares Jerusalem his capital

960 King Solomon builds the first Jewish temple

930 Israel splits into two nations

722 Assyria (modern-day Iraq) conquers the northern Jewish nation, exiling the survivors from their homeland

586 Babylon (modern-day Iraq) conquers the southern Jewish nation, exiling the survivors

470 Esther, a Jew and the new queen of Persia, stops an attempted holocaust

WORLD EVENTS

BC

7000 Cuicuilco pyramid built in Mexico, oldest man-made structure in North America

2575 Great Pyramid built in Egypt

2100 Ziggurat built in Abraham's Iraqi hometown of Ur

1440 Thutmose III, nicknamed the Napoleon of Egypt, rules as king

1279 Ramses II, pharaoh of Egypt, starts building statues and cities to honor himself

1184 Troy burns, Trojan War ends

1000 Sailors from southeast Asia begin settling in the Pacific islands

950 Rich Egyptians wear wigs

900 Accompanied by musicians, poets recite Homer's story: the *Odyssey*

776 First Olympic games in Greece

610 Ships from Phoenicia (modern-day Lebanon) sail around Africa

521 Buddha preaches his first sermon

432 Greeks in Athens build the Parthenon temple, devoted to the goddess Athena

BIBLE EVENTS

37 Herod the Great is appointed by Rome as king of the Jews

6 Jesus is born

4 Herod the Great dies

AD

27 Jesus begins his ministry

30 Jesus is crucified and resurrected

35 Paul becomes a Christian

43 Paul begins 10,000 miles of missionary trips

50 Paul writes what is probably the first book in the New Testament: 1 Thessalonians

64 Romans execute Paul

66 Jews rebel against the Roman occupying force, driving out the invaders

70 Rome mounts a counterstrike against the Jews, destroying Jerusalem and the Jewish temple—which is never rebuilt

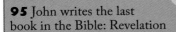

95 John writes the last book in the Bible: Revelation

WORLD EVENTS

30 Mark Antony and Cleopatra commit suicide after losing civil war against Rome

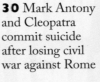

7 The planet Jupiter (representing kings) aligns with Saturn (representing Jews) in the Pisces constellation (representing what is now Israel)

5 A star explodes into a nova

AD

26 Pilate becomes governor of what is now southern Israel

30 Chinese use waterwheels as a power source, to operate bellows that fan iron furnaces

36 Two Vietnamese women launch a failed revolt against China

43 London is founded

50 The French (Gauls) introduce the Italians (Romans) to soap

64 Most of Rome burns; Nero blames Christians

68 Nero commits suicide

79 Mount Vesuvius erupts, destroying Pompeii near Naples, Italy

105 Paper is first made from tree bark, old rags, and fishnets

> Dates are approximate and often debated among experts.
>
> **BC** = Before Christ. Creator of this calendar got the date of Jesus' birth wrong by perhaps six years or more.
> **AD** = *Anno Domini*. That's Latin for "in the year of the Lord."

WHO WROTE THE BIBLE?

No one on the planet knows how many writers it took to produce the Bible—a writing project spread over more than a millennium.

There are 66 books in this sacred library. But few books identify their author. Even the four Gospels about Jesus were written anonymously. Church leaders about a century after Jesus attributed them to the apostle Matthew, to a missionary named John Mark, to a physician named Luke, and to the apostle John. That's where the Gospels got their names.

Even the books of Moses—the first five books in the Bible—may not have been written by him. Those books—Genesis, Exodus, Leviticus, Numbers, and Deuteronomy—are all anonymous. Though Jewish tradition says Moses wrote them, the book collection includes a report of his death followed by a fairly un-Moses-like brag: "There has never been another prophet in Israel like Moses" (Deuteronomy 34:10).

It's just speculation, but Abraham may have written some of his family history that's preserved in Genesis. After all, he came from the world's first known civilization, which invented wedge-shaped cuneiform writing: Sumer in what is now Iraq.

It's no speculation that Moses wrote. Talking about laws now preserved in Exodus through Deuteronomy, God told Moses to "write down all these instructions, for they represent the terms of the covenant I am making with you and with Israel" (Exodus 34:27). Raised in an Egyptian royal family, Moses had probably learned to write.

HOW WE GOT THE BIBLE

But how did these laws and the other Bible stories, poetry, and prophecies get compiled into a book?

Most Bible scholars guess that the earliest stories in our Bible were passed along by word of mouth from generation to generation, since most people couldn't read or write. When David became king, scholars speculate, palace officials started writing down these stories about their people—to preserve the history of how the Jews became a nation with David as their king.

Most of the Old Testament was probably finished in Iraq. That's where Jews were exiled after Babylonian invaders overran and decimated the Jewish nation.

The Jews couldn't offer sacrifices to God anymore, because the temple was destroyed. The temple was the only place Jewish law allowed them to offer animal sacrifices. But once Jewish scholars finished compiling the sacred Jewish writings, the people could offer sacrifices of prayer and praise by reading the sacred words—just as they had sung in one of their ancient songs. "Let my prayer be like incense placed before you, and my praise like the evening sacrifice" (Psalm 141:2 NCV).

By the time of Jesus, when the temple was rebuilt, devout Jews considered the Old Testament as God's Word. So did Jesus, who once quoted Deuteronomy to Satan: "People do not live by bread alone, but by every word that comes from the mouth of God" (Matthew 4:4, quoting Deuteronomy 8:3).

Jesus died in about AD 30. Within 65 years, the New Testament was completely written. It contains stories about Jesus, along with letters by Paul and other church leaders to Christians scattered throughout the Roman Empire.

Early Christians in the generations that followed never could agree on who wrote the books of the Bible. Many scholars even insist that some books identifying the writer were actually written by someone else, such as a student of the named author. That's what many Bible experts say about the book of 2 Peter, which claims the apostle Peter as its author. Writing under someone else's name was common in ancient times—a way of honoring a mentor; it was the opposite of plagiarism.

Christians did, however, agree on the source of inspiration behind these writings. They knew the Word of God when they saw it. And they agreed with something the apostle Paul wrote shortly before his execution. Paul was speaking just about his Bible, our Old Testament, but most Christians today would argue that it applies to the New Testament as well: "All Scripture is inspired by God and is useful to teach us what is true and to make us realize what is wrong in our lives" (2 Timothy 3:16).

In the centuries that followed, many Christians wrote religious books. But churches weeded through all the writings, keeping only the ones they believed accurately reported the message of God, as told by writers who had seen Jesus.

In AD 367 a bishop named Athanasius wrote an Easter letter, listing—for the first time in known history—all the books we now have in our New Testament. He added this note, confirming what churches throughout the world already believed: "These are the fountains of salvation, and they who thirst may be satisfied with the living words they contain."

A few years later, several church conferences considered the matter of which books belonged in the Holy Bible. And each one agreed with the sacred library we still read today.

THE BOOK OF

ISAIAH

1 The vision of Isaiah the son of Amoz, which he saw concerning Judah and Jerusalem in the days of Uzzi'ah, Jotham, Ahaz, and Hezeki'ah, kings of

your cities are burned with fire, in your very presence aliens devour your land; it is desolate, as overthrown by aliens.

8 And the daughter of Zion

13

THE BIBLE LIBRARY

OLD TESTAMENT

LAW
- ▶ Genesis
- ▶ Exodus
- ▶ Leviticus
- ▶ Numbers
- ▶ Deuteronomy

HISTORY
- ▶ Joshua
- ▶ Judges
- ▶ Ruth
- ▶ 1, 2 Samuel
- ▶ 1, 2 Kings
- ▶ 1, 2 Chronicles
- ▶ Ezra
- ▶ Nehemiah
- ▶ Esther

POETRY
- ▶ Job
- ▶ Psalms
- ▶ Proverbs
- ▶ Ecclesiastes
- ▶ Song of Songs

PROPHECY
- ▶ Isaiah
- ▶ Jeremiah
- ▶ Lamentations
- ▶ Ezekiel
- ▶ Daniel
- ▶ Hosea
- ▶ Joel
- ▶ Amos
- ▶ Obadiah
- ▶ Jonah
- ▶ Micah
- ▶ Nahum
- ▶ Habakkuk
- ▶ Zephaniah
- ▶ Haggai
- ▶ Zechariah
- ▶ Malachi

NEW TESTAMENT

GOSPELS
- Matthew
- Mark
- Luke
- John

HISTORY
- Acts of the Apostles

LETTERS BY PAUL TO CHURCHES
- Romans
- 1, 2 Corinthians
- Galatians
- Ephesians
- Philippians
- Colossians
- 1, 2 Thessalonians

LETTERS BY PAUL TO INDIVIDUALS
- 1, 2 Timothy
- Titus
- Philemon

GENERAL LETTERS TO THE CHURCH
- Hebrews
- James
- 1, 2 Peter
- 1, 2, 3 John
- Jude

PROPHECY
- Revelation

HALF A DOZEN OF THE EASIEST-READING BIBLES

Our English language flows like a river, constantly changing. That's why the Bible keeps getting a makeover, with major new versions coming out every few years.

Even the King James Version has been updated several times since it was introduced in 1611—while William Shakespeare was finishing up *The Tempest*. Here's a sample from the latest edition of the KJV:

> *Remember not the sins of my youth, nor my transgressions: according to thy mercy remember thou me for thy goodness' sake, O Lord.*
>
> PSALM 25:7

We still talk like that, right?

If we want to read from the King James Version, we need more than a fondness for Shakespearean English. We need a grade 12 education as well. Newspapers are written at about grade eight, on average.

The chart on the next page shows how several popular, easy-reading Bible versions translate Psalm 25:7.

> **A word of advice:** When choosing a Bible, pick one that's easy to understand and enjoyable to read. If you love Shakespeare, King James might be the one for you. Otherwise, there are plenty of great translations written in the style of English we speak at the moment. And new ones are coming—because the language flows on.

BIBLE VERSION	READING LEVEL	PSALM 25:7
NEW INTERNATIONAL READER'S VERSION	reading level at grade 2.9; published 1998 (revised edition)	Don't remember the sins I committed when I was young. Don't remember how often I refused to obey you. Remember me because you love me. Lord, you are good.
TODAY'S NEW INTERNATIONAL VERSION	targets young adults 18–34; reading level undetermined, but Psalm 25 is at grade 4.2; published 2005	Do not remember the sins of my youth and my rebellious ways; according to your love remember me, for you, Lord, are good.
CONTEMPORARY ENGLISH VERSION	grade 5.4; 1995	Forget each wrong I did when I was young. Show how truly kind you are and remember me.
NEW CENTURY VERSION	grade 5.6; 1991 (revised edition)	Do not remember the sins and wrong things I did when I was young. But remember to love me always because you are good, Lord.
NEW LIVING TRANSLATION	grade 6.3; 2004 (revised edition)	Do not remember the rebellious sins of my youth. Remember me in the light of your unfailing love, for you are merciful, O Lord.
THE MESSAGE	reading level runs all over the scale, often from about grade 5 to grade 10, but Psalm 25 is at grade 2.5; published 2002	Forget that I sowed wild oats; mark me with your sign of love. Plan only the best for me, God!

TWO BEST WAYS TO STUDY THE BIBLE

By the book or by the topic.

Those are the two most popular ways to study scripture.

The Bible isn't really a book that most people should study from front to back, in the order the books appear.

Someone starting at Genesis and hoping to work through to Revelation may well bail out about the time they hit the census report in Numbers—if they make it through the hundreds of out-dated laws in Leviticus.

Especially for Bible newcomers, it's best to start with a book or a topic of special interest.

BY THE BOOK

Want a quick intro about Jesus? Turn to the Gospel of Mark—the shortest and fastest-paced Gospel. Eager to know how Christians should behave? Read Ephesians or Philippians. What about how to put your faith into action? That's a no-brainer. Go straight to James.

People studying the Bible this way should consider getting a study Bible. These Bibles include notes in the margin, adding insightful background informa-tion and comments that help us better understand confusing statements.

For more inquisitive readers, there are single-book commentaries on the entire Bible. And for the really serious, there are books that offer verse-by-verse com-ments about individual books of the Bi-ble—an entire commentary book on just the Gospel of John, for example. Some of these are easy to understand, but oth-ers sound like they're written from one scholar to another—written in a language I not-so-fondly call academese (ACK uh duh MEEZE; rhymes with *sneeze*).

So look before you leap to the check-out counter.

BY THE TOPIC

Maybe you want to know what the Bi-ble says about a certain topic: abortion, drinking and drugs, forgiveness.

That's why so much of the *Student's Guide to the Bible* points out those passages.

Books that help us study topics like these are called topical concordances. The *Student's Guide to the Bible* contains just a condensed version, focusing only on some of the more important topics for students—and the most crucial Bible passages dealing with those topics. Other concordances are exhaustive, covering ev-ery word in the Bible. We can even look up every verse that includes the word *the*, though it's hard to imagine why anyone would want to. Most Bible software al-lows us to search the Bible by words, too.

But a topical concordance includes Bible passages that wouldn't turn up in a word search. If we want to know what the Bible says about gambling, for exam-ple, we should probably look at the bet Samson made with his wedding guests in Judges 14. But the words *gamble* and *gambling* don't show up in that story. So a topical concordance does what a word search can't.

HOW *NOT* TO READ THE BIBLE

It's easy to take a Bible idea out of context, especially if we're studying a topic that takes us to a single verse—and we read the verse without looking at the rest of the passage.

And it's even easier to warp the context if we already have our mind made up, and we're just looking for a verse to back us up.

For example, racist groups like the neo-Nazis and the Ku Klux Klan can cite Bible support for persecuting Jewish people:

> *"You [Jews] are the children*
> *of your father the devil."*
> —JESUS (JOHN 8:44)
> *"Jews killed their own prophets, and some*
> *even killed the Lord Jesus.*
> *Now they have persecuted us."*
> —PAUL (1 THESSALONIANS 2:15)

It's true that Jesus and Paul were talking about Jews. But they weren't criticizing the entire Jewish race—Jesus and Paul were Jews themselves. Both were criticizing a select group of Jewish leaders who used violence to silence people who disagreed with them.

RULES TO READ BY

1. *Look at the context.* The Jews whom Jesus and Paul criticized wanted nothing more than to see these two men lying dead in the dirt. So when we consider that context, the incredible irony is this: The words of Jesus and Paul—which hate groups have invoked to justify violence against the Jews—are the very words that argue against the violence of hate groups.

Many people take the Bible out of context when they're trying to prove a controversial position, such as their take on abortion, homosexuality, or a woman's role in church leadership. The best approach is to read the Bible with an open mind, searching for the truth instead of looking for a thumbs-up on our opinion.

2. *Consider the type of writing—the genre.* Among the many genres in the Bible are laws, history, poetry, wisdom sayings, prophecy, eyewitness stories about Jesus, and letters.

We need to take the genre into consideration when reading a passage.

If it's poetry, we should cut the writer some slack and allow for poetic license instead of reading it like it's a science book.

For example, when Joshua commanded the sun and moon to "stand still" (Joshua 10:12), he said it in the form of a poem. And it reads like he's quoting from a lost book of Hebrew poetry that the Bible says was the Book of Jashar. Joshua may simply have been asking for God's help to finish the long day's battle. Or maybe he wanted clouds to protect his army from the hot sun. "Stand still" translates a Hebrew word that can also mean "stop," as in "stop shining." If this is what Joshua meant, his prayer was certainly answered. Clouds rolled in and a hailstorm ended the battle, pummeling the enemy to death.

We should also be careful how we read the kind of end-time, apocalyptic prophecy we find in Revelation, Daniel, and Ezekiel. Some people take those words literally, even though the angel Gabriel told Daniel not to.

Daniel saw a vision of bizarre animals fighting each other, and he didn't have a clue what the vision meant. Gabriel came and explained that the animals represented the battling empires of Persia and Greece (Daniel 8:20–21). Without Gabriel's help, Daniel would have been stumped.

That should caution us to keep an open mind when we're reading Revelation, for example—unless we've had a visit from Gabriel.

WHERE TO FIND IT IN THE BIBLE

ABORTION

The Bible doesn't talk directly about abortion. But many Christians say there are important principles in the Bible that can guide us in this matter of life or death.

- [God] **knit me together in my mother's womb** (Psalm 139:13 NIV). Some Christians say this is when human life begins—when God puts a soul in us. But the Bible doesn't say when God places a soul within a human body, or even if he always follows the same timetable. What the Bible does say is that God created each one of us, and every life is valuable to him. This passage from Psalms isn't an attempt to define life's beginning. It's a poem thanking God for caring about us even before we were conceived.

- **"Do not murder"** (Deuteronomy 5:17 CEV). Many Christians say abortion is murder. But other Christians argue that every case of murder in the Bible refers to the killing of someone who has been born—not to the killing of an unborn child. Whether or not abortion is "murder," as the Bible uses the term, most people agree that a fetus is alive. And the command not to murder shows that life is important to God and should be important to us, as well.

- **As cheese is made from milk, you created my body from a tiny drop. Then you tied my bones together with muscles and covered them with flesh and skin. You, the source of my life, showered me with kindness and watched over me** (Job 10:10–12 CEV). Some Christians use this passage to teach that human life begins at conception: "from a tiny drop." But others argue that this passage isn't talking about when life begins. It's talking about

Job asking for God's help. Job appealed to God by arguing that it was God who created him in the first place.

- **GOD formed Man out of dirt from the ground and blew into his nostrils the breath of life. The Man came alive—a living soul!** (Genesis 2:7 THE MESSAGE). Some use this verse to teach that humans take on a soul with their first breath. But it's just a guess. The Bible doesn't say when God puts a soul in us. And it's possible that this moment can vary, depending on the circumstances. This verse does, however, confirm that God is the giver of life. And many Christians say that because of this, we should respect every human life, even the life of an unborn child.

- **"The punishment must match the injury: a life for a life"** (Exodus 21:23). That was the penalty in Moses' time for accidentally killing a pregnant woman.

Interestingly, many Bible translations say the attacker was only to be *fined* for accidentally hurting the woman enough to cause a miscarriage—as though the mother were more important than the fetus. This fine tracks with a similar law in practice at the time. Hammurabi's Code, named after a Babylonian king, ordered offenders executed for causing the death of a pregnant woman, but only fined them 10 silver coins for causing a miscarriage. Some Bible translations, however, say the death penalty was required if either the mother or the baby died. If that's the correct interpretation, it's out of sync with Hammurabi's Code. But the Bible has been known to pave new territory. The fact remains that Christian scholars don't agree on how to interpret this passage.

Breath of life. From dust of the earth God creates Adam, the first human. Then God "breathed the breath of life into the man's nostrils, and the man became a living person" (Genesis 2:7). Some students of the Bible wonder if this is a clue that humans are entrusted with a living soul only after they take their first breath. Unfortunately for the curious, the Bible doesn't say.

DOES GOD APPROVE OF ABORTION?

Even Christians don't agree on the answer.

The Bible doesn't talk about abortion—even though abortions were taking place when it was written. One Roman writer, Minucius Felix, spoke of "women who swallow drugs to stop the beginnings of a person inside their womb."

The Bible's silence on the subject doesn't mean God approved of the abortions that were going on. After all, the Bible doesn't take a stand against slavery either—and it was certainly going on at the time. And most of us would certainly agree that slavery isn't something that would earn God's stamp of approval.

The Bible does teach that life comes from God and that we should treat it with reverence and compassion. But the struggle comes over how to do that.

Many Christians argue that we need to extend this compassion not only to the unborn child but also to women who are considering abortion or who have had one.

These Christians say it's not compassionate to insist that a woman go through with the pregnancy if she got pregnant through rape or incest—or if pregnancy-related health problems threaten her life. On the other hand, there are many Christians who say it's callous to abort a child only because the pregnancy came at an inconvenient time. And most abortions fit this category.

The Roman Catholic Church permits abortion only if the pregnancy threatens a woman's life. And even then it describes abortion as both good and bad: good because it saves a life, bad because it takes a life.

CHRISTIAN TEACHINGS TO CONSIDER

God is the Creator. "Nothing was created except through him" (John 1:3). When we destroy life, we kill something God created.

Christians help the helpless. That's the lesson behind Jesus' story of the good Samaritan—the man who helped a robbery victim. In abortion cases, both the unborn child and the woman in a crisis pregnancy are in need of help. It's sometimes confusing to know how best to help. But this much is clear: Coercion and name-calling aren't helpful. Nor is callous disregard of the developing child. The woman and the child both need a support system.

We have no right to the control of our own bodies. "You do not belong to yourself, for God bought you with a high price. So you must honor God with your body" (1 Corinthians 6:19–20).

None of us, born or unborn, has a right to life. Life is a gift. "Relish life. . . each and every day of your precarious life. Each day is God's gift" (Ecclesiastes 9:9 THE MESSAGE).

Christians imitate Christ. He put others ahead of himself. He didn't live for his own comfort and convenience. And for that reason, many Christians argue that abortions of convenience are out of sync with the selfless example of Jesus.

The Holy Spirit is our guide. "I will ask the Father, and he will give you another Advocate, who will never leave you. He is the Holy Spirit, who leads into all truth" (John 14:16–17). The Bible doesn't spell out, in black and white, answers to all the tough questions we'll struggle with. But God sent us a personal Counselor to advise us in each situation. Many Christians believe that where the Bible stops its work, the Spirit begins.

ABORTION ADVICE

1. If you're considering abortion, consider adoption instead. Many infertile couples have to wait years to adopt a baby. And the meager supply with the heavy demand makes it an expensive venture.
2. If you've had an abortion, believe it was wrong, and can't get over the guilt, here are two Bible verses that might help:
   - "Do not remember the rebellious sins of my youth. Remember me in the light of your unfailing love, for you are merciful, O LORD" (Psalm 25:7).
   - "If we confess our sins to him, he is faithful and just to forgive us our sins and to cleanse us from all wickedness" (1 John 1:9). See *Forgiveness*
3. If you're angry with someone who had an abortion, consider how hard it must have been for her to go through with it—even if she doesn't show any signs of regret. And think about how you would act toward her if you obey what Jesus said is the Bible's most important law involving human relationships: "Do to others what you would like them to do to you" (Matthew 7:12).

ABSTINENCE

Sex belongs in a marriage relationship, according to the Bible. Sex outside of marriage is called "sexual immorality" in many Bible translations, and "fornication" in older versions.

- **Share your love only with your wife** (Proverbs 5:15). That's the advice of an elderly sage to young men.
- **Stay away from all sexual sin. Then each of you will control his own body and live in holiness and honor—not in lustful passion like the pagans who do not know God and his ways** (1 Thessalonians 4:3–5).
- **Run from sexual sin! No other sin so clearly affects the body as this one does. For sexual immorality is a sin against your own body** (1 Corinthians 6:18).
- **Guard the morality of sex and marriage** (Acts 15:20 THE MESSAGE).
- **Have nothing to do with sexual immorality, impurity, lust, and evil desires** (Colossians 3:5).

- **Avoid the evil things your bodies want to do that fight against your soul** (1 Peter 2:11 NCV).

ABUSE

- **"Do to others what you want them to do to you"** (Matthew 7:12 NCV). This is called the Golden Rule.
- **Eli was very old. He kept getting reports on how his sons were ripping off the people and sleeping with the women who helped out at the sanctuary** (1 Samuel 2:22 THE MESSAGE). Eli's sons were priests, abusing their authority.
- **Men of Sodom, young and old, came from all over the city and surrounded the house. They shouted to Lot, "Where are the men who came to spend the night with you? Bring them out to us so we can have sex with them"** (Genesis 19:4–5).
- **Don't rob the poor just because you can, or exploit the needy in court. For the LORD is their defender. He will ruin anyone who ruins them** (Proverbs 22:22–23).

- **Our dedication to Christ makes us look like fools. . . . We bless those who curse us. We are patient with those who abuse us** (1 Corinthians 4:10, 12).

See also *Exploitation*

ADDICTION

- **They let themselves go in sexual obsession, addicted to every sort of perversion. But that's no life for you. . . . Everything—and I do mean everything—connected with that old way of life has to go. It's rotten through and through. Get rid of it! And then take on an entirely new way of life—a God-fashioned life, a life renewed from the inside and working itself into your conduct as God accurately reproduces his character in you** (Ephesians 4:19–24 THE MESSAGE).
- **They make their appeal to the earthly longings of people's sinful nature. . . . They promise to give freedom. . . . But they themselves are slaves to sinful living. A person is a slave to anything that controls him** (2 Peter 2:18–19 NIrV). The writer is talking about false teachers trying to lure new Christians away from the church and into some unidentified destructive behavior. But the words could apply to anyone trying to lure us into any addictive behavior: drugs, premarital sex, pornography.

See also *Drinking and Drugs; Pornography*

ADULTERY

- **Save yourself for your wife and don't have sex with other women** (Proverbs 5:17 CEV).
- **Sexual drives are strong, but marriage is strong enough to contain them and provide for a balanced and fulfilling sexual life in a world of sexual disorder. The marriage bed must be a place of mutuality—the husband seeking to satisfy his wife, the wife seeking to satisfy her husband** (1 Corinthians 7:2–3 THE MESSAGE).
- **Give honor to marriage, and remain faithful to one another in marriage. God will surely judge people who are immoral and those who commit adultery** (Hebrews 13:4).
- **Come, let's make love until morning. . . . My husband is not home; he has gone on a long trip** (Proverbs 7:18–19 NCV). A woman's invitation to a young man—an invitation that the wise writer says is like inviting a bull into a butcher shop: "Many have died because of her" (Proverbs 7:26 NCV).

The forgiveness option.

Jewish leaders ask Jesus what they should do with a woman caught in adultery—reminding him that Jewish law said she should be stoned to death (John 8:4–5). Jesus offers an alternative: mercy and forgiveness.

ANGELS

Angels are divine beings God uses in many ways—to deliver messages, punish evil people, and even protect good people from danger.

Protection

- **If you honor the LORD, his angel will protect you** (Psalm 34:7 CEV).
- **"I could ask my Father for thousands of angels to protect us, and he would send them instantly"** (Matthew 26:53). This is Jesus talking to his disciples as he's being arrested.
- **The angel of God that usually traveled in front of Israel's army moved behind them. Also, the pillar of cloud moved from in front of the people and stood behind them. So the cloud came between the Egyp-**tians and the Israelites. This made it dark for the Egyptians but gave light to the Israelites. So the cloud kept the two armies apart all night (Exodus 14:19–20 NCV). An angel protects the Israelite refugees from the advancing Egyptian chariots.

Punishment

- **He dispatched against them a band of destroying angels** (Psalm 78:49).
- **"I will send an angel before you to drive out the Canaanites"** (Exodus 33:2).
- **GOD expelled them from the Garden of Eden. . .and stationed angel-cherubim. . .guarding the path to the Tree-of-Life** (Genesis 3:23–24 THE MESSAGE).

Delivery of messages

- **The angel said, "I am Gabriel! I stand in the very presence of God. It was he who sent me to bring you this good news!"** (Luke 1:19).

25

- **"He will send his angel ahead of you, and he will see to it that you find a wife there for my son"** (Genesis 24:7). Abraham assures his servant, who is being sent on a long trip to find a wife for Isaac.

ANGER

- **"Don't sin by letting anger control you." Don't let the sun go down while you are still angry** (Ephesians 4:26). Some kinds of anger are reasonable, and they won't fade when the sun does. If you get betrayed by an unfaithful boyfriend or girlfriend, you'll still be angry in the morning. And rightly so. But the point is to resolve as quickly as possible whatever problem caused the anger. And then move on with your life.

- **A fool is quick-tempered, but a wise person stays calm when insulted** (Proverbs 12:16).
- **Do not become angry easily, because anger will not help you live the right kind of life God wants** (James 1:19–20 NCV).
- **"If you are even angry with someone, you are subject to judgment! If you call someone an idiot, you are in danger of being brought before the court. And if you curse someone, you are in danger of the fires of hell"** (Matthew 5:22). Jesus said this. Most Bible experts insist there are exceptions to the rule. Jesus showed a few exceptions when he got angry at religious leaders and when he took a whip to merchants at the temple.

See also *Hate*

How to anger a pacifist.
Even Jesus—who taught us to turn the other cheek—flared up when he saw merchants turning the Temple courtyard into a strip mall. They had probably paid the priests a rental fee for the space. But this part of the Jerusalem hilltop was the main worship center for non-Jews who loved God—it was their sanctuary. Noisy and bustling with business, it was smelly and messy with animals for sale. Jesus chased off the merchants. By doing that he gave us at least one model for legitimate anger: It's natural to get upset when we see people in authority trashing the rights of others.

WHEN IS IT OKAY TO GET MAD?

Anger, when it gets the better of us, can make us crazy—temporarily insane. But there are times when it's crazy *not* to get angry.

Even the pacifist Jesus, who said we should turn the other cheek when hit, got angry enough to beat on merchants and to flip over their tables.

Here's the Bible's short course on anger: If our motive is to hurt someone, the anger is wrong. But if our motive is to protect someone or to stop an injustice, the anger makes perfect sense.

Consider these Bible examples of righteous anger.

- "Jesus traveled up to Jerusalem. He found the Temple teeming with people selling cattle and sheep and doves. . . . Jesus put together a whip out of strips of leather and chased them out of the Temple, stampeding the sheep and cattle, upending the tables of the loan sharks" (John 2:13–15 THE MESSAGE). Jesus' words explain his anger: "Get your things out of here! Stop turning my Father's house into a shopping mall!" Some history scholars say this was the last time merchants sold livestock in the temple courtyard.

- "Phinehas thrust the spear all the way through the man's body and into the woman's stomach" (Numbers 25:8). The couple was having sex at the time. Phinehas was a priest, violently putting a stop to idol-worship sex rituals during the Jewish Exodus out of Egypt. God had punished the Jewish people for taking part in these rituals by sending a plague on them. He said he would stop the plague only when the sex rituals stopped. The doomed couple had already ignored Moses' command to stop. So Phinehas decided to put a stop to them, an act that ended the plague—but not before 24,000 people died.

- "The Spirit of God suddenly took control of Saul and made him furious" (1 Samuel 11:6 CEV). King Saul got angry because a neighboring king was gouging out the right eye of every Israelite man. Saul led his nation to war.

- "He [Jesus] looked around at them angrily and was deeply saddened by their hard hearts. Then he said to the man, 'Hold out your hand.' So the man held out his hand, and it was restored!" (Mark 3:5). Jesus was angry that Jewish scholars didn't want him to heal a crippled man on the Sabbath. The Bible doesn't prohibit healing on the Sabbath, but scholars argued that healing was work—which was prohibited. Jesus was angry at their callous disregard for the man.

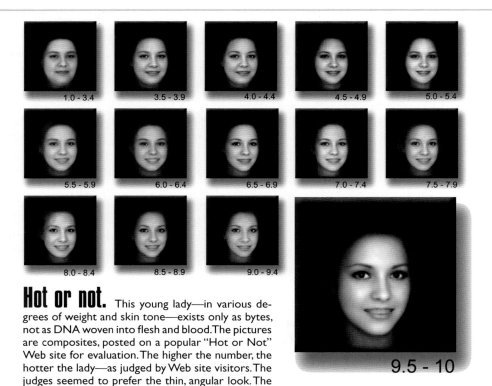

Hot or not. This young lady—in various degrees of weight and skin tone—exists only as bytes, not as DNA woven into flesh and blood. The pictures are composites, posted on a popular "Hot or Not" Web site for evaluation. The higher the number, the hotter the lady—as judged by Web site visitors. The judges seemed to prefer the thin, angular look. The Bible teaches that physical beauty doesn't last and that people should be more concerned about the beauty of a person's spirit and attitude.

APPEARANCE

- "Looks aren't everything. Don't be impressed with his looks and stature. . . . GOD judges persons differently than humans do. Men and women look at the face; GOD looks into the heart" (1 Samuel 16:7 THE MESSAGE). This was God's advice to the prophet Samuel when Samuel was about to anoint one of David's older brothers as king instead of anointing young David.
- Don't depend on things like fancy hairdos or gold jewelry or expensive clothes to make you look beautiful. Be beautiful in your heart by being gentle and quiet. This kind of beauty will last, and God considers it very special (1 Peter 3:3–4 CEV).
- Beauty does not last; but a woman who fears the LORD will be greatly praised (Proverbs 31:30).
- I want women to be modest in their appearance. They should wear decent and appropriate clothing and not draw attention to themselves by the way they fix their hair or by wearing gold or pearls or expensive clothes. For women who claim to be devoted to God should make themselves attractive by the good things they do (1 Timothy 2:9–10). What's good for the goose is good for the gander. That's an old saying. A *gander*, by the way, is a male.

ARGUMENTS

Avoid them in the first place

- It makes you look good when you avoid a fight—only fools love to quarrel (Proverbs 20:3 CEV).
- Stay away from stupid and senseless arguments. These only lead to trouble, and God's servants must not be troublemakers (2 Timothy 2:23–24 CEV).

Stop them quickly

- The start of a quarrel is like a leak in a dam, so stop it before it bursts (Proverbs 17:14 THE MESSAGE).
- "Settle your differences quickly. Otherwise, your accuser may hand you over to the judge, who will hand you over to an officer, and you will be thrown into prison" (Matthew 5:25).

How to stop them

- A kind answer soothes angry feelings, but harsh words stir them up (Proverbs 15:1 CEV).
- After a first and second warning, avoid someone who causes arguments (Titus 3:10 NCV).
- Regarding life together and getting along with each other, you don't need me to tell you what to do. You're God-taught in these matters. Just love one another! (1 Thessalonians 4:9 THE MESSAGE). We usually know how to end an argument. Often, the trick is to give ourselves the time and space to calm down and then to swallow our pride and say the tough words: "I'm sorry."

When it's good to argue

- When Peter came to Antioch, I [Paul] had to oppose him to his face, for what he did was very wrong (Galatians 2:11). Paul publicly criticized Peter for a public injustice. Peter had suddenly stopped eating with non-Jewish Christians. Peter did this right after a group of Jewish Christians arrived in town—Jews who felt it was wrong to mingle with non-Jews, even if those non-Jews were Christians. Paul stood up for what he believed was right.

Go ahead. Pull my ear.

A Staffordshire Bull Terrier, bred for fighting, licks its chops as a photographer moves in. Drawing from the canine world at a time when most dogs were wild, a sage offered this advice in a word picture: "Interfering in someone else's argument is as foolish as yanking a dog's ear" (Proverbs 26:17). In other words, it's a good way to get bit.

ASTROLOGY

Even though the wise men who followed the star of Bethlehem were probably astrologers who tried to predict the future by studying the stars, the Bible says astrology is fake.

- "Do not act like the other nations, who try to read their future in the stars. Do not be afraid of their predictions, even though other nations are terrified by them. Their ways are futile and foolish" (Jeremiah 10:2–3).
- "All the advice you receive. . .all your astrologers, those stargazers. . . they are like straw burning in a fire" (Isaiah 47:13–14).

See also *Occult*

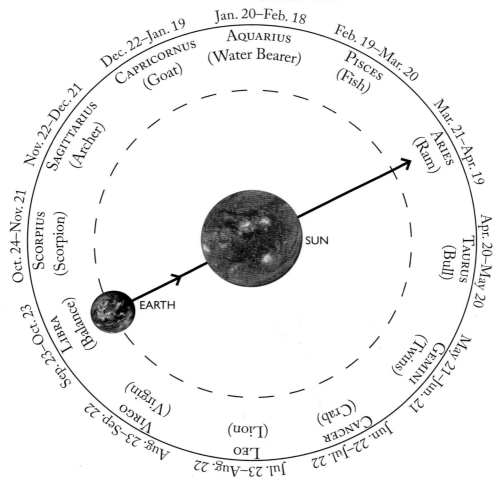

Signs of the zodiac. An imaginary line drawn from the earth through the sun to the constellations directly behind the sun determines the signs of the zodiac throughout the year. The constellation Aries, for example, lies behind the sun from March 21 to April 19. Astrologers say that people born during that time are born "under the sign of Aries." And astrologers plot the person's character and predict their day-to-day fate on that basis. The Bible says this is "futile and foolish."

ATHEISM

Atheists say they don't believe in God. The Bible says if they're serious, they're fools.

- **Only fools say in their hearts, "There is no God"** (Psalm 14:1).
- **Ever since the world was created, people have seen the earth and sky. Through everything God made, they can clearly see his invisible qualities—his eternal power and divine nature. So they have no excuse for not knowing God** (Romans 1:20). This is the classic argument for the existence of God. If we look at creation and deny it has a Creator, it's as though we're looking at a computer and arguing there was no computer programmer involved. The creation of a physical world defies the laws of physics. In physics, you can't create something from nothing. The conclusion seems obvious to many Christians: There was a nonphysical dimension involved in creation—a spiritual dimension. Even if the universe began with a Big Bang, someone had to pull the trigger. The brilliant physicist Albert Einstein said he felt "utter humility toward the unattainable secrets of the harmony of the cosmos." Atheists, he said, can't hear the "music of the spheres." He was talking about the spheres of science and religion. He explained that "science without religion is lame. Religion without science is blind."
- **The wicked are too proud to seek God. They seem to think that God is dead** (Psalm 10:4). These could include agnostics, people who say they don't know if God exists. So they don't commit themselves either way, and they end up ignoring God.
- **This is what makes an antichrist: denying the Father, denying the Son** (1 John 2:22 THE MESSAGE). John isn't talking about an end-time leader that some Christians expect to show up—a wicked man called the Antichrist. John is talking about all people who are against God and his Son.

ATTITUDE

- **A peaceful heart leads to a healthy body** (Proverbs 14:30). But don't count on it. At least not as a promise from God. Proverbs is a collection of advice from elderly men—general observations they've made over the years. They've noticed that easygoing people keep going longer.
- **Have the same attitude that Christ Jesus had. . . . He gave up his divine privileges; he took the humble position of a slave** (Philippians 2:5–7).
- **"God blesses those who are humble, for they will inherit the whole earth. God blesses those who hunger and thirst for justice, for they will be satisfied"** (Matthew 5:5–6). These are the words of Jesus, beginning his Sermon on the Mount with a prescription for spiritual happiness: the Beatitudes. Or as some have described them, the "Be Happy" Attitudes.
- **May God, who gives this patience and encouragement, help you live in complete harmony with each other, as is fitting for followers of Christ Jesus** (Romans 15:5).
- **Since Jesus went through everything you're going through and more, learn to think like him. Think**

of your sufferings as a weaning from that old sinful habit of always expecting to get your own way. Then you'll be able to live out your days free to pursue what God wants instead of being tyrannized by what you want (1 Peter 4:1–2 THE MESSAGE).

BACKSLIDING

Some Christians—including many Baptists—say that once you're saved, there's nothing you can do to lose your salvation. Other Christians disagree. Here are some key verses that Christians on both sides of the debate turn to for support.

Once saved, always saved

- "My sheep listen to my voice; I know them, and they follow me. I give them eternal life, and they will never perish. No one can snatch them away from me, for my Father has given them to me, and he is more powerful than anyone else. No one can snatch them from the Father's hand" (John 10:27–29). That's Jesus talking about his followers. Christians who don't believe in "once saved, always saved" argue that to keep from being "snatched away," we have to continue listening to Jesus and following him. If we don't, we can end up like a sheep that nibbles its way into a lion's den.
- We have a priceless inheritance— an inheritance that is kept in heaven for you, pure and undefiled, beyond the reach of change and decay. And through your faith, God is protecting you by his power until you receive this salvation (1 Peter

1:4–5). Christians who say it's possible to lose salvation say our spiritual security is based on the condition that we continue trusting God.

Believers can lose their salvation

- It is impossible to bring back to repentance those who were once enlightened—those who have experienced the good things of heaven and shared in the Holy Spirit, who have tasted the goodness of the word of God and the power of the age to come—and who then turn away from God (Hebrews 6:4–6). Some Christians who believe in "once saved, always saved" say the writer is talking about people who never fully believed—they "tasted" spiritual truth but never fully digested it. Others acknowledge that the people were true believers, but insist that they didn't lose their salvation. Instead, they just lost their ability to become "mature" believers, who are referred to at the beginning of the chapter. Some say the writer is exaggerating. The point of the book, many Bible experts say, is to stop Jewish Christians from going back to their old religion of Judaism. So the Hebrews writer seems to be saying, essentially, "If you leave, you can't come back."
- Some people have left the faith, because they wanted to get more money, but they have caused themselves much sorrow (1 Timothy 6:10 NCV). Christians favoring "once saved, always saved" acknowledge that we can leave the faith, but the faith won't leave us—we are saved regardless of what we do.
- Do not let those evil people lead you away by the wrong they do. Be careful so you will not fall from your

strong faith (2 Peter 3:17 NCV). But if you do fall, say the "once saved, always saved" folks, you'll fall into the arms of a loving Jesus who will carry you to heaven.

See also *Sin*

BAPTISM

In the ritual of baptism, a Christian is dipped into water—or sometimes sprinkled. This symbolizes that God has washed away our sins and given us new life. "Going under the water was a burial of your old life; coming up out of it was a resurrection, God raising you from the dead as he did Christ" (Colossians 2:12 THE MESSAGE). Christians rise from the baptismal water in a dramatic and public statement: I have become a new person—a Christian.

- **John the Baptist...was in the wilderness and preached that people should be baptized to show that they had repented of their sins and turned to God to be forgiven** (Mark 1:4). John started baptism, probably adapting the Jewish cleaning ritual that involved taking a bath before worshipping God.
- **After his baptism, as Jesus came up out of the water, the heavens were opened. . . . And a voice from heaven said, "This is my dearly loved Son, who brings me great joy"** (Matthew 3:16–17). Though Jesus had committed no sins, he insisted on being baptized—perhaps as an example for others to follow.
- **"Go into all the world and preach the Good News to everyone. Anyone who believes and is baptized**

will be saved" (Mark 16:15–16). Words like this, from Jesus, have led some Christians to conclude that we have to be baptized to make it into heaven. Most Christians, however, say that baptism is simply a helpful ritual to observe—not a requirement. Elsewhere, Jesus and the apostle Paul both made it clear that we are saved by faith in God, not by any rituals we perform.

- **On that day about three thousand believed his** [Peter's] **message and were baptized** (Acts 2:41 CEV). The church was born when Peter preached in Jerusalem several weeks after the crucifixion. Some 3,000 people believed what he said and took a public stand by getting baptized.
- **Even at that hour of the night, the jailer cared for them and washed their wounds. Then he and everyone**

Washing sins away. Water baptism is a Christian ritual brimming with symbolism. The Bible says it represents the cleansing of our sins. We rise from the water much as Jesus rose from the grave, declaring our victory over sin and death and clinging to the promise that we have been born again to live forever.

in his household were immediately baptized (Acts 16:33). This is from a story about Paul and Silas converting their jailer. Converts to the new Christian movement not only got baptized, they often had their entire family baptized, as well. That's one reason some churches baptize infants.

BIBLE

- Be prepared. You're up against far more than you can handle on your own. Take all the help you can get, every weapon God has issued, so that when it's all over but the shouting you'll still be on your feet. . . . God's Word is an indispensable weapon (Ephesians 6:13–17 THE MESSAGE).
- Since childhood, you have known the Holy Scriptures that are able to make you wise enough to have faith in Christ Jesus and be saved. Everything in the Scriptures is God's Word. All of it is useful for teaching and helping people and for correcting them and showing them how to live. The Scriptures train God's servants to do all kinds of good deeds (2 Timothy 3:15–17 CEV). Paul wrote this, referring to his Bible—the Old Testament. Within a few decades, Christians were calling the letters of Paul scripture, too.
- "People do not live by bread alone, but by every word that comes from the mouth of God" (Matthew 4:4). These are the words of Jesus.

BODY PIERCING

The Bible doesn't say anything directly about the kind of body piercing popular today, such as pierced ears—or the less common and more painful piercing of tongues, belly buttons, or genitals. But there are implied cautions. We see them in the Bible's respect for the human body as God's masterpiece.

- God created human beings in his own image. . . . And he saw that it was very good (Genesis 1:27, 31).
- You [God]. . .knit me together in my mother's womb. . . . Your workmanship is marvelous (Psalm 139:13–14).
- "Publicly pierce his ear" (Exodus 21:6). This permanently marked a person as a slave.

See also *Tattoos*

CAPITAL PUNISHMENT

God ordered Jews to execute people for certain crimes, including murder, adultery, and talking nasty to their parents. But many Christians say Jesus launched a new way of life that excludes killing killers— or anyone else.

Capital offenses (the short list)

- "If someone plans and murders another person on purpose, put him to death" (Exodus 21:14 NCV). God, however, spared two famous murderers: Cain, who killed his brother Abel, and King David, who arranged the death of Bathsheba's husband so David could marry his lover.
- "If a man is discovered committing adultery, both he and the woman must die" (Deuteronomy 22:22).
- "Anyone who says cruel things to his father or mother must be put to death" (Exodus 21:17 NCV).
- "Anyone who hits his father or his mother must be put to death" (Exodus 21:15 NCV).

- "Anyone who kidnaps someone... must be put to death" (Exodus 21:16 NCV).
- "The seventh day must be a Sabbath day of complete rest. . . . Anyone who works on that day must be put to death" (Exodus 35:2).

New commandments

- "You have heard that it was said, 'An eye for an eye, and a tooth for a tooth.' But I tell you, don't stand up against an evil person. If someone slaps you on the right cheek, turn to him the other cheek also" (Matthew 5:38–39 NCV). With this single statement, Jesus is declaring that the old Jewish law of retaliation is now obsolete. (See Exodus 21:24.)
- "Has no one judged you guilty? . . . I also don't judge you guilty. You may go now, but don't sin anymore" (John 8:10–11 NCV). The words of Jesus to a woman caught in adultery. Jesus talked religious leaders out of stoning her to death for this capital offense. Instead of punishing her, Jesus forgave her.
- "Love your enemies. Let them bring out the best in you, not the worst. When someone gives you a hard time, respond with the energies of prayer" (Matthew 5:44 THE MESSAGE).

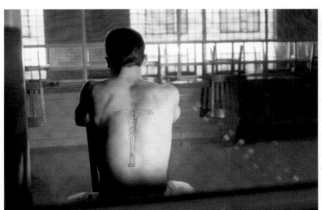

Death by lethal injection. Convicted of murdering a night clerk at a convenience store, 29-year-old J.D. Autry awaits execution at Huntsville prison in Texas. The homemade crucifixion tattoo on his back is a precursor to his painful death. Injected with drugs, it took him 10 minutes to die. He spent most of that time awake and complaining about intense pain. Physicians said he should have died much more quickly.

CHEATING

In the Bible, cheating is portrayed as a liar's way of getting ahead at the expense of others. Honesty is the Bible's policy.

- "If you are faithful in little things, you will be faithful in large ones. But if you are dishonest in little things, you won't be honest with greater responsibilities" (Luke 16:10).
- "You must not cheat" (Mark 10:19).
- Better to be poor and honest than to be dishonest and a fool (Proverbs 19:1).
- The LORD detests the use of dishonest scales, but he delights in accurate weights (Proverbs 11:1).

See also *Lying*

CHRISTIAN

- In Antioch [a city in Syria] the followers were called Christians for the first time (Acts 11:26 NCV). At first, converts to the teachings of Jesus called themselves "followers of the Way" (Acts 9:2). It wasn't until several years after the Crucifixion that people started calling them "Christians," from the Greek word *Christos* (Messiah) and the Latin ending *ianus*. The combo word meant "belonging to Christ." Originally, this was probably a degrading name. Perhaps a bit like calling followers of Sung Myung Moon "Moonies," when they prefer being identified as members of the Unification Church. In time, followers of Jesus grew to love the title "Christian" because it connected them to Christ.

- Anyone who belongs to Christ has become a new person. The old life is gone; a new life has begun! (2 Corinthians 5:17).
- It is no shame to suffer for being a Christian. Praise God for the privilege of being called by his name! (1 Peter 4:16).
- People who aren't spiritual can't receive these truths from God's Spirit. It all sounds foolish to them (1 Corinthians 2:14).
- Accept other believers who are weak in faith, and don't argue with them about what they think is right or wrong (Romans 14:1).

CHRISTIANITY

- "I am the way, the truth, and the life. No one can come to the Father except through me" (John 14:6). Because of passages like this, most Christians insist that people have to accept Jesus as Savior to make it into heaven. Others speculate that we may be able to accept him after we die, though most Christians consider this heresy that has no support in the Bible. For many, a troubling question is what God will do with the billions of people throughout history who never heard enough about Jesus to consider Christianity. "In God we trust," others answer. In other words, we trust in a God who perfectly blends fairness, justice, and love. We can count on him to do the right thing.

CHURCH

Christians didn't start building churches until the AD 300s, when Rome finally declared Christianity a legal religion. Before that, members of this outlawed faith met in small groups—often in homes.

Come to church

- **You should not stay away from the church meetings, as some are doing, but you should meet together and encourage each other** (Hebrews 10:25 NCV).

The church's job

- **"Go into all the world and preach the Good News to everyone"** (Mark 16:15). Known as the Great Commission, these are the last words of Jesus to his disciples.
- **Let us aim for harmony in the church and try to build each other up** (Romans 14:19).
- **A spiritual gift is given to each of us so we can help each other** (1 Corinthians 12:7).
- **Are any of you sick? You should call for the elders of the church to come and pray over you, anointing them with oil in the name of the Lord** (James 5:14).
- **I am told that a man in your church is living in sin with his stepmother. . . . It isn't my responsibility to judge outsiders, but it certainly is your responsibility to judge those inside the church who are sinning** (1 Corinthians 5:1, 12).

Leaders

- **It is true that anyone who desires to be a church official** [such as a pastor] **wants to be something worthwhile. That's why officials must have a good reputation and be faithful in marriage. They must be self-controlled, sensible, well-behaved, friendly to strangers, and able to teach. They must not be heavy drinkers or troublemakers. Instead, they must be kind and gentle and not love money** (1 Timothy 3:1–3 CEV).
- **"I say to you that you are Peter. . . and upon this rock I will build my church, and all the powers of hell will not conquer it"** (Matthew 16:18). These are the words of Jesus

Megachurch.

Pope John Paul II celebrates Easter Sunday Mass from the balcony of one of the world's largest churches: Saint Peter's Basilica in Rome. The crowds are so massive that they gather outside in the sprawling courtyard.

to his leading disciple. Roman Catholics say this is when Jesus appointed Peter to become what amounts to the first in a long line of popes. Many Protestants say Jesus was referring to the leadership Peter would give to the Christian movement, beginning with a sermon that would produce 3,000 converts in Jerusalem (Acts 2).

See also *Worship*

COMPASSION

- "A despised Samaritan came along, and when he saw the man, he felt compassion for him. Going over to him, the Samaritan soothed his wounds with olive oil and wine and bandaged them. Then he put the man on his own donkey and took him to an inn, where he took care of him" (Luke 10:33–34). In the famous parable of the good Samaritan, Jesus teaches the importance of compassion. He links it with what he calls the most important commandment of all: loving God and our neighbors. The Samaritan shows how to do it—he honors God by helping someone in need.

- "They will reply, 'Lord, when did we ever see you hungry or thirsty or a stranger or naked or sick or in prison, and not help you?' And he will answer, 'I tell you the truth, when you refused to help the least of these my brothers and sisters, you were refusing to help me'" (Matthew 25:44–45). Jesus says that when we

Mercy in the Guatemala mountains.

Nursing student Becca Miller, left, assesses a young patient in one of many health screenings that volunteers conducted in mountain churches throughout Guatemala. With the little girl's mother serving as translator, the patient tells Miller she has a tummyache. All the children attending this clinic are treated for parasites, which they get from the water.

help others, it's the same as helping him. He adds later that helping people in need is something God expects of those who call themselves his people.

- **"Go and sin no more"** (John 8:11). That's what Jesus told a married woman caught having an affair. Instead of punishing her, as Jewish law allowed, he forgave her.

COMPLAINING

- **It's better to live alone in the desert than with a quarrelsome, complaining wife** (Proverbs 21:19). Or husband. This book was written for young men, offering them advice from older men. But we can probably count on this: Given a chance, the older women would have warned younger women about crabby husbands.
- **Do everything without complaining and arguing, so that no one can criticize you** (Philippians 2:14–15).
- **"What did I do to deserve the burden of all these people? . . . They keep whining. . . . If this is how you intend to treat me, just go ahead and kill me. Do me a favor and spare me this misery!"** (Numbers 11:11, 13, 15). The constant complaining of the Exodus Israelites frustrates Moses so much that he asks God to put him out of his misery. God later offers to kill the Israelites instead—an offer Moses rejects.
- **I will wait to see what the LORD says and how he will answer my complaint** (Habakkuk 2:1). A prophet complains to God about what seems to be God's unfair treatment of the Jews. God graciously listens and responds.

See also *Criticism*

CONFESSION

> The Bible says we should confess our sins not only to God, but to the people we hurt, as well.

Confess to God
- **If we confess our sins to him, he is faithful and just to forgive us our sins and to cleanse us from all wickedness** (1 John 1:9). After we confess, God removes all traces of our guilt. There may be consequences we have to face from others, but Judge God strikes his gavel on the desk and declares us "not guilty."
- **Purify me from my sins, and I will be clean; wash me, and I will be whiter than snow** (Psalm 51:7).
- **When I refused to confess my sin, my body wasted away, and I groaned all day long** (Psalm 32:3). Guilt does that to us.
- **David prayed, "I am your servant. But what I did was stupid and terribly wrong. Please forgive me"** (1 Chronicles 21:8 cev). The Bible portrays King David as a man who was quick to confess after being confronted with his sin.

Confess to each other
- **Confess your sins to each other and pray for each other so that you may be healed** (James 5:16). This doesn't mean we should tell everyone how bad we've been. They've got their own problems. But it does mean we should try to work things out with the people who have been hurt by our bad behavior.

CRITICISM

As far as the Bible is concerned, criticism is something best given to and from friends—in a spirit of loving concern, without anger or hypocrisy.

When to keep quiet
- "Why do you notice the little piece of dust in your friend's eye, but you don't notice the big piece of wood in your own eye?" (Luke 6:41 NCV).
- Welcome all the Lord's followers, even those whose faith is weak. Don't criticize them for having beliefs that are different from yours.... Only their Lord can decide if they are doing right, and the Lord will make sure that they do right (Romans 14:1, 4 CEV).
- Do not correct those who make fun of wisdom, or they will hate you. But correct the wise, and they will love you (Proverbs 9:8 NCV).

Listen to constructive criticism
- If you listen to constructive criticism, you will be at home among the wise (Proverbs 15:31).
- It is better to be criticized by a wise person than to be praised by a fool (Ecclesiastes 7:5).
- If you ignore criticism, you will end in poverty and disgrace; if you accept correction, you will be honored (Proverbs 13:18).

How to disarm your critics
- Keep a clear conscience so that those who speak evil of your good life in Christ will be made ashamed (1 Peter 3:16 NCV).

CURSING

Some Christians say it's okay to use profane words in anger, as long as we don't use God's name that way. Others argue just the opposite. They see nothing wrong with the complaint, "Oh, God!" But they would never say, "Oh, [fill in the blank with a hammer-hits-thumb cussword]. Actually, in the Bible profanity and cursing mean something different than they do today. In the Bible, a curse is a prayer that something bad will happen to someone. To profane means to treat something that's sacred as though it's not—like God's name. Christians aren't supposed to curse others or abuse God's name. They're also to drop nasty words from their vocabulary.

- "You must not misuse the name of the LORD your God. The LORD will not let you go unpunished if you misuse his name" (Exodus 20:7). This is number three of the 10 Commandments. If God ranks swear words, the abuse of his name is probably the worst offense since it's important enough to make it on his Top Ten list of don'ts.
- Don't use foul or abusive language (Ephesians 4:29).
- You know better now, so make sure it's all gone for good: bad temper, irritability, meanness, profanity, dirty talk (Colossians 3:8 THE MESSAGE).
- Don't yell at one another or curse each other (Ephesians 4:31 CEV).
- "A good person produces good things from the treasury of a good heart, and an evil person produces evil things from the treasury of an evil heart" (Matthew 12:35).

DATING

There's not a lot of dating going on in the Bible—at least it's not reported. Parents usually arranged the marriages of their children. When Abraham, father of the Jewish people, decided that his 40-year-old son, Isaac, needed a wife, Abraham sent his trusted servant out on a wife hunt. And that was that. "Isaac, meet Rebekah, your wife." Though the Bible has no how-to section on dating, it does talk about the kind of person worth getting to know better. And it talks about sexual boundaries.

Dating prospects

- **I choose as my friends everyone who worships you and follows your teachings** (Psalm 119:63 CEV).
- **Charm can fool you, and beauty can trick you, but a woman who respects the LORD should be praised** (Proverbs 31:30 NCV). And dated.
- **Don't team up with those who are unbelievers. How can righteousness be a partner with wickedness? How can light live with darkness? . . . How can a believer be a partner with an unbeliever?** (2 Corinthians 6:14–15). Bible experts debate what Paul means by this. Some say, in the context of Paul's letter to Christians in Corinth, that he's telling them they shouldn't worship at shrines of idols and then expect to worship in church, too. Others say he's warning Christians against any kind of partnership with unbelievers—in business or romance—since Christians and non-Christians live by radically different principles.

Boundaries

- **Don't allow love to turn into lust, setting off a downhill slide into sexual promiscuity** (Ephesians 5:3 THE MESSAGE). The Bible doesn't provide specific boundaries, such as what body parts are off-limits, or how long we can hold a kiss. But it repeatedly reminds us that sexual intimacy is reserved for marriage. We have to set limits that allow us to reach that goal.
- **Keep yourselves from sexual promiscuity. Learn to appreciate and give dignity to your body, not abusing it, as is so common among those who know nothing of God** (1 Thessalonians 4:3–5 THE MESSAGE).
- **"Do to others whatever you would like them to do to you"** (Matthew 7:12). This is the Golden Rule that sums up all Bible teachings about how to handle relationships. In the context of dating, it's not a license to kiss someone we would like to kiss us. That's taking the "do unto others" a bit too literally. Instead, Jesus means we shouldn't impose our will on someone else—with nagging, force, or any other tool of manipulation. After all, we wouldn't want to be treated that way.
- **Respect everyone** (1 Peter 2:17).

See also *Abstinence*

Dater's scrapbook.

In the cramped privacy of a photo booth, a young couple exercise their facial muscles. It's a cheap date, but fun.

DEATH

Plenty of people have quit the faith after watching loved ones die. It's common for the folks left behind to wonder why God didn't step into human history and save the person. But the Bible's message is that God did just that. He sent his Son, Jesus, to save us. Death is not the end of the road. For believers, it's the doorway into a spiritual dimension that never ends.

- **Even when I walk through the darkest valley, I will not be afraid, for you are close beside me. Your rod and your staff protect and comfort me** (Psalm 23:4). This chapter in the Bible is read to the dying perhaps more than any other words ever written.
- **The length of our days is seventy years—or eighty, if we have the strength. . .they quickly pass, and we fly away** (Psalm 90:10 NIV).
- **The Christians who have died will rise from their graves** (1 Thessalonians 4:16).
- **Those who have died will be raised to live forever. . .transformed. . . . Our mortal bodies must be transformed into immortal bodies** (1 Corinthians 15:52–53). Many speculate that our "transformed bodies" will be like that of the resurrected Jesus—able to eat, touch, be recognized, disappear, walk through walls, and levitate.
- **When these bodies of ours are taken down like tents and folded away, they will be replaced by resurrection bodies in heaven** (2 Corinthians 5:1 THE MESSAGE).
- **Each person is destined to die once**

and after that comes judgment (Hebrews 9:27). This verse seems to refute the idea of reincarnation.
- **God will wipe away every tear from their eyes; there shall be no more death** (Revelation 21:4 NKJV).
- **They mourned and wept and fasted all day for Saul and his son Jonathan** (2 Samuel 1:12). Sorrow is a natural response to the death of someone we love.

DECISION-MAKING

- **If you need wisdom, ask our generous God, and he will give it to you** (James 1:5).
- **"Keep on asking, and you will receive what you ask for. Keep on seeking, and you will find"** (Matthew 7:7). That's Jesus' advice.
- **I praise the LORD because he advises me. Even at night, I feel his leading** (Psalm 16:7 NCV).
- **Jesus went up on a mountain to pray, and he prayed to God all night. At daybreak he called together all of his disciples and chose twelve of them to be apostles** (Luke 6:12–13). Before making the key decision about which disciples to select from among his many followers, Jesus spends the night in prayer.
- **One day as these men** [a group of five from the same church] **were worshiping the Lord and fasting, the Holy Spirit said, "Dedicate Barnabas and Saul for the special work to which I have called them"** (Acts 13:2). The Bible doesn't say how the Spirit communicated. But apparently all the men felt assured that Barnabas and Saul—better known today by his Greek name: Paul—needed to begin missionary

work. Maybe the men had been discussing it and were seeking God's direction in prayer.

- **Paul and Silas traveled through the area of Phrygia and Galatia, because the Holy Spirit had prevented them from preaching the word in the province of Asia** [in what is now western Turkey] (Acts 16:6). Somehow—again in a way the Bible doesn't describe—the Holy Spirit communicated to Paul and Silas. Perhaps the Spirit spoke as a quiet, inner voice. Or maybe it was more dramatic.

See also *Prayer*

DEPRESSION

It's normal to get depressed from time to time. In some cases, the Bible offers spiritual encouragement—reminding us that God is in control. Sometimes the treatment is rest, food, and a fresh perspective on our situation—that's how God treated Elijah's depression (see at right). Sometimes the problem is a physical one, caused by brain chemical imbalances that exaggerate our troubles. God gave us doctors and medications to help with that.

Depressed Bible heroes
- **"I would rather be strangled—rather die than suffer like this. I hate my life and don't want to go on living"** (Job 7:15–16). After tragically losing his children, his riches, and his health, Job is bitterly depressed. He tells God exactly how he feels, and in time God replies.
- **The Spirit of GOD left Saul and in its place a black mood sent by GOD settled on him. He was terrified.**

Saul's advisors said, **"This awful tormenting depression from God is making your life miserable. O Master, let us help. Let us look for someone who can play the harp. When the black mood from God moves in, he'll play his music and you'll feel better"** (1 Samuel 16:14–16 THE MESSAGE). Music therapy for treating depression is nothing new. The help it gave King Saul, however, was only temporary.

- **Elijah was afraid and fled for his life. . . . He sat down under a solitary broom tree and prayed that he might die** (1 Kings 19:3–4). God's treatment for Elijah's depression: food, rest, and a fresh challenge that offered hope.
- **"Now I am deeply troubled, and I don't know what to say. But I must not ask my Father to keep me from this time of suffering. In fact, I came into the world to suffer"** (John 12:27 CEV). This is Jesus talking, shortly before his crucifixion.
- **The God who lifts up the downcast lifted our heads and our hearts with the arrival of Titus** (2 Corinthians 7:6 THE MESSAGE). Paul is discouraged by problems he faces—until a friend arrives.
- **Why am I discouraged? Why is my heart so sad? I will put my hope in God! I will praise him again—my Savior and my God!** (Psalm 42:11). A poet admits his depression, but he puts his hope in God.

Hope for the depressed
- **The LORD is there to rescue all who are discouraged and have given up hope** (Psalm 34:18 CEV).
- **Darkness and despair will not go on forever. . . . The people who walk in darkness will see a great light**

(Isaiah 9:1–2). This prophecy points to Jesus. "A child is born to us, a son is given to us. . . . Wonderful Counselor, Mighty God, Everlasting Father, Prince of Peace" (Isaiah 9:6).

- **"In this godless world you will continue to experience difficulties. But take heart! I've conquered the world"** (John 16:33 THE MESSAGE). The words of Jesus to his followers.

- **Even though the fig trees have no blossoms, and there are no grapes on the vines; even though the olive crop fails, and the fields lie empty and barren; even though the flocks die in the fields, and the cattle barns are empty, yet I will rejoice in the LORD! I will be joyful in the God of my salvation! The Sovereign LORD is my strength! He makes me as surefooted as a deer, able to tread upon the heights** (Habakkuk 3:17–19). This is one of the Bible's most powerful statements of faith—offered by a man whose nation is about to be wiped off the map. On the brink of an invasion, the prophet vows to trust in God no matter what.

DEVOTIONS

Private devotions are times we set aside to read the Bible, think about it, and talk with God. When we do that, we're imitating Jesus, who knew the Scriptures well and who prayed often—sometimes "all night" (Luke 6:12).

- **I treasure your word above all else; it keeps me from sinning against you. . . . I will study your teachings and follow your footsteps** (Psalm 119:11, 15 CEV).

- **Study to shew thyself approved unto God, a workman that needeth not to be ashamed, rightly dividing the word of truth** (2 Timothy 2:15 KJV). Pardon the Shakespearian English from the 1600s, but the more recent versions take out the word "study." Paul is advising his friend, Pastor Timothy, to understand the Bible well enough to live it and explain it correctly. And that takes study.

- **By your words I can see where I'm going; they throw a beam of light on my dark path** (Psalm 119:105 THE MESSAGE).

- **Listen to my voice in the morning, LORD. Each morning I bring my requests to you and wait expectantly** (Psalm 5:3). This writer was apparently a morning person. Others in the Bible had their devotions at midday or in the evening.

- **You have accepted Christ Jesus as your Lord. Now keep on following him. Plant your roots in Christ and let him be the foundation for your life. Be strong in your faith, just as you were taught** (Colossians 2:6–7 CEV). To grow in our relationship with Christ, we need to spend time with him.

DISAPPOINTMENT

- **Nothing you do for the Lord is ever useless** (1 Corinthians 15:58).

See also *Depression*

DISCRIMINATION

- **How can you claim to have faith in our glorious Lord Jesus Christ if you favor some people over others? For example, suppose someone comes into your meeting dressed in fancy clothes and expensive jewelry, and another comes in who is poor and dressed in dirty clothes. If you give special attention and a good seat to the rich person, but you say to the poor one, "You can stand over there, or else sit on the floor"—well, doesn't this discrimination show that your judgments are guided by evil motives?** (James 2:1–4).

- **In Christ, there is no difference between Jew and Greek, slave and free person, male and female. You are all the same in Christ Jesus** (Galatians 3:28 NCV).

- **"I am the LORD, and I consider all people the same, whether they are Israelites or foreigners"** (Numbers 15:15 CEV).

- **"You must not mistreat or oppress foreigners in any way. . . . You must not exploit a widow or an orphan. If you exploit them in any way and they cry out to me, then I will certainly hear their cry. My anger will blaze against you"** (Exodus 22:21–24). Throughout the Bible, God is especially concerned about one group of people: the powerless. In Bible times, these included immigrants, orphans, and widows.

Waiting for trash delivery.
At the city dump of Matamoros, Mexico, near the U.S. border, eight-year-old Marisol Ortiz waits with her mother and eight brothers and sisters for the evening arrival of dump trucks. The family survives by selling castaway items while Marisol's father works in the U.S. Though he's a legal immigrant, the only way he knows how to get his family into the U.S. is to lead them across the border, illegally. There, they become migrant farmworkers, living on the fringe of poverty and being exploited by employers who manipulate them with threats of deportation.

DIVORCE

Bible verses about divorce veer off in more directions than a freshman's term paper. It's because each passage seems to address a different situation. Even Jesus, in one sermon, forbids divorce—without making any exceptions (Luke 16:18). Other times he allows divorce in cases involving sexual immorality. Paul goes further. He allows divorce when a non-Christian spouse abandons a Christian spouse. This much is clear in the Bible: There's nothing okay with divorce. It's caused by sin. And God hates it because it hurts people. Yet even after divorce, there are forgiveness and healing. Unfortunately, there are scars from the wounds, as well.

God's plan didn't include divorce

- **"I hate divorce!" says the LORD, the God of Israel. "To divorce your wife is to overwhelm her with cruelty"** (Malachi 2:16).
- **"God has joined the two together, so no one should separate them"** (Matthew 19:6 NCV).
- **"Moses wrote this command** [allowing divorce] **only as a concession to your hardhearted ways"** (Mark 10:5 THE MESSAGE). Debating Jewish scholars, Jesus argues that even though the laws that God gave through Moses permitted divorce (see Deuteronomy 24:1), God intended marriage to last a lifetime.

When it's allowed

- **"Let us now make a covenant with our God to divorce our pagan wives and to send them away with their children"** (Ezra 10:3). Fearing a repeat of losing the land of Israel to invaders—a punishment the nation suffered after worshipping other gods—a priest convinces fellow Jewish men who are rebuilding their nation to divorce their non-Jewish wives. Some Bible experts say this was harsh and unnecessary—not a principle worth following then or now.

- **"Whoever divorces his wife and marries someone else commits adultery—unless his wife has been unfaithful"** (Matthew 19:9). Jesus allows "unfaithfulness" as a justifiable reason for divorcing. But scholars debate what "unfaithfulness" means. There are three popular options: adultery, premarital sex, and illegal marriages such as a man marrying his sister or his aunt. But even in cases of adultery, Jesus would have urged forgiveness and healing.

- **If the husband or wife who isn't a believer insists on leaving, let them go. In such cases the Christian husband or wife is no longer bound to the other** (1 Corinthians 7:15). Paul is dealing with a problem Jesus didn't address: believers married to nonbelievers. Offering his opinion and admitting, "I do not have a direct command from the Lord," Paul advises Christians to let the non-Christians go if they want out of the marriage. Paul considers the agreement between God and his people more important than any marriage agreement. We aren't to compromise our faith to save our marriage.

When it's not allowed

- **If a Christian man has a wife who is not a believer and she is willing to continue living with him, he must not leave her. And if a Christian woman has a husband who is not a believer and he is willing to continue living with her, she must not leave** him (1 Corinthians 7:12–13). Paul explains that by staying, the Christian might be able to convert the spouse and raise Christian children.

See also *Marriage*

DOUBT

- "Is anything too hard for the LORD?" (Genesis 18:14). This is God's response to 90-year-old Sarah, laughing at news that she would have a son.

- If you need wisdom, ask our generous God. . . . But when you ask him, be sure that your faith is in God alone. . . . For a person with divided loyalty is as unsettled as a wave of the sea that is blown and tossed by the wind. Such people should not expect to receive anything from the Lord. Their loyalty is divided between God and the world, and they are unstable in everything they do (James 1:5–8).

See also *Faith*

DRINKING AND DRUGS

Some people in Bible times abused drugs, just as many folks do today. The drug of choice back then was alcohol—mainly wine in Israel, where vineyards flourished. The Bible talks about wine as both a blessing and a curse—and sometimes as part of the reason for crime, violent behavior, and injustice. Still, it's tough to argue from the Bible that Christians shouldn't drink alcoholic beverages when Jesus' first miracle was turning water into wine (John 2) and when he drank wine himself (Matthew 11:19; Mark 14:23). Even children sometimes drank watered-down wine because alcohol killed bacteria and parasites in the water, making it safer than plain water. That doesn't mean young people today should drink alcohol. For one thing, there are safer alternatives. And for another, our country has laws against underage drinking, and the Bible tells Christians to obey the laws of the land (Romans 13:1–2). Though the Bible allows for some drinking, it raises a bunch of warnings. And it has nothing good to say about getting drunk or addicted.

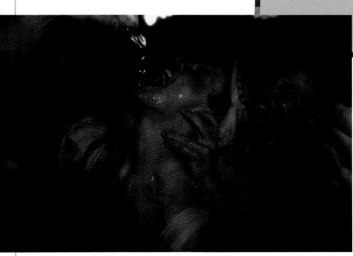

Just say "Ah-h-h."

College students at State University of New York in Albany chug beer at a party. Binge drinking, a popular pastime among college students, contributes to the about 1,700 deaths and half a million injuries among students each year, according to a federally funded study published in the *Annual Review of Public Health*. Info link: collegedrinkingprevention.gov.

The troubles it causes

- **Wine makes you mean, beer makes you quarrelsome—a staggering drunk is not much fun** (Proverbs 20:1 THE MESSAGE).
- **Who are the people who are always crying the blues? Who do you know who reeks of self-pity? Who keeps getting beat up for no reason at all? Whose eyes are bleary and blood-shot? It's those who spend the night with a bottle, for whom drinking is serious business. Don't judge wine by its label, or its bouquet, or its full-bodied flavor. Judge it rather by the hangover it leaves you with— the splitting headache, the queasy stomach. Do you really prefer seeing double, with your speech all slurred, reeling and seasick, drunk as a sailor?** (Proverbs 23:29–34 THE MESSAGE).
- **Don't be drunk with wine, because that will ruin your life. Instead, be filled with the Holy Spirit** (Ephesians 5:18).
- **Rulers should not crave alcohol. For if they drink, they may forget the law and not give justice to the oppressed** (Proverbs 31:4–5).

Don't party too hearty

- **Everyone must submit to governing authorities. For all authority comes from God, and those in positions of authority have been placed there by God. So anyone who rebels against authority is rebelling against what God has instituted** (Romans 13:1–2). Underage drinking is illegal. And God expects us to obey the law.
- **We must live decent lives for all to see. Don't participate in the dark-ness of wild parties and drunkeness** (Romans 13:13).
- **It is better not to eat meat or drink wine or do anything else if it might cause another believer to stumble. You may believe there's nothing wrong with what you are doing, but keep it between yourself and God** (Romans 14:21–22). This doesn't mean that Christian adults of legal drinking age should abstain from alcohol just because others feel it's wrong. But a sensitive Christian wouldn't knowingly drink in front of a person who feels uncomfortable with drinking—and certainly not in front of a recovering alcoholic.
- **You say, "I am allowed to do any-thing"—but not everything is good for you. And even though "I am al-lowed to do anything," I must not become a slave to anything** (1 Corinthians 6:12).

Famous Bible drinkers and nondrinkers

- **Noah began to cultivate the ground, and he planted a vineyard. One day he drank some wine he had made, and he became drunk and lay naked inside his tent** (Genesis 9:20–21). Not one of his shining moments.
- **Go ahead and drink a little wine, for instance; it's good for your diges-tion, good medicine for what ails you** (1 Timothy 5:23 THE MESSAGE). Paul's advice to Pastor Timothy, who was having stomach problems.
- **"If any of you, man or woman, wants to make a special Nazirite vow, consecrating yourself totally to GOD, you must not drink any wine or beer, no intoxicating drink of any kind"** (Numbers 6:2–3 THE MESSAGE). Strongman Samson and the prophet Samuel were both lifetime Nazirites. Others, such as the apostle Paul, took the Nazirite vow for a short time—much like

many Christians today who give up something for Lent as a way of honoring Christ.

- **They gave Jesus some wine mixed with a drug to ease the pain. But when Jesus tasted what it was, he refused to drink it** (Matthew 27:34 CEV). Even during the crucifixion, Jesus apparently wanted a clear head. So he refused a painkiller commonly given to victims of this lingering method of execution.

See also *Addiction*

The dilemma. Good for the heart, bad for the soul? Many doctors say red wine in moderation can be good for the cardiovascular system—when you're old enough to drink it. But many Christians argue that it's better to avoid it because alcoholic beverages tag team with some destructive behaviors: drunk driving, eroded sexual inhibition, addiction.

WHY SOME CHRISTIANS DON'T DRINK ALCOHOL

Researchers today say that a drink of red wine every day or two, for some people, can help prevent heart disease and improve digestion. The health benefits weren't news in ancient times. Even the apostle Paul told his friend, a pastor named Timothy, "Don't drink only water. You ought to drink a little wine for the sake of your stomach because you are sick so often" (1 Timothy 5:23).

In spite of any possible health benefits, some Christians adamantly refuse to drink alcohol—for a variety of reasons.

Some Christians don't drink because they were raised on preaching that said it was always wrong and that incorrectly insisted that wine in Bible times didn't have a kick—that it was grape juice. Grapes were harvested in the August heat of a desert region. They started to ferment right away. The wine kicked, all right. Exceptions were new wine freshly pressed, or fresh grape juice boiled—which stopped the fermenting process.

Other Christians avoid alcohol for different reasons.

Health risks. Some researchers aren't sure if the benefits of even mild drinking outweigh the risks, which can include high blood pressure, diseased livers, and injury caused by drowsiness. And there is new evidence suggesting that red grapes and grape juice may offer the same benefit for the heart as red wine does.

Family addicts. Many Christians have noticed that their extended family includes several alcoholics or drug addicts. So they conclude that they may have a genetic code that raises their risk of slipping into alcoholism once they start down that path. Wisely, they decide not to go there.

Drunk drivers. Most people who drive after taking a couple of drinks genuinely think they can handle the highway. Christians don't want to be counted among those believers.

EDUCATION

Even in a culture where few people could read or write, the Bible was already promoting the value of a good education.

- **Gold there is, and rubies in abundance, but lips that speak knowledge are a rare jewel** (Proverbs 20:15 NIV).
- **The instruction of the wise is like a life-giving fountain; those who accept it avoid the snares of death** (Proverbs 13:14).
- **He [Apollos] refuted the Jews with powerful arguments in public debate. Using the Scriptures, he explained to them that Jesus was the Messiah** (Acts 18:28).
- **One day as he saw the crowds gathering, Jesus went up on the mountainside and sat down. His disciples gathered around him, and he began to teach them** (Matthew 5:1–2). What follows is the most famous lecture in history: the Sermon on the Mount. Teaching was a big part of Jesus' ministry.

The sea gives up its dead.

Heavenbound, a family rises from the ocean waters, along with the corpses of other godly people lost at sea. The painting is from a vision at the end of the Bible: "The sea gave up its dead, and death and the grave gave up their dead. And all were judged according to their deeds" (Revelation 20:13).

ETERNAL LIFE

Our bodies aren't built to last forever, but our spirits inside those bodies certainly are. The Bible promises that those who die with faith in Jesus will inherit resurrection bodies—perhaps like the body of Jesus after his resurrection. He could walk, talk, and eat. But he could also suddenly appear and disappear and even levitate.

Resurrection bodies
- **Our earthly bodies are planted in the ground when we die, but they will be raised to live forever** (1 Corinthians 15:42).
- **Jesus himself was suddenly standing there among them** [the disciples after Jesus' resurrection]. **"Peace be with you," he said. But the whole**

group was startled and frightened, thinking they were seeing a ghost! "Why are you frightened?" he asked. . . . "Touch me and make sure that I am not a ghost." . . . Then he asked them, "Do you have anything here to eat?" They gave him a piece of broiled fish, and he ate it as they watched (Luke 24:36–43).

Who will live forever?

- "I tell you the truth, those who listen to my message and believe in God who sent me have eternal life. They will never be condemned for their sins, but they have already passed from death into life" (John 5:24). For believers, eternal life has already started.

- "God loved the world so much that he gave his one and only Son, so that everyone who believes in him will not perish but have eternal life" (John 3:16).

- Keep thinking about the message you first heard, and you will always be one in your heart with the Son and with the Father. The Son has promised us eternal life (1 John 2:24–25 CEV).

- "Many of those whose bodies lie dead and buried will rise up, some to everlasting life and some to shame and everlasting disgrace" (Daniel 12:2). Written just a few hundred years before Jesus, this is the first clear reference in the Old Testament to a resurrection and eternal life. Most people in earlier days apparently didn't realize that their souls were built to last forever. But the archangel Michael revealed this insight to the prophet Daniel.

EVOLUTION

The Bible says God created everything that exists. But it doesn't say how, answering only the question of *who*. Some Christians interpret the Genesis version of a six-day creation literally. Others take it figuratively, arguing that it wasn't until the fourth day that God created the sun and moon—which are essential for measuring a day as we know it. For many Christians, "day" simply means some span of time, which could stretch for eons.

- A day is like a thousand years to the Lord, and a thousand years is like a day (2 Peter 3:8).

- In the beginning God created the heavens and the earth (Genesis 1:1).

- In the beginning the Word already existed. The Word was with God, and the Word was God. He existed in the beginning with God. God created everything through him, and nothing was created except though him (John 1:1–3). The Word means Jesus—God's message delivered in the flesh.

- Through him [Christ] God created everything in the heavenly realms and on earth. . . . Everything was created through him and for him. He existed before anything else, and he holds all creation together (Colossians 1:16–17).

- Don't let anyone capture you with empty philosophies and high-sounding nonsense that come from human thinking (Colossians 2:8). The theory of evolution is just that— a theory, though one that's widely accepted among scientists. Many

Christians are repulsed by the idea that they evolved from primordial slime. Others see no serious problem with evolution, arguing that at some point in human development God "breathed into his nostrils the breath of life; and man became a living soul" (Genesis 2:7 KJV).

EXPLOITATION

- A final word to you arrogant rich.... Your money is corrupt and your fine clothes stink.... You thought you were piling up wealth. What you've piled up is judgment. All the workers you've exploited and cheated cry out for judgment. The groans of the workers you used and abused are a roar in the ears of the Master Avenger. You've looted the earth and lived it up. But all you'll have to show for it is a fatter than usual corpse (James 5:1–5 THE MESSAGE).
- "You have ruined Israel, my vineyard. Your houses are filled with things stolen from the poor. How dare you crush my people, grinding the faces of the poor into the dust?" demands the Lord (Isaiah 3:14–15).
- "Do not oppress widows, orphans, foreigners, and the poor" (Zechariah 7:10).
- The LORD demands accurate scales and balances; he sets the standards for fairness (Proverbs 16:11).
- I tried to understand why the wicked prosper. But what a difficult task it is! Then I went into your sanctuary, O God, and I finally understood the destiny of the wicked. Truly, you put them on a slippery path and send them sliding over the cliff to destruction (Psalm 73:16–18).

See also *Abuse*

FAITH

Faith is another word for trust. In the Bible it usually refers to trust in God. This trust in God grows a bit like the trust we develop with our closest friends. Over time, our friends prove they are worthy of our trust. God does the same.

The Bible's definition
- Faith means being sure of the things we hope for and knowing that something is real even if we do not see it (Hebrews 11:1 NCV). This is the Bible's classic definition of faith.

Putting faith to work
- Faith by itself isn't enough. Unless it produces good deeds, it is dead and useless (James 2:17). People who have faith in God show it by their actions—by doing what God says, such as helping the poor and doing the best they can to live honorable lives.
- "If you had faith even as small as a mustard seed, you could say to this mountain, 'Move from here to there,' and it would move. Nothing would be impossible" (Matthew 17:20). Jesus is using exaggeration to make his point that it's important to trust in God's power. He's not saying it's mind over matter and that we can get anything we want if we believe enough. It's God who does the giving. We do the asking—and we ask for his will, not ours. Jesus did the same thing on the night of his arrest: "My Father! If it is possible, let this cup of suffering be taken away from me. Yet I want your will to be done, not mine" (Matthew 26:39).

Faith leads to salvation

- **You cannot make God accept you because of something you do. God accepts sinners only because they have faith in him** (Romans 4:5 CEV). We don't earn our salvation by doing good deeds for others. Salvation is God's gift for trusting in him. The writer was referring to Abraham, the father of the Jews and the Bible's most famous man of faith: "Abram believed the LORD, and the LORD counted him as righteous because of his faith" (Genesis 15:6).

- **The people of Israel, who tried so hard to get right with God by keeping the law, never succeeded. Why not? Because they were trying to get right with God by keeping the law instead of by trusting in him** (Romans 9:31–32).

FAITH MAKES MIRACLES HAPPEN

Jesus said the greatest faith he ever saw in all of Israel was from a Roman officer.

The soldier asked Jesus to heal his young servant. When Jesus agreed to go to the soldier's house, the man replied, "Just say the word from where you are, and my servant will be healed" (Matthew 8:8). Jesus healed the servant right then—from a distance.

Faith played a critical role in some of the miracles Jesus performed. One woman worked her way through a crowd and touched Jesus' robe, hoping the touch would heal her from the excessive menstrual bleeding that she had suffered for a dozen years. Jesus turned to her and said, "Your faith has made you well" (Matthew 9:22).

Sometimes, lack of faith limited what Jesus did. When he returned to his hometown of Nazareth, most people saw only the grown-up son of a carpenter. They couldn't accept him as the Messiah. "So he did only a few miracles there because of their unbelief" (Matthew 13:58).

A spoonful of faith. Mustard seeds are some of the smallest garden seeds around. At a millimeter in diameter, a mustard seed is no thicker than the edge of a worn-out dime. But Jesus said a speck of faith can move mountains. Yet Jesus matched his faith to his Father's will—which is what faith really is: trusting God.

FAMILY

The Bible says surprisingly little about how to raise a family. In fact, most families that the Bible describes in detail were troubled—with problems ranging from petty rivalries to adultery, incest, and murder.

Honor, obey your parents

- **"Respect your father and your mother"** (Exodus 20:12 CEV). This is one of the 10 Commandments—a fundamental rule for God's people.
- **Children must always obey their parents. This pleases the Lord** (Colossians 3:20 CEV). "Always" presumes that the parents are asking their children to do things that please the Lord.
- **Jesus** [twelve years old] **went back to Nazareth with his parents and obeyed them** (Luke 2:51 CEV).

Earn the respect of your children

- **Parents, don't be hard on your children. If you are, they might give up** (Colossians 3:21 CEV).
- **Church officials must be in control of their own families, and they must see that their children are obedient and always respectful. If they don't know how to control their own families, how can they look after God's people?** (1 Timothy 3:4–5 CEV). Unmarried Paul wrote this advice to Pastor Timothy, without adding qualifiers that many parents would like to see. Most parents agree that they shouldn't let their young children walk all over them and over others. But there's a limit to how much control parents can exert over their children—especially during the teen and young adult years. Parents can't always be held responsible for the dumb decisions their kids make. After all, we adults don't hold God responsible for the dumb decisions that we make.

Don't cause trouble for your family

- **Those who bring trouble on their families inherit the wind** (Proverbs 11:29). As a general rule, if we make life miserable for our family, we shouldn't expect much from them when we need it.

Take care of each other

- **If a widow has children or grandchildren, they should learn to serve God by taking care of her, as she once took care of them. This is what God wants them to do. . . . People who don't take care of their relatives, and especially their own families, have given up their faith. They are worse than someone who doesn't have faith in the Lord** (1 Timothy 5:4, 8 CEV). In Bible times, there was no Social Security, Medicare, or private insurance policies covering assisted living for the elderly. Christian families looked out for each other.

See also *Marriage; Parents*

FEAR

- "Don't be afraid, because the LORD your God will be with you every-where you go" (Joshua 1:9 NCV).
- "Don't be afraid of those who want to kill your body; they cannot touch your soul. Fear only God, who can destroy both soul and body in hell" (Matthew 10:28).
- God is our protection and our strength. He always helps in times of trouble. So we will not be afraid even if the earth shakes, or the mountains fall into the sea (Psalm 46:1–2 NCV).
- Fearing people is a dangerous trap, but trusting the LORD means safety (Proverbs 29:25).

FELLOWSHIP

- "Where two or three gather to-gether as my followers, I am there among them" (Matthew 18:20).
- They were like family to each other. . . . They broke bread together in dif-ferent homes and shared their food happily and freely (Acts 2:42, 46 CEV). This is a description of the early church, shortly after Jesus returned to heaven and the disciples began preaching about him in Jerusalem.
- Dear friend, when you extend hos-pitality to Christian brothers and sisters, even when they are strang-ers, you make the faith visible (3 John 1:5 THE MESSAGE).

See also *Friendship*

FORGIVENESS

Forgiveness works two ways in the Bible. God forgives us, but we're supposed to forgive each other, too.

Forgiveness from God

- "Though your sins are like scarlet, I will make them as white as snow. Though they are red like crimson, I will make them as white as wool" (Isaiah 1:18).
- If we confess our sins to God, he can always be trusted to forgive us and take our sins away (1 John 1:9 CEV).
- "Through this man Jesus there is forgiveness for your sins. Everyone who believes in him is declared right with God" (Acts 13:38–39).
- He has taken our sins away from us as far as the east is from west (Psalm 103:12 NCV).

Forgiving each other

- "If you forgive those who sin against you, your heavenly Father will forgive you. But if you refuse to forgive others, your Father will not forgive your sins" (Matthew 6:14–15). It's unthinkable, Jesus says, that his followers would have the nerve to ask God for forgiveness but would not forgive people who sinned against them. That's hypocrisy. Cer-tainly, Jesus understands that some sins are harder to forgive than others. But forgiving those people should be our goal. It's self-destructive to hang on to bitter feelings.
- Peter came to Jesus and asked, "Lord, when my fellow believer sins against me, how many times must I forgive him? Should I forgive him

as many as seven times?" Jesus answered, "I tell you, you must forgive him more than seven times. You must forgive him even if he wrongs you seventy times seven" (Matthew 18:21–22 NCV). This is a metaphor. Jesus' point: we should never stop forgiving. Even after sin number 490.

- **Make allowance for each other's faults, and forgive anyone who offends you. Remember, the Lord forgave you, so you must forgive others** (Colossians 3:13).

FRIENDSHIP

Our best friends, the Bible teaches, are the people who stay with us when everyone else leaves.

- **A friend loves you all the time** (Proverbs 17:17 NCV).
- **Some friends may ruin you, but a real friend will be more loyal than a brother** (Proverbs 18:24 NCV).
- **Wounds from a sincere friend are better than many kisses from an enemy** (Proverbs 27:6). True friends tell us the truth, even when it hurts us. But people who don't care about us tell us whatever we want to hear—if it benefits them.
- **I choose as my friends everyone who worships you and follows your teachings** (Psalm 119:63 CEV).
- **My enemies are not the ones who sneer and make fun. I could put up with that. . . . But it was my closest friend, the one I trusted most** (Psalm 55:12–13 CEV).
- **Jonathan thought as much of David as he did of himself, so he asked**

How to spot a real friend. Some people we hang out with are just acquaintances who stick with us only in the good times. A true friend, the Bible says, sticks with us no matter what—whether we're sad, mad, or bad. And in the process, they'll tell us the truth instead of feeding us a line.

David to promise once more that he would be a loyal friend (1 Samuel 20:17 CEV). In words and actions, David and Jonathan are a great example of what it means to be best friends. Prince Jonathan even protected David from Jonathan's father, King Saul.

GAMBLING

The Bible doesn't condemn gambling, but in those rare instances when gambling shows up, the scene turns violent. Many Christians oppose gambling because they don't like what they've seen it do to people. It can become addictive. It tends to exploit the poor who desperately want to break out of their poverty. And it encourages greed.

Bible gamblers
- "Let's make a bet: I'll tell you a riddle, and if you can tell me the right answer before the party is over, I'll give each one of you a shirt and a full change of clothing" (Judges 14:12 CEV). That's Samson betting the Philistine guests at his wedding that they can't solve his riddle. They threaten Samson's bride into nagging the answer out of him. Samson gets so angry that he leaves his wife and then kills Philistines in a neighboring city to steal their clothes and pay off his debt.
- "We will gamble to see who gets it" (John 19:24 CEV). Roman soldiers gambled to see who would get the robe of their crucifixion victim, Jesus.

Bible principles against gambling
- Wealth from get-rich-quick schemes quickly disappears (Proverbs 13:11). The Bible's prescription

for getting ahead in the world is to work hard. Or as one wise writer put it: "Take a lesson from the ants, you lazybones" (Proverbs 6:6).
- "Do not want anything that belongs to someone else" (Exodus 20:17 CEV). This is one of the 10 Commandments.
See also *Addiction*

GOALS

- Most people are motivated to success because they envy their neighbors (Ecclesiastes 4:4). This isn't a recommendation, but a sad observation.
- I do not mean that I am already as God wants me to be. I have not yet reached that goal, but I continue trying to reach it and to make it mine (Philippians 3:12 NCV).
- "Whoever wants to be a leader among you must be your servant, and whoever wants to be first among you must be the slave of everyone else" (Mark 10:43–44).
- So I run with purpose in every step (1 Corinthians 9:26). Paul is talking about the "eternal prize" that awaits us for persevering in the Christian faith.

GOD

The first of three persons in the Trinity: Father, Son, and Holy Spirit.

What God is like

- **God is love** (1 John 4:8).
- **"Is anything too hard for the LORD?"** (Genesis 18:14). That's what God said after Sarah laughed when she heard God say that she and Abraham would soon have a son. Sarah was age 90 at the time. Abraham was almost 100.
- **"I AM WHO I AM." . . . This is my eternal name"** (Exodus 3:14–15). God's reply when Moses asked for God's name.
- **I am everywhere—both near and far, in heaven and on earth** (Jeremiah 23:23–24 CEV).
- **"No other god is like you. We're safer with you than on a high mountain"** (1 Samuel 2:2 CEV).
- **God's way is perfect. All the LORD's promises prove true. He is a shield for all who look to him for protection** (Psalm 18:30).

What God wants from us

- **"This is what the LORD your God wants you to do: Respect the LORD your God, and do what he has told you to do. Love him. Serve the LORD your God with your whole being"** (Deuteronomy 10:12 NCV).
- **"Worship no other gods, for the LORD. . . is a God who is jealous about his relationship with you"** (Exodus 34:14).
- **"Don't desecrate my holy name. I insist on being treated with holy reverence"** (Leviticus 22:32 THE MESSAGE).

See also *Jesus Christ; Holy Spirit*

HOW CAN THREE GODS BE ONE GOD?

The Bible does strange math.

It says there's just one God: "GOD the one and only!" (Deuteronomy 6:4 THE MESSAGE). Then along comes his Son, Jesus Christ, who says, "The Father and I are one" (John 10:30).

That's one plus one equals one. Then when Jesus leaves, the Holy Spirit arrives. And one plus one plus one still equals one.

How's that possible?

Even Jesus didn't try to explain it. Perhaps he knew that we physics-bound humans couldn't possibly understand.

But we've tried. For centuries, Bible scholars debated the relationship between God the Father, Son, and Holy Spirit. Some said there was just one God and that Jesus was God on earth and the Holy Spirit is God at work in the world.

Yet Jesus prayed to his Father. Jesus also spoke of the deities as though they're distinct—for he told his disciples to baptize converts "in the name of the Father and the Son and the Holy Spirit" (Matthew 28:19).

Scholars, for the most part, gave up trying to figure out the Trinity in the AD 400s. That's when a theologian named Augustine summed up the scholarly consensus: "The Father is God, the Son is God, the Holy Spirit is God. . . yet we do not say that there are three gods, but one God, the most exalted Trinity."

They couldn't explain it. But they decided to believe it anyway because it's in the Bible.

GOSSIP

Gossip is a favorite pastime for many people—even in the church. But the Bible has nothing good to say about it.

- **They. . .get into the habit of going from house to house. Next, they will start gossiping and become busybodies, talking about things that are none of their business** (1 Timothy 5:13 CEV). The apostle Paul is warning Timothy, pastor of a church, about how people who have nothing to do often tend to fill their idle time with gossip.
- **"Do not spread slanderous gossip"** (Leviticus 19:16).
- **"Don't spread harmful rumors"** (Exodus 23:1 CEV).
- **Gossip separates the best of friends** (Proverbs 16:28).
- **Remind the believers to. . .speak no evil about anyone, to live in peace, and to be gentle and polite to all people** (Titus 3:1–2 NCV).
- **Take control of what I say, O LORD, and guard my lips** (Psalm 141:3).

GRACE

Grace is a word describing kindness or mercy that's undeserved. In the Bible it usually refers to God's mercy toward sinful people. Grace is God loving us where we are, but not being willing to leave us there. He loves us even while we're enslaved by sin, but he's working to set us free. Salvation that Christians experience is because of God's grace.

- **Sin is no longer your master. . . . Instead, you live under the freedom of God's grace** (Romans 6:14).
- **"I will now have mercy on you through my grace"** (Isaiah 60:10).
- **"My grace is all you need. My power works best in weakness"** (2 Corinthians 12:9). This is a promise Jesus gave to the apostle Paul when Paul was struggling with an undisclosed, humiliating personal problem.
- **May God our Father and the Lord Jesus Christ give you grace and peace** (Romans 1:7). This was a common prayerful greeting among early Christians.

Out of proportion.

Gossip is the art of telling all we know and more. The Bible portrays it as a disease. And the cure is a cork: "Stop. . . spreading vicious rumors!" (Isaiah 58:9).

GRUDGES

- "Do not seek revenge or bear a grudge against a fellow Israelite, but love your neighbor as yourself" (Leviticus 19:18).
- Stop being bitter and angry and mad at others (Ephesians 4:31 CEV).
- Don't go to bed angry (Ephesians 4:26 CEV).

See also *Anger; Revenge*

GUILT

- "There is no one who always does what is right, not even one" (Romans 3:10 NCV).
- "Through this man Jesus there is forgiveness for your sins. Everyone who believes in him is declared right with God" (Acts 13:38–39).
- If we confess our sins, he will forgive our sins, because we can trust God to do what is right. He will cleanse us from all the wrongs we have done (1 John 1:9 NCV).
- Clean the slate, God. . . . Then I can start this day sun-washed, scrubbed clean of the grime of sin (Psalm 19:13 THE MESSAGE).
- Purify me from my sins, and I will be clean; wash me, and I will be whiter than snow. . . . Don't keep looking at my sins. Remove the stain of my guilt. Create in me a clean heart, O God (Psalm 51:7–10).

See also *Confession; Forgiveness*

HAPPINESS

- Children with good sense make their parents happy, but foolish children make them sad (Proverbs 10:1 CEV).
- If you obey and do right, a light will show you the way and fill you with happiness (Psalm 97:11 CEV).
- "God blesses those who hunger and thirst for justice, for they will be satisfied" (Matthew 5:6). This is Jesus in his Sermon on the Mount, teaching the Beatitudes—sometimes called the "Be Happy" Attitudes.
- If we please God, he will make us wise, understanding, and happy. But if we sin, God will make us struggle for a living, then he will give all we own to someone who pleases him (Ecclesiastes 2:26 CEV).

HATE

- Better a bread crust shared in love than a slab of prime rib served in hate (Proverbs 15:17 THE MESSAGE).
- "You have heard the law that says, 'Love your neighbor' and hate your enemy. But I say, love your enemies! Pray for those who persecute you! . . . If you love only those who love you, what reward is there for that? . . . Even pagans do that" (Matthew 5:43–47).
- People may cover their hatred with pleasant words, but they're deceiving you. They pretend to be kind, but don't believe them. Their hearts are full of many evils. While their hatred may be concealed by trickery, their wrongdoing will be exposed in public (Proverbs 26:24–26).
- My enemies are strong and healthy, and many hate me for no reason. They repay me with evil for the good I did. They lie about me because I try to do good. Lord, don't leave me; my God, don't go away. Quickly come and help me, my Lord and Savior (Psalm 38:19–22 NCV).

HEAVEN

When John described heaven, after seeing it in a vision reported in the last book of the Bible—Revelation—he spoke of pearl gates, golden streets, and jasper walls. But most scholars say these are just symbols—that John was using the most precious objects on earth to describe the indescribable majesty of an eternal and spiritual dimension that shatters the boundaries of understanding in this physical world.

- "There is more than enough room in my Father's home. If this were not so, would I have told you that I am going to prepare a place for you? When everything is ready, I will come and get you, so that you will always be with me where I am" (John 14:2–3). Hours before Jesus is arrested, he comforts his disciples by promising that they will live forever with him in heaven.

- I saw the holy city, the new Jerusalem, coming down from God out

Out of this world. Radiant with light, quasars form at the center of galaxies, and are built of star clusters, stardust, and sheets of gas. This artist's impression shows how quasars—which scientists say are supermassive black holes—may have looked in the early days of the universe. Christians have looked to the skies for heaven ever since Jesus ascended after his resurrection. Some say heaven is a physical place that God will one day set up on earth. Others speculate that it's a super-physical dimension, blending the best of two worlds—physical and spiritual. The Bible is clear about this: it's the home of God and his people forever. "There will be no night there—no need for lamps or sun-for the Lord God will shine on them. And they will reign forever and ever" (Revelation 22:5).

of heaven like a bride beautifully dressed for her husband. I heard a loud shout from the throne, saying, "Look, God's home is now among his people! He will live with them, and they will be his people. God himself will be with them. He will wipe every tear from their eyes, and there will be no more death or sorrow or crying or pain. All these things are gone forever" (Revelation 21:2–4). Wherever heaven is, or whatever it's like, heartache and death don't exist there. But God does.

• The City shimmered like a precious gem, light-filled, pulsing light. . . . The twelve gates were twelve pearls, each gate a single pearl. The main street of the City was pure gold, translucent as glass. . . . The City doesn't need sun or moon for light. God's Glory is its light, the Lamb its lamp! . . . Nothing dirty or defiled will get into the City, and no one who defiles or deceives. Only those whose names are written in the Lamb's Book of Life will get in (Revelation 21:12–27 THE MESSAGE). An excerpt from John's description of heaven.

• "Look down from your holy dwelling place in heaven and bless your people Israel" (Deuteronomy 26:15). From the beginning of Jewish history, people believed that God lived somewhere in the heavens. Yet some Christians say that the Bible's description of heaven suggests that it doesn't have a galactic address but that it exists in a nonphysical, spiritual dimension.

HELL

Christians can't agree on how literally to take the Bible's teaching about hell.

• "In hell. . .the fire is never put out. Every person will be salted with fire" (Mark 9:48–49 NCV). Jesus is warning people about the reality of hell.

Hell's guest. The ghost of Roman poet Virgil, left, leads Italian nobleman Dante on a tour of hell. Dante wrote about this fictional journey in the late 1200s, in a story called *The Divine Comedy.* In Dante's version of hell, demons dump sinners into designated zones. Angry souls land in the zone of wrath where they fight each other forever.

- **"Don't be afraid of those who want to kill your body; they cannot touch your soul. Fear only God, who can destroy both soul and body in hell"** (Matthew 10:28). A "destroyed soul" suggests to some that hell means eternal death, not eternal torment.
- **"You're good for nothing but the fires of hell"** (Matthew 25:41 THE MESSAGE). With a parable about a king separating goats from sheep, Jesus says—with perhaps only a bit of exaggeration—that hell is the destiny of people who refuse to help the poor. God will cut them from the herd that's headed for heaven.

Home for fallen angels

- **God did not have pity on the angels that sinned. He had them tied up and thrown into the dark pits of hell until the time of judgment** (2 Peter 2:4 CEV).
- **Then the devil. . .was thrown into the fiery lake of burning sulfur, joining the beast and the false prophet. There they will be tormented day and night forever and ever** (Revelation 20:10).

IS HELL A REAL PLACE?

Hell has an address. We can actually send mail there, if we take the original language of the Bible literally.

Hell is the English translation of *Gehenna*, which is a valley outside the walled city of Jerusalem. For some reason, this valley became a symbol of God's judgment—and no one is sure why. Perhaps it's because this is where the Bible says Jews sacrificed their children to idols—a sin God eventually punished by deporting the Jews from their homeland. Or maybe the Jews used the valley as a dump, to burn their ever-smoldering garbage. But somewhere along the way this valley became a symbol of God's judgment—just as September 11, 2001, came to symbolize terrorism.

Bible experts have many theories about hell. That's partly because of the mysterious symbolism behind the word *hell*. And it's partly because of the confusing descriptions of this place—sometimes called "dark" and other times called a place brightened by "fire."

- *Physical fire.* It's a real place where souls suffer forever in fire.
- *Separation from God.* God wouldn't torture someone forever. When he punishes someone in the Bible, it's with the good intention of helping people—even if he strikes someone dead as an object lesson to show others that sin leads to death. Eternal torture, however, seems to serve no redemptive purpose. For this reason, some say, hell is more likely a place where sinners are separated from God. In life, they had wanted nothing to do with him. And in death, he grants their wish.
- *Eternal death.* Fires of hell refer to annihilation. It's not the torture that lasts forever; it's the punishment. Since fire destroys what it touches, this is a symbolic way of saying God destroys sinners.
- *Everyone will be saved.* God keeps reaching out to sinners, even in the next life. He keeps them alive, not to punish them but to reconcile with them. Through Jesus "God reconciled everything to himself. He made peace with everything in heaven and on earth by means of Christ's blood on the cross" (Colossians 1:19–20). Reconciliation with everyone can't happen, some say, if there are people in hell. Most Christians, however, call this heresy. They say the Bible teaches that our eternal destiny is determined in this life.

HOLINESS

- **God called us to be holy and does not want us to live in sin** (1 Thessalonians 4:7 NCV).
- **You were taught to be made new in your hearts, to become a new person. That new person is made to be like God—made to be truly good and holy. So you must stop telling lies. . . . Those who are stealing must stop stealing and start working. . . . Never do anything evil. Be kind and loving to each other, and forgive each other just as God forgave you in Christ** (Ephesians 4:23–32 NCV).
- **"Make them holy by your truth"** (John 17:17). Jesus' prayer for his disciples.
- **May the God of peace make you holy in every way, and may your whole spirit and soul and body be kept blameless until our Lord Jesus Christ comes again. God, who calls you, will make this happen, for he is faithful** (1 Thessalonians 5:23–24). Drawing from passages like this, some churches teach that after we are saved we can experience a deeper work of God. In that second work, God defeats sin's power over us and changes our spiritual programming—getting rid of our tendency to sin. Some call this "entire sanctification" and say that it opens the door to holiness in this lifetime. But others say we can't be perfectly holy in this lifetime.
- **Now you are free from the power of sin and have become slaves of God. Now you do those things that lead to holiness and result in eternal life** (Romans 6:22).
- **You are citizens along with all of God's holy people. You are members of God's family** (Ephesians 2:19).
- **"Who will not fear you, Lord, and glorify your name? For you alone are holy"** (Revelation 15:4).

See also *Sin*

HOLY SPIRIT

The Holy Spirit is the third person of the Trinity, along with God the Father and God the Son. In the Old Testament, it's hard to tell the difference between God the Father and God the Holy Spirit. Their names usually seem woven together: "Spirit of God." Back then, the Holy Spirit was sent to empower only key spiritual leaders, such as kings like David: "The Spirit of the LORD came powerfully upon David" (1 Samuel 16:13). But the prophets quoted God as promising that one day "I will pour out my Spirit upon all people" (Joel 2:28). The New Testament teaches that this time came after the resurrection and ascension of Jesus.

- **"I will ask the Father, and he will give you another Helper to be with you forever—the Spirit of truth. The world cannot accept him, because it does not see him or know him. But you know him, because he lives with you and he will be in you"** (John 14:16–17 NCV).
- **The Holy Spirit produces this kind of fruit in our lives: love, joy, peace, patience, kindness, goodness, faithfulness, gentleness, and self-control** (Galatians 5:22–23).
- **You are not ruled by your sinful selves. You are ruled by the Spirit, if that Spirit of God really lives in you. . . . If you use your lives to do the wrong things your sinful selves want, you will die spiritually. But if**

you use the Spirit's help to stop doing the wrong things you do with your body, you will have true life (Romans 8:9, 13 NCV).

- "The Holy Spirit comes and fills you with power from heaven" (Luke 24:49).
- There are different kinds of spiritual gifts, but the same Spirit is the source of them all (1 Corinthians 12:4).

See also *God; Jesus Christ*

HOW CAN HUMANS BE HOLY WHEN WE'RE ONLY HUMAN?

"You must. . .be holy, because I am holy" (Leviticus 11:44).

God said that to the Jews.

Jesus said much the same thing to his followers: "You are to be perfect, even as your Father in heaven is perfect" (Matthew 5:48).

Scholars are still trying to figure out what that means. The problem is that like the rest of us, they know we humans tend not to be perfectly behaved unless we're unconscious.

One theory is that holiness and perfection are the goal of a lifetime—that we should try to follow the example of Jesus, especially in matters of loving others since that's the context of Jesus' statement. It's as though Jesus is saying: "You know right from wrong; now act like it. I know it takes time to learn how to love your neighbor and especially your enemy. But practice makes perfect."

Another theory is that God and Jesus weren't talking mainly about perfect behavior, but about complete devotion to God. When a temple utensil, such as a bowl, was dedicated for use only in service to God, it was no longer considered common. It was separate and distinct from other bowls, just as God is transcendent and one-of-a-kind. The bowl was holy—devoted completely to God. We, too, are holy when we dedicate ourselves to God. We become a one-of-a-kind people devoted to the one-of-a-kind God.

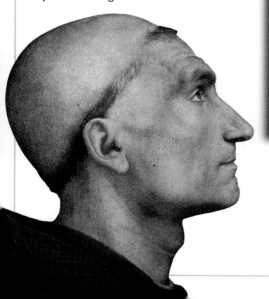

Holy as a monk. Many monks, like Baldassare Vallombrosano shown in this portrait from the 1500s, have tried to achieve holiness by separating themselves from the sinful world. But most Bible experts say there's nothing to achieve—that God's people are holy not because of how they live, but because of who they live for. They've set themselves aside for God's use. And because of that, God considers them his holy people. They'll make mistakes. But for the imperfectly holy, there's forgiveness.

HOMOSEXUALITY

- "Do not practice homosexuality.... It is a detestable sin" (Leviticus 18:22).
- God left them and let them do the shameful things they wanted to do. Women stopped having natural sex and started having sex with other women. In the same way, men stopped having natural sex and began wanting each other (Romans 1:26–27 NCV).

- Those who indulge in sexual sin. . . or commit adultery, or are male prostitutes, or practice homosexuality. . . none of these will inherit the Kingdom of God (1 Corinthians 6:9–10).
- God created humans to be like himself; he made men and women. God gave them his blessing and said: Have a lot of children! (Genesis 1:27–28 CEV). God designed men and women as heterosexuals. Homosexuality is discouraged every time it's mentioned in the Bible.

The Bible tells me so.

People protest the Pope's opposition to homosexuality during his visit to San Francisco. Most Bible experts agree that Jesus loves gay people. They agree, too, that as far as the Bible is concerned there's nothing wrong with having homosexual desires. But most scholars insist that the Bible advises people not to act on those desires—just as the Bible says single heterosexuals shouldn't have sex outside of marriage.

WHAT'S WRONG WITH HOMOSEXUALITY?

Only about half a dozen short Bible passages refer to homosexual behavior. And all of them call it sin.

The Bible doesn't come right out and say what's wrong with the gay lifestyle. But it does describe homosexuality with words that give us a clue—words like "unnatural" and "perversion."

This implies homosexuality is wrong because it's the opposite of what God intended for human sexuality. The creation story reveals that God designed us as heterosexuals. And it's this design that keeps our species alive.

Not all Christians agree that homosexuality is wrong. That's why some churches ordain gay ministers and conduct same-sex marriages.

Here are three key arguments some Christians make, with counterpoints by others.

1. Genetic factors contribute to homosexuality, and it would be unfair of God the Creator to condemn people for doing what he programmed them to do.

COUNTERPOINT

Unmarried heterosexuals face the same challenge. So do alcoholics, who have a genetic predisposition to alcoholic addiction. The only Christian response is abstinence. Jesus and Paul each abstained from sex.

2. Paul wasn't condemning homosexuality, but heterosexuals experimenting with it. That's what he meant by saying they "exchanged natural relations for unnatural ones" (Romans 1:26 NIV).

COUNTERPOINT

Paul was pointing back to the creation story and to all of scripture, which says God intended sex to be shared between a man and a woman.

3. Just as old Jewish laws about kosher food and circumcision became obsolete when Jesus arrived with his message of God's love and mercy, so did legalistic rules about sex.

COUNTERPOINT

New Testament writers declare that the moral laws of the Old Testament—such as those about murder, stealing, and sexual sins—are still in force.

Though most Christians insist that practicing homosexuality is wrong, they stop short of saying it's sinful to have homosexual desires. Sin comes to life when sex is performed outside the boundaries God set up: marriage with a partner of the opposite sex.

Should homosexuals be allowed to join churches and even serve as church leaders? Think of it this way. Substitute "homosexuals" with "greedy people," "liars," or another category of sin—because the Bible describes homosexual behavior as just one of many sins. It doesn't rate sin on a scale of 1 to 10, with homosexuality as a 10 and cheating on a test as a 1.

Based on this kind of reasoning, many Christians answer yes. If the homosexuals are willing to make the same pledge as other sinners in the church—a pledge to allow the teachings of Jesus to mold them into new creatures, which in their case would involve living a disciplined life of abstinence—then they should be welcomed into the church. There, they can sing with the rest of us an old Charles Wesley hymn about a God who "breaks the power of canceled sin; He sets the prisoner free."

That doesn't mean every Christian homosexual will be "cured" of the homosexual desire any more than the rest of us are cured of our harmful desires. But it does mean that they don't have to be enslaved by their sin and that they can devote each day to living for God.

HONESTY

- "If you are dishonest in little things, you won't be honest with greater responsibilities" (Luke 16:10).
- The LORD detests the use of dishonest scales, but he delights in accurate weights (Proverbs 11:1).
- It is better to be poor and honest than to be dishonest and a fool (Proverbs 19:1).
- Corrupt tax collectors came to be baptized and asked, "Teacher, what should we do?" He replied, "Collect no more taxes than the government requires" (Luke 3:12–13).

See also *Cheating; Lying*

HOPE

- LORD, don't hold back your tender mercies from me. Let your unfailing love and faithfulness always protect me. For troubles surround me—too many to count! My sins pile up so high I can't see my way out (Psalm 40:11–12).
- Many are saying about me, "God won't rescue him." But, LORD, you are my shield, my wonderful God who gives me courage (Psalm 3:2–3 NCV).
- Let all that I am wait quietly before God, for my hope is in him. He alone is my rock and my salvation, my fortress where I will not be shaken (Psalm 62:5–6).
- You are the God who saves me. All day long I put my hope in you (Psalm 25:5).
- We do not want you to. . .grieve like the rest of men, who have no hope. We believe that Jesus died and rose again. . . . The Lord himself will come down from heaven, with a loud command, with the voice of the archangel and with the trumpet call of God, and the dead in Christ will rise first. After that, we who are still alive and are left will be caught up together with them in the clouds to meet the Lord in the air. And so we will be with the Lord forever. Therefore encourage each other with these words (1 Thessalonians 4:13–18 NIV).

HUMILITY

This is a character trait the Bible encourages. It's the opposite of self-absorbed pride.

- Don't try to impress others. Be humble, thinking of others as better than yourselves (Philippians 2:3).
- Think the same way that Christ Jesus thought. . . . He became like one of us. Christ was humble (Philippians 2:5–8 CEV).
- "Anyone who becomes as humble as this little child is the greatest in the Kingdom of Heaven" (Matthew 18:4). This is Jesus talking.
- During the meal Jesus stood up and took off his outer clothing. Taking a towel, he wrapped it around his waist. Then he poured water into a bowl and began to wash the followers' feet. . . . When he had finished washing their feet, he put on his clothes and sat down again. He asked, "Do you understand what I have just done for you? . . . I did this as an example so that you should do as I have done for you" (John 13:4–15 NCV). Jesus is practicing what he preached—a rabbi master acting like a servant.

- "Look, your King is coming to you. He is humble, riding on a donkey" (Matthew 21:5).
- "When you are invited to a wedding feast, don't sit in the seat of honor. What if someone who is more distinguished than you has also been invited? . . . Instead, take the lowest place at the foot of the table. Then when your host sees you, he will come and say, 'Friend, we have a better place for you!' Then you will be honored in front of all the other guests. For those who exalt themselves will be humbled, but those who humble themselves will be exalted" (Luke 14:8–11). Jesus takes advantage of dinner guests jostling for position to teach an object lesson about spiritual etiquette.

See also *Pride*

HYPOCRISY

One of the sins that fired the anger of Jesus most of all was hypocrisy—especially in people who claimed to serve God but who were serving only themselves.

- "I hate all your show and pretense—the hypocrisy of your religious festivals and solemn assemblies. . . . Away with your noisy hymns of praise! I will not listen to the music of your harps. Instead, I want to see a mighty flood of justice, an endless river of righteous living" (Amos 5:21–24). Worship is nothing but interactive theater if we don't take it with us.
- "You're hopeless, you religion scholars and Pharisees! Frauds! You're like manicured grave plots, grass clipped and the flowers bright, but six feet down it's all rotting bones and worm-eaten flesh" (Matthew 23:27 THE MESSAGE). This is Jesus talking.
- "You hypocrites! Isaiah was right when he prophesied about you, for he wrote, 'These people honor me with their lips, but their hearts are far from me. Their worship is a farce' " (Matthew 15:7–9). Jesus is criticizing religion scholars. He uses the word *hypocrite* many times during his frequent clashes with them.
- "How can you think of saying, 'Friend, let me help you get rid of that speck in your eye,' when you can't see past the log in your own eye? Hypocrite!" (Luke 6:42).
- "When you give a gift to someone in need, don't do as the hypocrites do. . .to call attention to their acts of charity! I tell you the truth, they have received all the reward they will ever get" (Matthew 6:2). This is Jesus preaching in the famous Sermon on the Mount.
- "When you pray, don't be like the hypocrites who love to pray publicly . . .where everyone can see them" (Matthew 6:5).

INCEST

- **"You must never have sexual relations with a close relative"** (Leviticus 18:6). Jewish law clarifies what a "close relative" is: parent, stepparent, brother or sister, stepbrother or stepsister, aunt, uncle, daughter-in-law, son-in-law, or the child or grandchild of someone with whom a person has had sex. Marriage between cousins was allowed.
- **I can hardly believe the report about the sexual immorality going on among you—something that even the pagans don't do. I am told that a man in your church is living in sin with his stepmother. . . . You should remove this man from your fellowship** (1 Corinthians 5:1–2). Some translations use the term "father's wife" instead of "stepmother."
- **"It is against God's law for you to marry your brother's wife"** (Mark 6:18). Quoting Jewish law, that's what John the Baptist told Herod Antipas, ruler of Galilee. Herod had married his brother's ex-wife. John got decapitated for that remark. Herod's new wife insisted on it.

ABRAHAM MARRIES HIS HALF SISTER

Oddly enough, the father and mother of the Jewish race were brother and sister. Abraham married his half sister Sarah. They had the same father but different mothers.

Under Jewish law—which didn't come until almost 1,000 years later—such marriages were forbidden, considered incest. And yet this marriage started the Jewish race, God's chosen people.

Why would God allow such a marriage for Abraham and then forbid it later?

The Bible doesn't say.

We like tidy rules we can understand and follow, but God doesn't always work in ways that make sense to us. Perhaps for this pivotal marriage in Jewish history, Sarah's spirit was more important than her genetics. The vast majority of people in Abraham's hometown of Ur, in what is now southern Iraq, worshipped idols.

JEALOUSY

- **Get the satisfaction of a job well done, and you won't need to compare yourself to anyone else** (Galatians 6:4).
- **A peaceful heart leads to a healthy body; jealousy is like cancer in the bones** (Proverbs 14:30).
- **When some of the Jews saw the crowds, they were jealous; so they slandered Paul and argued against whatever he said** (Acts 13:45).

JESUS CHRIST

"Jesus Christ" isn't just a name. It's a name and a title—a bit like "Jesus, Ph.D." Only in this case it's "Jesus, Messiah." The title means "Anointed One," which refers to someone chosen by God for special service, such as a king. The Bible calls King David an anointed one. But Jesus is more than just another king. The Bible portrays him as the King of kings.

A king is born

- "You will conceive and give birth to a son, and you will name him Jesus. He will be very great and will be called the Son of the Most High. The Lord God will give him the throne of his ancestor David. And he will reign over Israel forever; his Kingdom will never end!" (Luke 1:31–33). Gabriel to Mary.

- Mary asked the angel, "But how can this happen? I am a virgin." The angel replied, "The Holy Spirit will come upon you, and the power of the Most High will overshadow you. So the baby to be born will be holy, and he will be called the Son of God" (Luke 1:34–35).

- "Where is the newborn king of the Jews? We saw his star as it rose, and we have come to worship him"

Here's the man. Pilate, Roman governor in Jerusalem, introduced the freshly whipped Jesus to the crowd who still demanded the Crucifixion. A Roman historian from that century, Josephus, confirmed in a history book that Pilate ordered Jesus crucified. Josephus added that Jesus' disciples said their teacher rose from the dead: "that he had appeared to them three days after his crucifixion, and that he was alive."

(Matthew 2:2). Wise men from the East, speaking to King Herod—who had already executed two of his own sons for threatening his power.

Teacher and healer

- **Jesus was about thirty years old when he began his public ministry. Jesus was known as the son of Joseph** (Luke 3:23).
- **Jesus traveled throughout the region of Galilee, teaching in the synagogues and announcing the Good News about the Kingdom. And he healed every kind of disease and illness. News about him spread as far as Syria, and people soon began bringing to him all who were sick. And whatever their sickness or disease, or if they were demons possessed or epileptic or paralyzed—he healed them all** (Matthew 4:23–24).
- **" 'You must love the LORD your God with all your heart, all your soul, and all your mind.' This is the first and greatest commandment. A second is equally important: 'Love your neighbor as yourself' "** (Matthew 22:37–39).

Savior

- **"God loved the world so much that he gave his one and only Son, so that everyone who believes in him will not perish but have eternal life. God sent his Son into the world not to judge the world, but to save the world through him"** (John 3:16–17).
- **He was pierced for our rebellion, crushed for our sins. He was beaten so we could be whole. He was whipped so we could be healed. All of us, like sheep, have strayed away. We have left God's paths to follow our own. Yet the LORD laid on him the sins of us all** (Isaiah 53:5–6). A

prophecy of Jesus' death, written 700 years before Jesus.

- **"You are looking for Jesus of Nazareth, who was crucified. He isn't here! He is risen from the dead!"** (Mark 16:6). An angel, talking to women who have come to Jesus' grave to finish preparing his body for burial.

Coming again

- **"Don't let your hearts be troubled . . . . If this were not so, would I have told you that I am going to prepare a place for you? When everything is ready, I will come and get you, so that you will always be with me"** (John 14:1–3). After telling his disciples that he will die, Jesus comforts them with assurances that he will return.
- **"In the future you will see the Son of Man seated in the place of power at God's right hand and coming on the clouds of heaven"** (Matthew 26:64). Jesus, speaking at his trial.

See also *God; Holy Spirit*

JESUS IN A ROMAN HISTORY BOOK

The Bible isn't the only book from Jesus' century that talks about him.

A Roman historian—Josephus—born in AD 37 had this to say about him: "There was a wise man who was called Jesus, and his conduct was good. . . . Pilate condemned him to be crucified and to die. And those who had become his disciples did not abandon their loyalty to him. They reported that he had appeared to them three days after his crucifixion, and that he was alive."

JOKES (DIRTY)

- Obscene stories, foolish talk, and coarse jokes—these are not for you (Ephesians 5:4).
- **Let nothing foul or dirty come out of your mouth** (Ephesians 4:29 THE MESSAGE).
- **Now is the time to get rid of anger, rage, malicious behavior, slander, and dirty language** (Colossians 3:8).

JUDGING OTHERS

There's a time to judge others and a time to mind our own business and leave the judging to God. The Bible talks about both situations. Christians have a right—even an obligation—to judge sin among their congregation and to impose discipline. But only God has the right to judge a person's motives and spiritual condition.

Time to judge

- I am told that a man in your church is living in sin with his stepmother . . . . **You should remove this man from your fellowship** (1 Corinthians 5:1–2). Paul says that a church member who is having sex with his own stepmother needs expelled from membership. Perhaps then he will come to his spiritual senses, repent, and change his lifestyle. That's the intent—restoration, not punishment.
- **"If your fellow believer sins against you, go and tell him in private what he did wrong. . . . But if he refuses to listen, go to him again and take one or two other people with you. . . . If he refuses to listen to them, tell the church. If he refuses to listen to the**

church, then treat him like a person who does not believe in God" (Matthew 18:15–17 NCV).

- **Tell those who continue sinning that they are wrong. Do this in front of the whole church so that the others will have a warning** (1 Timothy 5:20 NCV). This is Paul's advice to Timothy, pastor of a church.
- **If you have legal disputes. . .why go to outside judges who are not respected by the church?. . . Isn't there anyone in all the church who is wise enough to decide these issues? But instead, one believer sues another—right in front of unbelievers!** (1 Corinthians 6:4–6). Paul pleads with Christians in the same congregation to work out their differences.

Time to mind our own business

- **"Do not judge others, and you will not be judged. For you will be treated as you treat others. The standard you use in judging is the standard by which you will be judged. And why worry about a speck in your friend's eye when you have a log in your own? How can you think of saying to your friend, 'Let me help you get rid of that speck in your eye,' when you can't see past the log in your own eye? Hypocrite! First get rid of the log from your own eye; then you will see well enough to deal with the speck in your friend's eye"** (Matthew 7:1–5). In his famous Sermon on the Mount, Jesus warns that if we're harsh in our judgments of others, people will tend to judge us harshly, too. And he reminds us that we've got faults of our own.
- **"All right, but let the one who has never sinned throw the first stone!"** (John 8:7). Jesus is talking to a group of Jews asking his permission to

stone a woman to death. She was caught having sex with a man other than her husband. The men eventually drop their stones and walk away.

- **Who are you to condemn someone else's servants? They are responsible to the Lord, so let him judge whether they are right or wrong. And with the Lord's help, they will do what is right** (Romans 14:4). Paul is telling Christians not to condemn each other over debatable subjects, such as whether or not to eat only kosher meat.
- **Don't make judgments about anyone ahead of time—before the Lord returns. For he will bring our darkest secrets to light and will reveal our private motives. Then God will give to each one whatever praise is due** (1 Corinthians 4:5).

LAZINESS

There were apparently a lot of lazy people in Bible times, because there are plenty of verses about laziness—about 20 in Proverbs alone. Every Bible verse about laziness condemns it. Here are a few of the more interesting.

- **Just as a door turns on its hinges, so a lazybones turns back over in bed** (Proverbs 26:14 THE MESSAGE).
- **You lazy fool, look at an ant. Watch it closely; let it teach you a thing or two** (Proverbs 6:6 THE MESSAGE).
- **Lazy people irritate their employers, like. . .smoke in the eyes** (Proverbs 10:26).
- **The lazy person claims, "There's a lion out there! If I go outside, I might be killed!"** (Proverbs 22:13).
- **Lazy people want much but get little, but those who work hard will**

prosper (Proverbs 13:4).
- **Never be lazy, but work hard and serve the Lord enthusiastically** (Romans 12:11).

LEADERSHIP

- **"Whoever wants to be a leader among you must be your servant, and whoever wants to be first among you must become your slave. For even the Son of Man came not to be served but to serve others"** (Matthew 20:26–28).
- **It's important that a church leader, responsible for the affairs in God's house, be looked up to—not pushy, not short-tempered, not a drunk, not a bully, not money-hungry. He must welcome people, be helpful, wise, fair, reverent, have a good grip on himself, and have a good grip on the Message, knowing how to use the truth to either spur people on**

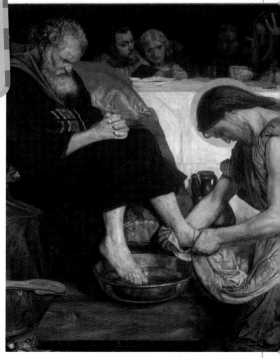

in knowledge or stop them in their tracks if they oppose it (Titus 1:7–9 THE MESSAGE). This is Paul's advice to Titus, who is starting churches and selecting church leaders on the island of Crete.

LIVING TOGETHER

Many young Christians say there's nothing wrong with unmarried members of the opposite sex living together without having sex. But others disagree. They say living together is like taking an obese friend to study with you in a donut shop and telling him he won't have a problem if he stays away from the donuts.

- **Run from temptations that capture young people** (2 Timothy 2:22 CEV).
- **"Pray for strength against temptation. The spirit wants to do what is right, but the body is weak"** (Matthew 26:41 NCV).
- **"Do not lead us into temptation"** (Matthew 6:13 NKJV). This is from the Lord's Prayer.

Servant leader.
Peter isn't happy about Jesus stooping to wash his feet. But it's a lesson Jesus wanted to teach his disciples—that leaders should humbly serve the people who depend on them.

- **"What sorrow awaits the world, because it tempts people to sin. Temptations are inevitable, but what sorrow awaits the person who does the tempting"** (Matthew 18:7).

Just friends.
Is it okay for an unmarried man and woman to live together so they can save on rent—as long as they don't have sex? Some young Christians wonder. But many older, more experienced Christians would refer them to another section in this book: Temptation.

LONELINESS

- God has said, "I will never fail you. I will never abandon you." So we can say with confidence, "The Lord is my helper, so I will have no fear" (Hebrews 13:5–6).
- God is in his holy Temple. He is a father to orphans, and he defends the widows. God gives the lonely a home (Psalm 68:5–6 NCV).

Alone with God. Jesus spent a lot of time alone. Before starting his ministry, he slipped off into Israel's rocky badlands to pray for 40 days. Throughout his ministry he often slipped away from the crowds and his disciples to pray. Constantly criticized by top religious leaders, he must have felt isolated and lonely even when crowds surrounded him.

LOVE

> Love isn't just a feeling. It's a decision to act in the best interest of someone else because we want that person to be happy.

The greatest love of all
- "This is the very best way to love. Put your life on the line for your friends" (John 15:13 THE MESSAGE). Fortunately, most of us never have to do this. But many have—often on the battlefield or in other moments of extreme danger.
- We know what real love is because Jesus gave up his life for us. So we also ought to give up our lives for our brothers and sisters (1 John 3:16). Using Jesus as the ultimate example of selflessness, John urges Christians to follow Christ's example of putting others first.

Romantic love
- A bowl of vegetables with someone you love is better than steak with someone you hate (Proverbs 15:17).
- Kiss me and kiss me again, for your love is sweeter than wine (Song of Songs 1:2).
- My lover is mine, and I am his (Song of Songs 2:16).
- The passion of love bursting into flame is more powerful than death, stronger than the grave. Love cannot be drowned by oceans or floods; it cannot be bought, no matter what is offered (Song of Songs 8:6–7 CEV).

The importance of love
- " 'Love the Lord your God with all your heart, all your soul, and all your mind.' This is the first and most important command. And the

second command is like the first: 'Love your neighbor as you love yourself'" (Matthew 22:37–39 NCV). This is the answer Jesus gives to a scholar asking which of the hundreds of commandments in the Bible is the most important.

- **These three things continue forever: faith, hope, and love. And the greatest of these is love** (1 Corinthians 13:13 NCV). In an entire chapter praising the value of love, Paul says there's no trait better than love.

God's love for us

- **"God loved the people of this world so much that he gave his only Son, so that everyone who has faith in him will have eternal life and never really die"** (John 3:16 CEV). This is the Bible's message summed up in one sentence.
- **Nothing in all creation will ever be able to separate us from the love of God that is revealed in Christ Jesus our Lord** (Romans 8:39).
- **His faithful love endures forever** (Psalm 106:1). Repeated dozens of times throughout the Old Testament, this is one of the Bible's most popular ways of describing God—which may be why a New Testament writer concluded: "God is love" (1 John 4:8).

Love others

- **"This is my commandment: Love each other in the same way I have loved you"** (John 15:12).
- **"Your love for one another will prove to the world that you are my disciples"** (John 13:35).
- **Don't just pretend to love others. . . . Love each other with genuine affection, and take delight in honoring each other** (Romans 12:9–10).

- **"Love your enemies! Do good to those who hate you"** (Luke 6:27).
- **Most important of all, continue to show deep love for each other, for love covers a multitude of sins** (1 Peter 4:8). We can make big mistakes that hurt others. But if the people know we love them, they'll overlook a lot.

WHEN WE ONLY *THINK* IT'S LOVE

Sometimes it's hard to tell the difference between love and lust.

At first, they may feel a lot alike. Whether we're in love or in lust, we want to be with the person we desire.

But love and lust approach that goal in radically different ways.

Love is selfless and will actually let go—if that's what the other person wants. When we love another, we put that person's wishes ahead of our own.

Lust is selfish. It tries to figure out ways to manipulate the target. And that's what the person is to us, just a target.

In the Bible, a prince named Amnon fell in lust with his half sister—though he called it love. Pretending to be sick, he arranged for her to come to his bedroom and feed him. He raped her. Afterward, "he hated her even more than he had loved her" (2 Samuel 13:15).

For those wondering if it's love or lust, here's a clue. It's from the Bible's famous essay on the nature of love: "Love is patient and kind. Love is not jealous or boastful or proud or rude. It does not demand its own way" (1 Corinthians 13:4–5).

LUST

- **Run from anything that stimulates youthful lusts** (2 Timothy 2:22).
- **Keep your minds on whatever is true, pure, right, holy, friendly, and proper** (Philippians 4:8 CEV).
- **If they can't control themselves, they should go ahead and marry. It's better to marry than to burn with lust** (1 Corinthians 7:9). That's Paul's advice to unmarried people.
- **"Anyone who even looks at a woman with lust has already committed adultery with her in his heart"** (Matthew 5:28). Jesus teaches that sin begins in the mind and works its way out, to behavior. But even before we act on a lustful thought, merely dwelling on it is dangerous and harmful.
- **"I made a covenant with my eyes not to look with lust at a young woman"** (Job 31:1).
- **Have nothing to do with sexual immorality, impurity, lust, and evil desires** (Colossians 3:5).

See also *Love; Sex*

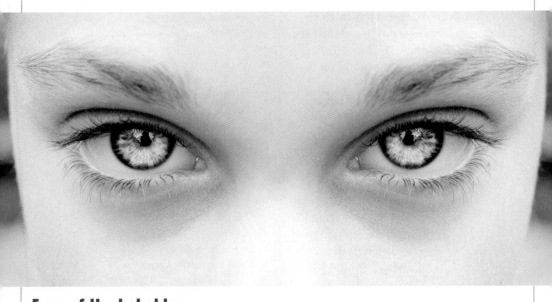

Eyes of the beholder. Seen through eyes of love, another person is our master—someone we want only to please. Seen through the eyes of lust, another person is our servant—someone we want only to please us.

IS MASTURBATION WRONG?

No, say some Christians—to the angry objection of others.

Unfortunately for both groups, the Bible skips the debate altogether. It says nothing about masturbation.

Some Christians argue that masturbation was the sin of Onan, who "spilled the semen on the ground" (Genesis 38:9). But they're wrong. *Coitus interruptus* is the technical term for what Onan was doing. He was withdrawing from his wife's vagina before ejaculating. God killed him for it because Onan was deliberately denying his wife the child she desperately wanted.

If any Bible passage speaks even indirectly about masturbation, it's the one that says, "Whenever a man has an emission of semen, he must wash his entire body in water, and he will remain ceremonially unclean until the next evening" (Leviticus 15:16). Most scholars, however, say this probably refers to wet dreams, or sex with a spouse. Yet the passage might include masturbation—at least it doesn't exclude it. Nor does it describe the sexual experience that produced the emission as sinful. The discharge of semen simply requires a short time of ritual purification—similar to when a Jew touched a corpse, or when a woman had a menstrual period. They weren't allowed to worship God until the time of purification was over.

Because the Bible skips the *M* word, Christians have to search for answers elsewhere.

Arguments in FAVOR

- It's too common to be unnatural, especially among boys after the sudden release of body-altering testosterone—sometime between the ages of 9 and 14.
- Since the Bible doesn't say anything about it, and since surveys reveal that nearly all teen boys (and most girls) masturbate, young people don't need guilt added to the sexual tension they're already experiencing.
- It's a healthy way to release pent-up sexual tension, without risking sexual disease, pregnancy, or destructive relationships.

Argument AGAINST

- The Bible clearly opposes lust, and boys tend to masturbate with girls in mind—and vice versa. It's not like anyone would masturbate to a sunset.

Whether masturbation is right or wrong, our thought life matters. Yet without a direct word from the Bible about masturbation, God apparently intends the Holy Spirit to guide each of us toward a tailor-made, healthy sexuality. God understands our physical desires. We can trust him to work with us in providing a healthy way for dealing with them.

LYING

- Telling lies about others is as harmful as hitting them with an ax, wounding them with a sword, or shooting them with a sharp arrow (Proverbs 25:18).
- "Do not tell lies about others" (Exodus 20:16 CEV). This is one of the 10 Commandments.
- Riffraff and rascals talk out of both sides of their mouths (Proverbs 6:12 THE MESSAGE).

See also *Cheating; Honesty*

MARRIAGE

God's plan for marriage
- A man leaves his father and mother and is joined to his wife, and the two are united into one (Genesis 2:24).
- "They are no longer two people, but one. And no one should separate a couple that God has joined together" (Mark 10:8–9 CEV).
- "God has joined the two together, so no one should separate them" (Matthew 19:6 NCV).

Keeping the marriage healthy
- Submit to one another out of reverence for Christ. For wives, this means submit to your husbands as to the Lord. . . . For husbands, this means love your wives, just as Christ loved the church. He gave up his life for her (Ephesians 5:21–22, 25).
- Honor marriage, and guard the sacredness of sexual intimacy between wife and husband (Hebrews 13:4 THE MESSAGE).
- The marriage bed must be a place of mutuality—the husband seeking to satisfy his wife, the wife seeking to satisfy her husband. Marriage is not a place to "stand up for your rights." Marriage is a decision to serve the other, whether in bed or out (1 Corinthians 7:3–4 THE MESSAGE).
- "A newly married man must not be drafted into the army or be given any other official responsibilities. He must be free to spend one year at home, bringing happiness to the wife he has married" (Deuteronomy 24:5).

Christians married to non-Christians
- If a Christian man has a wife who is not a believer, and she is happy to live with him, he must not divorce her. And if a Christian woman has a husband who is not a believer, and he is happy to live with her, she must

Rx for a happy marriage.

Submission is the key, according to the Bible. Not submission by the wife alone. But mutual submission—by husband and wife—out of love for each other.

not divorce him. . . . Wife, you don't know; maybe you will save your husband. And husband, you don't know; maybe you will save your wife (1 Corinthians 7:12–13, 16 NCV).

Surprising facts

• "Marriage is for people here on earth. But in the age to come, those worthy of being raised from the dead will neither marry nor be given in marriage" (Luke 20:34–35). Answering a question about who in heaven will be the husband of a widow who remarried, Jesus says in heaven we will be unmarried, "like angels."

See also *Divorce; Family*

WHY SHOULDN'T CHRISTIANS MARRY NON-CHRISTIANS?

The Bible gives two compelling reasons why Christians should marry Christians.

1. Christians and non-Christians have radically different rules for living—and the rules clash.

"You are not the same as those who do not believe. So do not join yourselves to them," Paul told Christians in the Greek town of Corinth. "What can a believer have together with a nonbeliever?" (2 Corinthians 6:14–15 NCV).

2. The smartest man on earth lost his faith because of a bad marriage choice.

When Solomon became king of Israel, he asked God for just one thing: wisdom. God replied, "I'll make you wiser than anyone who has ever lived or ever will live" (1 Kings 3:12 CEV).

Smart as Solomon was, though, he broke the Jewish law that prohibited marriage to non-Jews. Solomon did what the prevailing Middle Eastern culture said was smart. Kings were supposed to grow huge harems as a show of power. And these kings married the daughters of neighboring kings to seal peace and trade agreements. Solomon married 1,000 women.

Many of those women worshipped idols.

"As Solomon got older, some of his wives led him to worship their gods" (1 Kings 11:4 CEV).

The smartest man in human history stopped worshipping God. It happened because of who he chose as his intimate partners.

MODESTY

- I want women to be modest in their appearance. They should wear decent and appropriate clothing and not draw attention to themselves by the way they fix their hair or by wearing gold or pearls or expensive clothes. For women who claim to be devoted to God should make themselves attractive by the good things they do (1 Timothy 2:9–10). This is Paul's advice, which he wants Pastor Timothy to pass along to the congregation.

See also *Temptation*

MONEY

We're fond of money, and most of us want as much as we can get. But the Bible plants warning signs all around money.

Dangers

- Those who love money will never have enough. How meaningless to think that wealth brings true happiness! The more you have, the more people come to help you spend it. So what good is wealth—except perhaps to watch it slip through your fingers! (Ecclesiastes 5:10–11).
- "Don't store treasures for yourselves here on earth where moths and rust will destroy them and thieves can break in and steal them. But store your treasures in heaven. . . . Your heart will be where your treasure is" (Matthew 6:19–21 NCV).
- Keep your lives free from the love of money, and be satisfied with what you have (Hebrews 13:5 NCV).

- "It is easier for a camel to go through the eye of a needle than for a rich person to enter the Kingdom of God!" (Mark 10:25). Most Bible experts say Jesus was exaggerating a bit to make his point that money often lures people away from God.
- "You cannot serve God and money" (Luke 16:13 CEV).
- The love of money causes all kinds of evil. Some people have left the faith, because they wanted to get more money, but they have caused themselves much sorrow (1 Timothy 6:10 NCV).

Be generous

- Remind the rich to be generous and share what they have (1 Timothy 6:18 CEV).

MUSIC

Music was important to worshippers in Bible times. Psalms is actually a collection of lyrics once set to music. If the words are any clue, the music covered a wide range of styles.

- My heart is confident in you, O God. . . . No wonder I can sing your praises! Wake up, my heart! Wake up, O lyre and harp! I will wake the dawn with my song (Psalm 57:7–8).
- Sing praises to God, our strength. . . . Sing! Beat the tambourine. Play the sweet lyre and the harp. Blow the ran's horn (Psalm 81:1–3).
- Clap your hands and shout joyful praises to God (Psalm 47:1 CEV).
- Miriam. . .led the other women out to play their tambourines and to dance. Then she sang to them: "Sing praises to the LORD for his great victory! He has thrown the horses

and their riders of the sea" (Exodus 15:20–21 CEV).

- The LORD sent a tormenting spirit that filled him with depression and fear. Some of Saul's servants said to him. . ."Let us find a good musician to play the harp whenever the tormenting spirit troubles you. He will play soothing music, and you will soon be well again" (1 Samuel 16:14–16). Shepherd boy David was a music therapist for King Saul before he became a giant killer.

- About midnight Paul and Silas were praying and singing praises to God, while the other prisoners listened (Acts 16:25 CEV).

- David chose some people to be in charge of the music in the house of the LORD (1 Chronicles 6:31 NCV). After King David set up a worship center in Jerusalem, he assigned singers and instrumentalists—nearly 300—to help lead worship there.

- Whatever you do or say, do it as a representative of the Lord Jesus (Colossians 3:17). That applies to the kind of music we listen to.

See also *Worship*

OBESITY

Obesity wasn't nearly the problem in Bible times that it is in most developed nations today. That's because most people back then had to sweat through hard physical labor to survive. They burned off the calories, and they didn't have nearly as many rich foods to eat as we do today.

- All they want is easy street. . . . Those who live there make their bellies their gods; belches are their praise; all they can think of is their appetites (Philippians 3:18–19 THE MESSAGE). Paul is talking about people who worship the pleasures of life instead of worshipping God.

- Your body is a sacred place, the place of the Holy Spirit. Don't you see that you can't live however you please, squandering what God paid such a high price for? The physical part of you is not some piece of property belonging to the spiritual part of you. God owns the whole works. So let people see God in and through your body (1 Corinthians 6:19–20 THE MESSAGE).

- Here's what I want you to do, God helping you: Take your everyday, ordinary life—your sleeping, eating, going-to-work, and walking-around life—and place it before God as an offering (Romans 12:1 THE MESSAGE).

- "I will destroy those who are fat and powerful. I will feed them, yes—feed them justice!" (Ezekiel 34:16). Most people described in the Bible as overweight—as in this case—are the rich who get their wealth by exploiting the poor. Many poorer nations of the world today complain that this is exactly what wealthier nations are doing to them—getting rich and fat off the products they produce at slave wages.

- You women of Samaria are fat cows! You mistreat and abuse the poor and needy, then you say to your husbands, "Bring us more drinks!" (Amos 4:1 CEV).

OCCULT

It's wrong to consult fortune-tellers or psychics who try to conjure up the dead. The Bible makes that clear. But as is often the case, the Bible doesn't bother to explain why. One guess: There are good and bad spirits out there—the Bible says so—and the only way we can be sure we're getting advice from a good spirit is to consult God. We don't need a psychic for that.

- **We are not fighting against humans. We are fighting against forces and authorities and against rulers of darkness and powers in the spiritual world** (Ephesians 6:12 CEV). Though these forces aren't part of the physical dimension, they are as real as we are—and they can affect us for better or worse.
- **"There's a woman at Endor who can talk to spirits of the dead"** (1 Samuel 28:7 CEV). The night before a battle, King Saul asks a psychic to call up the spirit of the prophet Samuel to find out how the battle will end. To the psychic's horror, Samuel appears and correctly predicts that when the battle is over, Saul and his sons will be dead.
- **"I will be against anyone who goes to mediums and fortune-tellers for advice, because that person is being unfaithful to me"** (Leviticus 20:6 NCV).
- **"Don't let anyone use magic or witchcraft, or try to explain the meaning of signs. Don't let anyone try to control others with magic, and don't let them be mediums or try to talk with the spirits of dead**

people. The LORD hates anyone who does these things"** (Deuteronomy 18:10–12 NCV).
- **"I will put an end to all witchcraft, and there will be no more fortune-tellers"** (Micah 5:12).

See also *Astrology*

PARENTS

There are 10 basic laws on which all other laws in the Bible are based. And one of the 10 tells children to respect their parents. The Bible also calls on parents to earn that respect by loving their children.

- **"Honor your father and mother"** (Exodus 20:12). That's one of the 10 Commandments.
- **Children, obey your parents because you belong to the Lord, for this is the right thing to do. "Honor your father and mother." This is the first commandment with a promise: If you honor your father and mother, "things will go well for you, and you will have a long life on the earth"** (Ephesians 6:1–3).
- **My child, listen when your father corrects you. Don't neglect your mother's instruction. What you learn from them will crown you with grace and be a chain of honor around your neck** (Proverbs 1:8–9).
- **My son, keep your father's commands, and don't forget your mother's teaching. Keep their words in mind forever as though you had them tied around your neck. They will guide you** (Proverbs 6:20–22 NCV).
- **Don't be a fool and disobey your parents. Be smart! Accept correction** (Proverbs 15:5 CEV).

- **Children, always obey your parents, for this pleases the Lord. Fathers, do not aggravate your children, or they will become discouraged** (Colossians 3:20–21).

Like mother, like daughter. Kids imitate their parents. That's one of the ways they learn—for better or worse. The Bible tells parents to serve as models of good behavior and to teach their children about God's laws: "Repeat them again and again to your children" (Deuteronomy 6:7). The Bible also tells kids to show respect to their parents; it's one of the 10 Commandments, the solid-rock foundation on which all the other rules in the Bible are based.

PARTYING

God wants us to enjoy life, just as our loved ones want us to. But there's such a thing as going overboard.

- **We must live decent lives for all to see. Don't participate in the darkness of wild parties and drunkenness** (Romans 13:13).
- **In the past you wasted too much time doing what nonbelievers enjoy. You were guilty of sexual sins, evil desires, drunkenness, wild and drunken parties** (1 Peter 4:3 NCV).
- **Whether you eat or drink, or whatever you do, do it all for the glory of God** (1 Corinthians 10:31).

See also *Drinking and Drugs*

PATIENCE

God is patient with us, and he expects us to be patient with others. But like any other character trait, patience has to be cultivated. We've got to work at it.

God's patience with us
- **Don't you see how wonderfully kind, tolerant, and patient God is with you? Does this mean nothing to you? Can't you see that his kindness is intended to turn you from your sin?** (Romans 2:4).

Wait patiently on God's timing
- **Be still in the presence of the LORD, and wait patiently for him to act. Don't worry about evil people who prosper or fret about their wicked schemes** (Psalm 37:7).

Learn patience
- **Be patient with each other, making**

allowance for each other's faults (Ephesians 4:2).

- **Better to be patient than powerful** (Proverbs 16:32).
- **Don't lose a minute in building on what you've been given, complementing your basic faith with good character, spiritual understanding, alert discipline, passionate patience. . . . With these qualities active and growing in your lives. . . no day will pass without its reward as you mature in your experience of our Master Jesus** (2 Peter 1:5–8 THE MESSAGE).
- **Be patient with each person, attentive to individual needs. And be careful that when you get on each other's nerves you don't snap at each other** (1 Thessalonians 5:14–15 THE MESSAGE).
- **A servant of the Lord must not quarrel but must be kind to everyone. . .patient with difficult people** (2 Timothy 2:24).
- **Be patient in trouble, and keep on praying** (Romans 12:12).
- **God blesses those who patiently endure testing and temptation. Afterward they will receive the crown of life that God has promised to those who love him** (James 1:12).

PEER PRESSURE

- **Don't be like the people of this world, but let God change the way you think. Then you will know how to do everything that is good and pleasing to him** (Romans 12:2 CEV).
- **My child, if sinners entice you, turn your back on them! They may say, "Come and join us. . . . We'll all share the loot." My child, don't go along with them! . . . They are trying**

to get themselves killed (Proverbs 1:10–18).

- **God blesses those people who refuse evil advice and won't follow sinners** (Psalm 1:1 CEV).
- **"Do not act like the people in Egypt, where you used to live, or like the people of Canaan, where I am taking you. You must not imitate their way of life. You must obey all my regulations and be careful to obey my decrees, for I am the LORD your God"** (Leviticus 18:3–4).
- **They quit following the LORD. . . . They began to worship the gods of the people who lived around them, and that made the LORD angry** (Judges 2:12 NCV).

PERSECUTION

- **"Count yourself blessed every time someone cuts you down or throws you out, every time someone smears or blackens your name to discredit me. What it means is that the truth is too close for comfort and that that person is uncomfortable. You can be glad when that happens—skip like a lamb, if you like!—for even though they don't like it, I do. . .and all heaven applauds. And know that you are in good company; my preachers and witnesses have always been treated like this"** (Luke 6:22–23 THE MESSAGE). That's Jesus talking.
- **Troubles produce patience. And patience produces character** (Romans 5:3–4 NCV).
- **Consider it a sheer gift, friends, when tests and challenges come at you from all sides. You know that under pressure, your faith-life is forced into the open and shows its true colors. So don't try to get out**

of anything prematurely. Let it do its work so you become mature and well-developed, not deficient in any way (James 1:2–4 THE MESSAGE).

POLLUTION

• "Let us make humans beings in our image, to be like us. They will reign over the fish in the sea, the birds in the sky, the livestock, all the wild animals on the earth, and the small animals" (Genesis 1:26). God made us caretakers of his creation. We might not know all the answers to the question, "Why are we here?" But at least we know one of the answers.

POPULARITY

• "There's trouble ahead when you live only for the approval of others, saying what flatters them, doing what indulges them. Popularity contests are not truth contests. . . . Your task is to be true, not popular" (Luke 6:26 THE MESSAGE). This is Jesus preaching to a crowd.

He only looks popular. Brad Miller was visiting Kent State University when a group of cheerleaders attending a conference asked him to take their picture. Then they returned the favor, taking this picture with his camera. It's normal to want to be accepted by our peers and to become popular. But the Bible says there's danger ahead for anyone who lives mainly for the approval of others and who loves "human praise more than the praise of God" (John 12:43).

PORNOGRAPHY

Sketchy drawings of sex acts existed in Bible times, but nothing close to the photos and films we have today. And very few people had access to those early, cartoonish-looking sketches. So the Bible doesn't talk about pornography as we know it. But it does condemn the lust and addiction that pornography produces—as well as the immodesty and sexual immorality it glamorizes. Pornography also creates unrealistic images of what people should look like, spurring dangerous body sculpting and destroying the marriages of couples who think their sex life doesn't measure up.

- **Oholibah saw images of Babylonian men carved into walls and painted red. . . . As soon as she looked at them, she wanted to have sex with them. And so, she sent messengers to bring them to her. Men from Babylonia came and had sex with her so many times that she got disgusted with them** (Ezekiel 23:14–17 CEV). Even in ancient times, pictures stimulated destructive sexual behavior. Though this story is symbolic, it draws from that fact. Oholibah represents the Jews. The point of this symbolism is that the Jews abandoned God by putting their trust in the world's superpower, Babylon— and in Babylon's idols.
- **Your old life is dead. . . . And that means killing off everything connected with that way of death: sexual promiscuity, impurity, lust, doing whatever you feel like whenever you feel like it, and grabbing whatever attracts your fancy. That's a life shaped by things and feelings instead of by God** (Colossians 3:3, 5 THE MESSAGE).
- **I want women to be modest in their appearance. They should wear decent and appropriate clothing and not draw attention to themselves** (1 Timothy 2:9). This is Paul's advice to Timothy, pastor of a church.
- **Late one afternoon, after his midday rest, David got out of bed and was walking on the roof of the palace. As he looked out over the city, he noticed a woman of unusual beauty taking a bath** (2 Samuel 11:2). Though the story of King David and Bathsheba isn't about pornography, there are similarities. David sees a married woman who's naked. He lusts for her, meets her for sex, and gets her pregnant. Her husband is away at war. So to cover up the affair, David has her husband killed and he marries Bathsheba.

See also Abstinence; Addiction

PRAYER

Prayer isn't just a chat with a do-nothing God. Prayer has the power to change reality just as effectively as a child's sincere request to Mom or Dad can change things. It's probably not that the request changes God's mind. After all, how could someone who knows everything change his mind? It's more likely that the request somehow changes us, and so God changes his plans to match the changes in us.

How to pray
- **"When you come before God, don't turn that into a theatrical production either. All these people making**

a regular show out of their prayers, hoping for stardom! Do you think God sits in a box seat?" (Matthew 6:5 THE MESSAGE). Jesus is criticizing religious leaders who use public prayer to draw attention to themselves.

- "Our Father in heaven, reveal who you are. Set the world right; do what's best—as above, so below. Keep us alive with three square meals. Keep us forgiven with you and forgiving others. Keep us safe from ourselves and the Devil. You're in charge! You can do anything you want! You're ablaze in beauty! Yes. Yes. Yes" (Matthew 6:9–13 THE MESSAGE). This is the Lord's Prayer. Jesus taught it to his disciples to show them how to keep their prayers short and simple.

- Pray every way you know how, for everyone you know. Pray especially for rulers and their governments to rule well (1 Timothy 2:1–2 THE MESSAGE).

- Jesus went up on a mountain to pray, and he prayed to God all night (Luke 6:12). This was on the night before he chose his disciples.

Prayer changes things

- "If you believe, you will get anything you ask for in prayer" (Matthew 21:22 NCV). Jesus is assuming we will do what he did on the night of his arrest and ask according to God's will. Jesus didn't want to be tortured on the cross, and he told God so. But he was willing to die if necessary. And it was. (See "When God's answer is no" at right.)

- We are confident that he hears us whenever we ask for anything that pleases him (1 John 5:14).

- Hezekiah got sick and was almost dead. Isaiah the prophet went in and told him, "The LORD says you won't ever get well. You are going to die, so you had better start doing what needs to be done." Hezekiah turned toward the wall and prayed (2 Kings 20:1–2 CEV). God's reply: "I heard you pray, and I saw you cry. I will let you live fifteen years more."

- Moses begged the LORD his God and said, "LORD, don't let your anger destroy your people." . . . So the LORD changed his mind and did not destroy the people as he had said he might (Exodus 32:11, 14 NCV).

- "Don't be afraid, Daniel. Since the first day you began to pray for understanding and to humble yourself before your God, your request has been heard in heaven. I have come in answer to your prayer" (Daniel 10:12). The words of an angel.

When God's answer is no

- "Father, if it is possible, don't let this happen to me! Father, you can do anything. Don't make me suffer by having me drink from this cup. But do what you want, and not what I want" (Mark 14:36 CEV). A few hours after Jesus prayed this prayer, he was hanging on the cross.

- So I wouldn't get a big head, I was given the gift of a handicap to keep me in constant touch with my limitations. . . . At first I didn't think of it as a gift, and begged God to remove it. Three times I did that, and then he told me, My grace is enough; it's all you need (2 Corinthians 12:7–9 THE MESSAGE).

- Never stop praying. Be thankful in all circumstances, for this is God's will for you who belong to Christ Jesus (1 Thessalonians 5:17–18).

- I waited patiently for the LORD to help me, and he turned to me and

heard my cry (Psalm 40:1). Sometimes the answer isn't yes or no, but wait.

- **God has no use for the prayers of the people who won't listen to him** (Proverbs 28:9 THE MESSAGE).

PRIDE

- **Pride leads to conflict** (Proverbs 13:10).
- **Pride leads only to shame; it is wise to be humble** (Proverbs 11:2 NCV).
- **Pride ends in humiliation, while humility brings honor** (Proverbs 29:23).
- **Pride leads to destruction; a proud attitude brings ruin. It is better to be humble and be with those who suffer** (Proverbs 16:18–19 NCV).
- **Though the LORD is great, he cares for the humble, but he keeps his distance from the proud** (Psalm 138:6).
- **"Let's build a great city for ourselves with a tower that reaches into the sky." . . . The LORD scattered them all over the world, and they stopped building the city** (Genesis 11:4, 8). The city was Babel, short for Babylon. In the Jewish language of Hebrew, the name means "confusion."

See also *Humility*

RAPE

- **If an engaged woman is raped out in the country, only the man will be put to death. Do not punish the woman at all; she has done nothing wrong. . . . This crime is like murder, because the woman was alone out in the country when the man attacked her. She screamed, but there was no one to help her** (Deuteronomy 22:25–27 CEV). This is one of the ancient Jewish laws.
- **Shechem's rape of Jacob's daughter was intolerable in Israel and not to be put up with** (Genesis 34:5 THE MESSAGE).
- **Amnon wouldn't listen to her [Tamar], and since he was stronger than she was, he raped her. Then suddenly Amnon's love turned to hate, and he hated her even more**

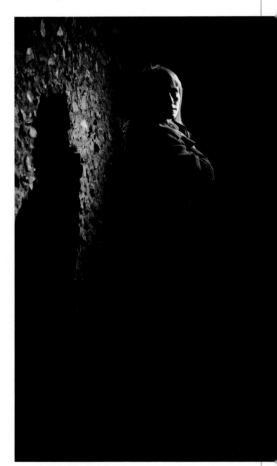

Risky walk. Don't walk alone at night. That's one piece of advice that rape counseling centers offer to young women—the most common victims of sexual assault.

than he had loved her (2 Samuel 13:14–15). This is King David's son raping his own half sister because she refused to have sex with him. David didn't punish Amnon, but Tamar's full brother, Absalom, did. Absalom had the rapist assassinated.

- **"He came into my room to rape me, but I screamed"** (Genesis 39:14).

This was a lie that an Egyptian official's wife told about Joseph, who refused her invitation to have sex with her. The official put Joseph in prison—a mild punishment, suggesting that the official didn't believe his wife.

RAPE: A FEW SURPRISING FACTS

No one knows how many people are raped each year. Not a clue.

That's because more than half the rapes probably aren't reported. Some surveys say the number of rapes is five times higher than those the police hear about.

Why not report the crime?

Shame, for one. Fear, for another. About 8 out of 10 victims know their rapist. And about 1 in 10 is someone considered a close friend—as if a rapist could actually be a friend to the victim. So the victim fears that people might think the sex was consensual. And the victim fears retaliation from the attacker.

Raw stats

- Every two and a half minutes someone is sexually assaulted in America.
- One in six American women is a victim of sexual assault and one in 33 men.
- About 200,000 people reported they were victims of rape, attempted rape, or sexual assault in the most recent year on record as this book went to press.
- About half of all rape victims are under age 18; and 80 percent are under age 30.

Tips for avoiding rape

- Stay in control of your surroundings. Don't walk alone at night, accept a ride from a new acquaintance, or get drunk on a date.
- Don't let someone talk you into sex when you really don't want to have sex.
- Trust your instincts about people. If you sense a threat, back away from the person.
- Learn some self-defense techniques. For women, this includes the ever-effective foot, knee, fist, or fully loaded purse to the attacker's groin.

How not to treat a rape victim

After the rape, some victims get emotionally assaulted—by the very people who should be helping them: family, friends, police, and health-care providers.

Some of these people react with suspicion, even asking if the victim was to blame by inviting the attack.

Others minimize the rape as no big deal—when it's a very big deal.

And some think it's best to pretend the rape never happened. So they don't mention it again. But this rape may have been the most traumatic experience the victim has ever faced. And as much as a person needs to talk about the pain of getting dumped by a boyfriend or a girlfriend, a person needs to talk about the agony and lingering effects of a rape.

Sources: U.S. National Library of Medicine; National Institutes of Health; the Rape, Abuse, and Incest National Network (RAINN; Hotline: 1-800-656-HOPE).

REPENTANCE

- "If my people, who are called by my name, will humble themselves, if they will pray and seek me and stop their evil ways, I will hear them from heaven. I will forgive their sin" (2 Chronicles 7:14 NCV).
- "Turn to God! Give up your sins, and you will be forgiven. Then that time will come when the Lord will give you fresh strength" (Acts 3:19–20 CEV).
- For the kind of sorrow God wants us to experience leads us away from sin and results in salvation. There's no regret for that kind of sorrow (2 Corinthians 7:10).

See also *Forgiveness*

RESTITUTION

- "When a man or woman does something wrong to another person, that is really sinning against the LORD. That person is guilty and must admit the wrong that has been done. The person must fully pay for the wrong that has been done, adding one-fifth to it, and giving it to the person who was wronged" (Numbers 5:6–7 NCV). This was a Jewish law in the time of Moses.

REVENGE

- If someone takes unfair advantage of you, use the occasion to practice the servant life. No more tit-for-tat stuff. Live generously (Matthew 5:41–42 THE MESSAGE).
- Don't repay evil for evil. Don't retaliate with insults when people insult you. Instead, pay them back with

a blessing. That is what God has called you to do, and he will bless you for it (1 Peter 3:9).
- Do all that you can to live in peace with everyone. Dear friends, never take revenge. Leave that to the righteous anger of God. For the Scriptures say, "I will take revenge; I will pay them back," says the LORD (Romans 12:18–19).
- "I only did to them what they did to me" (Judges 15:11). Samson defending himself after neighbors complained that his attacks sparked a Philistine invasion of the Jewish homeland.

See also *Grudges*

RULES

Jesus respected the basic rules that God gave, like the 10 Commandments. Those rules are intended to help people. They work like warning signs about danger ahead. But Jesus didn't think much of rules that religious leaders invented to control people—especially rules that hurt people who needed help.

Rules that help
- "The Sabbath was made to meet the needs of the people, and not people to meet the requirements of the Sabbath" (Mark 2:27). Some Jewish scholars taught that it was wrong to heal people on the Sabbath. The Bible says to avoid working on the Sabbath, but it doesn't say that tending the sick is work—the Jewish scholars jumped to that conclusion and made it law. When they criticized Jesus for breaking their law, Jesus gave this terse reply.

- "Here is a simple, rule-of-thumb guide for behavior: Ask yourself what you want people to do for you, then grab the initiative and do it for them" (Matthew 7:12 THE MESSAGE). Known as the Golden Rule, this sums up all the other Bible rules about how to behave.
- **Athletes cannot win the prize unless they follow the rules** (2 Timothy 2:5).

Rules that hurt

- "You skillfully sidestep God's law in order to hold on to your own tradition. For instance, Moses gave you this law from God: 'Honor your father and mother.' . . . But you say it is all right for people to say to their parents, 'Sorry, I can't help you. For I have vowed to give to God what I would have given to you'" (Mark 7:9–11). Jesus is criticizing a financial loophole that religious leaders created so adult children wouldn't have to give money to help their own parents. The leaders were creating rules like this that undermined God's most basic laws.
- **The Jewish law had many commands and rules, but Christ ended that law. His purpose was to make the two groups of people become one new people in him and in this way make peace** (Ephesians 2:15 NCV). The old Jewish laws about circumcision, kosher foods, and other rules that distinguished God's people from others are now obsolete. Those rules served their purpose of guiding people, but now the Holy Spirit has that assignment.

SALVATION

- "God loved the people of this world so much that he gave his only Son, so that everyone who has faith in him will have eternal life and never really die" (John 3:16 CEV). Condensed to a single verse, this is the message of the New Testament.
- **If you confess with your mouth that Jesus is Lord and believe in your heart that God raised him from the dead, you will be saved** (Romans 10:9).
- "Everyone who calls on the name of the LORD will be saved" (Romans 10:13).
- **God saved you by his grace when you believed. And you can't take credit for this; it is a gift from God. Salvation is not a reward for the good things we have done** (Ephesians 2:8–9).

See also *Faith; Grace*

SALVATION ROAD

Romans isn't just a letter Paul wrote to Christians in Rome; it's the most carefully thought-out system of belief in the New Testament—like a mini theology book. In this letter, Paul explains how to find salvation. Many Bible experts call the following collection of verses the Roman Road to Salvation.

- "Everyone has sinned fallen short of God's glorious standard" (Romans 3:23 NCV).
- "The wages of sin is death" (Romans 6:23).
- "God showed his great love for us by sending Christ to die for us while we were still sinners" (Romans 5:8).
- "It is by believing in your heart that you are made right with God, and it is by confessing with your mouth that you are saved" (Romans 10:10).

SATAN

An all-too-real evil spirit, Satan is described in the Bible as the leader of an army of evil spirits.

- The Spirit who lives in you is greater than the spirit who lives in the world (1 John 4:4).
- Put on all of God's armor so that you will be able to stand firm against all strategies of the devil. For we are not fighting against flesh-and-blood enemies, but against evil rulers and authorities of the unseen world, against mighty powers in this dark world, and against evil spirits in the heavenly places (Ephesians 6:11–12).
- Then the devil. . .was thrown into the fiery lake of burning sulfur, joining the beast and the false prophet. There they will be tormented day and night forever and ever (Revelation 20:10).
- "Get out of here, Satan," Jesus told him. "For the Scriptures say, 'You must worship the LORD your God'" (Matthew 4:10). This is what Jesus said when Satan offered to let him rule the world in exchange for worshipping Satan.

SEX

The Bible devotes an entire book to love and sex—Solomon's Song of Songs, an intimate and sometimes erotic conversation between a man and woman in love. Sex in the Bible is considered a good thing—as long as it's within marriage, within the species, and with the opposite sex.

When to say no

- Potiphar's wife grabbed hold of his [Joseph's] coat and said, "Make love to me!" Joseph ran out of the house, leaving her hanging onto his coat (Genesis 39:12 CEV).
- "Do not practice homosexuality. . . . It is a detestable sin" (Leviticus 18:22).
- "You must not have sexual relations with an animal. . . . It is not natural" (Leviticus 18:23 NCV).
- God wants you to be holy and to stay away from sexual sins. He wants each of you to learn to control your own body in a way that is holy and honorable. Don't use your body for sexual sin like the people who do not know God (1 Thessalonians 4:3–5 NCV).
- "I promised myself never to stare with desire at a young woman" (Job 31:1 CEV).

When to say yes

- The husband should fulfill his wife's sexual needs, and the wife should fulfill her husband's needs. . . . Do not deprive each other of sexual relations, unless you both agree to refrain from sexual intimacy for a limited time so you can give yourselves more completely to prayer. Afterward, you should come together again so that Satan won't be able to tempt you because of your lack of self-control (1 Corinthians 7:3–5).
- You are tall and supple, like the palm tree, and your full breasts are like sweet clusters of dates. I say, "I'm going to climb that palm tree! I'm going to caress its fruit!" (Song of Songs 7:7–8 THE MESSAGE). Unapologetically sensual, Solomon's Song of Songs reports the love talk of a young couple praising one

another's physical features and expressing their shared fantasies about making love.

See also *Homosexuality; Marriage*

SIN

Christians define sin in different ways—two ways, mainly. Many among Baptists, Presbyterians, and Lutherans say it's sin if we do something wrong in God's eyes—whether we realize it's wrong or not. So they say we sin every day. Other Christians—including many Methodists, Nazarenes, and those in the Salvation Army—say we have to know it's wrong before it's sin. So they say we can live above sin if we choose not to do what we know is wrong.

- **Remember, it is sin to know what you ought to do and then not do it** (James 4:17).
- **Everyone has sinned and fallen short of God's glorious standard, and all need to be made right with God by his grace, which is a free gift** (Romans 3:23–24 NCV).
- **The payment for sin is death. But God gives us the free gift of life forever in Christ Jesus our Lord** (Romans 6:23 NCV).
- **Your sins. . .have cut you off from God. Because of your sins, he has turned away and will not listen anymore** (Isaiah 59:2). Persistent sin builds a wall between us and God.
- **If the power of sin within me keeps sabotaging my best intentions, I obviously need help! I realize that I don't have what it takes. . . . I decide to do good, but I don't really do it; I decide not to do bad, but then I do it anyway. . . . I've tried everything**

and nothing helps. I'm at the end of my rope. Is there no one who can do anything for me? . . . The answer, thank God, is that Jesus Christ can and does (Romans 7:17–25 THE MESSAGE). This describes how sin can overpower our desire to do what's right. Alone, we're no match for sin. But with Christ, sin doesn't stand a chance. Christ rules—sin doesn't.

- **Everyone who sins is breaking God's law, for all sin is contrary to the law of God. And you know that Jesus came to take away our sins, and there is no sin in him. Anyone who continues to live in him will not sin. But anyone who keeps on sinning does not know him or understood who he is** (1 John 3:4–6). John is warning against a sinful lifestyle, not the occasional sin that trips us up on our Christian journey. A person who persistently "opposes the law of God" is no friend of God.

See also *Forgiveness; Salvation*

THE UNFORGIVABLE SIN

If you're worried you committed it—and many Christians are—you can stop. Worrying is a sure sign you're not guilty.

The problem is the way Jesus phrased what became a sound byte: "Every sin and blasphemy can be forgiven—except blasphemy against the Holy Spirit, which will never be forgiven" (Matthew 12:31).

Taken by itself, this sounds like we're doomed to toast if we swear at the Holy Spirit. One curse, doomed forever.

But that's not so.

Jesus was talking to Jewish scholars who hated him so much they insisted his miracles came from the devil. They looked at the Son of God and called him the son of Satan. They were hopeless; nothing could convince them to repent.

That's the unforgivable sin. God won't forgive us if we don't repent.

SMOKING

The Bible doesn't talk about smoking, since the practice wasn't picked up from American natives until the time of Christopher Columbus in the 1400s. But the Bible encourages us to take good care of our bodies. And smoking—which is a bit like sucking on the tailpipe of a '57 Chevy—is the opposite of that. Rare exceptions would include when smoking delivers helpful medication to someone who's sick. One more thing: Smoking is an incredibly difficult habit to break. With that in mind, Christians should probably cut smokers some slack: "Be patient with each other, making allowance for each other's faults" (Ephesians 4:2).

- **Your body is a temple for the Holy Spirit who is in you. . . . So honor God with your bodies** (1 Corinthians 6:19–20 NCV).
- **Give your bodies to God because of all he has done for you. Let them be a living and holy sacrifice—the kind he will find acceptable. This is truly the way to worship him** (Romans 12:1).

STEALING

- **"You must not steal"** (Exodus 20:15). This is one of the 10 Commandments.
- **"The thief's purpose is to steal. . . . My purpose is to give"** (John 10:10). These are the words of Jesus, the example Christians are to follow.
- **If you are a thief, quit stealing. Instead, use your hands for good hard work, and then give generously to others in need** (Ephesians 4:28).
- **"Do you think you can rob. . .and then march into this Temple, set apart for my worship, and say, 'We're safe!' . . . Do you think you can turn this Temple, set apart for my worship, into something like that? Well, think again"** (Jeremiah 7:9–11 THE MESSAGE).

See also *Honesty*

One tough habit to break.

Smoking doesn't show up on any of the don't-do lists in the Bible. No surprise. Smoking wasn't introduced to the civilized world until about 600 years ago. But it's deathly unhealthy and extremely addictive. Apostle Peter warns, "You are a slave to whatever controls you" (2 Peter 2:19).

SUCCESS

Success for a Christian doesn't look anything like success in the material world—exactly the opposite, in fact. Spiritual success is worldly success turned inside out, upside down, and backward.

- I observed that most people are motivated to success because they envy their neighbors. But this, too, is meaningless—like chasing the wind (Ecclesiastes 4:4). The reason that success is meaningless: We die and our success dies with us. "We all come to the end of our lives as naked and empty-handed as on the day we were born" (Ecclesiastes 5:15).

- "You can't worship God and Money both" (Matthew 6:24 THE MESSAGE)

- "You've observed how godless rulers throw their weight around, how quickly a little power goes to their heads. It's not going to be that way with you. Whoever wants to be great must become a servant. Whoever wants to be first among you must be your slave. That is what the Son of Man has done: He came to serve, not be served" (Matthew 20:25–28 THE MESSAGE).

- Commit your actions to the LORD, and your plans will succeed (Proverbs 16:3).

SUFFERING

- Our physical body is becoming older and weaker, but our spirit inside us is made new every day. We have small troubles for a while now, but they are helping us gain an eternal glory that is much greater than the troubles. We set our eyes not on what we see but on what we cannot see. What we see will last only a short time, but what we cannot see will last forever (2 Corinthians 4:16–18 NCV).

- You're suffering now, but justice is on the way. When the Master Jesus appears out of heaven in a blaze of fire with his strong angels, he'll even up the score by settling accounts with those who gave you such a bad time (2 Thessalonians 1:5–6 THE MESSAGE).

- There's a lot of suffering to be entered into in this world—the kind of suffering Christ takes on. I welcome the chance to take my share in the church's part of that suffering (Colossians 1:24 THE MESSAGE). Paul writes this from jail, arrested for preaching about Jesus.

When God uses suffering for good

- "Why was this man born blind? Was it because of his own sins or his parents' sins?" (John 9:2). That's a question the disciples asked Jesus. His reply: "He was born blind so the power of God could be seen in him." Then Jesus healed the man.

- "You intended to harm me, but God intended it all for good. He brought me to this position so I could save the lives of many people" (Genesis 50:20). Joseph reassures his brothers that he won't kill them for selling him to slave-traders years earlier. Joseph said God used this bad situation to elevate him to a high office in Egypt, which allowed him to invite the 70 people in his extended family to come down and weather out a seven-year drought that was scorching Israel.

WHY DO WE HAVE TO SUFFER?

Suffering is one of the biggest reasons people reject Christianity. Many can't understand why a loving God would allow suffering.

Perhaps God asks the same about us—why we do little or nothing to help all the people suffering around us.

As for why God allows suffering, the Bible doesn't give us a full answer. He didn't even give old, suffering Job a clue, except to imply, "Trust me. I know what I'm doing." Job had lost his children, wealth, and health.

The Bible does show that God often uses suffering as a springboard for helping people, as he did with Joseph, who got sold to slave-traders. God also sends suffering sometimes as punishment, to get our attention and to point us toward holy living.

But much of our suffering—such as growing older and dying—seems to stem from what happened when sin entered God's perfect creation and somehow mysteriously changed it for the worse. Until then, death didn't seem to be on the agenda.

Even so, the Bible says that our life on Earth is just a speck on the calendar. We will suffer some. But eternal joy is coming: "There will be no more death or sorrow or crying or pain. All these things are gone forever" (Revelation 21:4).

SUICIDE

Suicide doesn't appear to have been very common in Bible times. In one rare exception, King Saul fell on his sword after getting mortally wounded in battle. Though the Bible doesn't directly condemn suicide, many people argue that Scripture opposes it in several passages.

- **"You must not murder anyone"** (Exodus 20:13 NCV). That includes ourselves, according to Bible experts even from early Christian centuries—such as Augustine in the AD 400s.
- **Why am I discouraged? Why is my heart so sad? I will put my hope in God!** (Psalm 42:5). Suicide suggests we've lost all hope—even our hope in God.

DOES SUICIDE LEAD TO HELL?

Some people think that anyone who commits suicide is doomed to eternity in hell.

Passages like the following lead them to believe that: "Don't you know that you are God's temple and that God's Spirit lives in you? If anyone destroys God's temple, God will destroy that person" (1 Corinthians 3:16–17 NCV).

Yet suicide isn't the topic in this letter. The writer, Paul, is pleading for unity in a fractured church. Most Bible experts say Paul is talking about people who run a church into the ground, destroying it.

The Bible doesn't say what happens to a person who commits suicide. In fact, speaking from the realm of the dead, the prophet Samuel had this to say to King Saul, who killed himself a few hours later: "Tomorrow. . .you and your sons will be here with me" (1 Samuel 28:19).

When it comes to judging the eternal destiny of suicide victims—or anyone else—it's best to leave that to God. He knows people better than we do. Even we know that many of the people who take their own lives are physically ill and not thinking rationally. God knows that, too.

TATTOOS

Jews weren't supposed to scar or tattoo their bodies. Though early Christians ignored many Jewish laws—like those about circumcision and kosher food—they agreed with Jews that the human body was God's masterpiece. Christians called it God's temple. Because of this, some Christians today say that wearing a tattoo is a bit like spray-painting graffiti on the walls of the Grand Canyon—to improve the looks. Or maybe like giving a Rembrandt to a kindergartner with a crayon.

- "Do not cut your bodies for the dead, and do not mark your skin with tattoos. I am the LORD" (Leviticus 19:28).
- I plead with you to give your bodies to God. . . . Let them be a living and holy sacrifice—the kind he will find acceptable (Romans 12:1).
- Don't you realize that your body is the temple of the Holy Spirit? (1 Corinthians 6:19).

See also *Body Piercing*

Colorized and pierced. A young woman wears a brilliant tattoo on her back and shoulder, while gauging (stretching) her earlobe to enlarge one of the holes. Tattoos and body piercing have become popular fads. The Bible doesn't condemn the practice or encourage it. But it does describe the canvas on which we're working—the human body—as one of God's masterpieces.

TEMPER

- It's smart to be patient, but it's stupid to lose your temper (Proverbs 14:29 CEV).
- Hot-tempered people must pay the penalty. If you rescue them once, you will have to do it again (Proverbs 19:19).

See also *Anger*

TEMPTATION

- Run away from the evil desires of youth (2 Timothy 2:22 NCV)
- The temptations in your life are no different from what others experience. And God is faithful. He will not allow the temptation to be more than you can stand. When you are tempted, he will show you a way out so that you can endure (1 Corinthians 10:13).
- Don't blame God when you are tempted! . . . We are tempted by

our own desires that drag us off and trap us. Our desires make us sin, and when sin is finished with us, it leaves us dead (James 1:13–15 CEV).

- The devil came to Jesus to tempt him, saying, "If you are the Son of God, tell these rocks to become bread." Jesus answered, "It is written in the Scriptures, 'A person lives not on bread alone by everything God says'" (Matthew 4:3–4 NCV). When Jesus is tempted while praying and fasting in the desert, he fights off the temptation by quoting relevant Bible verses.

TITHING

Jews in Old Testament times gave a tenth of their income to the temple. This paid for temple upkeep and the salaries of temple workers, and it helped the poor. Tithing isn't on the list of Christian obligations. In fact, early Christians refused to tithe. They said it represented Jewish legalism and was one of the many laws that became obsolete after Jesus came—like eating only kosher food. Instead of tithing, Christians gave offerings. In the 1800s, some Christian preachers began raising money for missionary work by teaching that the tithe was required of all Christians. The idea caught on and became a main way of funding local church ministries. Many Bible scholars say tithing is still a good and practical idea, because it takes money to run the church ministries. But they say it's wrong to insist that the Bible requires Christians to give 10 percent of their income. The apostles didn't teach that. Instead, they taught the first generation of Christians to give generous offerings.

Jewish tithes

- "One tenth of the produce of the land, whether grain from the fields or fruit from the trees, belongs to the LORD and must be set apart to him as holy" (Leviticus 27:30). This applied to animals and other goods, too. Animals, crops, and currency were all presented as gifts to God at the worship center.

- "Should people cheat God? Yet you have cheated me! But you ask, 'What do you mean? When did we ever cheat you?' You have cheated me of the tithes" (Malachi 3:8). Some Jews were skipping the tithes. Others were giving injured or diseased livestock instead of healthy animals as the law required.

- "Hypocrites! For you are careful to tithe even the tiniest income from your herb gardens, but you ignore the more important aspects of the law—justice, mercy, and faith" (Matthew 23:23). That's Jesus talking to Jewish religion scholars.

Christian offerings

- Believers in Macedonia and Achaia have eagerly taken up an offering for the poor among the believers in Jerusalem (Romans 15:26).

- You must each decide in your heart how much to give. Don't give reluctantly or in response to pressure. "For God loves a person who gives cheerfully." And God will generously provide all you need. Then you will always have everything you need and plenty left over to share with others. As the Scriptures say, "They share freely and give generously to the poor" (2 Corinthians 9:7–9). This is part of Paul's fund-raising letter for an offering he was collecting for believers in Jerusalem.

- All the believers were united in heart and mind. And they felt that what they owned was not their own, so they shared everything they had. . . . There were no needy people among them, because those who owned land or houses would sell them and bring the money to the apostles to give to those in need (Acts 4:32–35).
- Teach those who are rich in this world not to be proud and not to trust in their money. . . . Tell them to use their money to do good. They should be rich in good works and generous to those in need, always being ready to share with others (1 Timothy 6:17–18).

VIRGIN BIRTH

- God sent the angel Gabriel to Nazareth. . .to a virgin named Mary. . . . Gabriel appeared to her and said. . . "You will conceive and give birth to a son, and you will name him Jesus. . . . Mary asked the angel, "But how can this happen? I am a virgin" (Luke 1:26–34).
- Mary was engaged to be married to Joseph. But. . .while she was still a virgin, she became pregnant through the power of the Holy Spirit (Matthew 1:18).
- "The virgin will conceive a child! She will give birth to a son and will call him Immanuel (which means 'God is with us')" (Isaiah 7:14). Though the Hebrew word translated "virgin" in this passage can also mean "young woman," New Testament writers say this prophecy from about 700 BC points to the birth of Jesus. The Greek word translated "virgin" in the New Testament refers to a woman who has never had sex.

WAR

God led so many battles in Old Testament times that many people—some Jews included—thought of him as the god of war. Jesus came with a new message about how to deal with enemies.

God at war
- "Do not be afraid as you go out to fight your enemies today! Do not lose heart or panic. . . . For the LORD your God is going with you! He will fight for you against your enemies, and he will give you victory!" (Deuteronomy 20:3–4). These are the words of Moses shortly before the Jews invade what is now Israel.
- "In those towns that the LORD your God is giving you as a special possession, destroy every living thing. . .just as the LORD your God has commanded you" (Deuteronomy 20:16–17). Moses warned if the Jews didn't obey, enemy survivors would teach them to worship idols—which is exactly what happened.

Jesus calling for peace
- "Love your enemies! Pray for those who persecute you!" (Matthew 5:44). This is what Jesus told his fellow Jews after nearly a century of occupation by Roman forces. Jewish freedom fighters rebelled against Rome about 35 years later and were crushed.
- "Blessed are the peacemakers, for they will be called sons of God" (Matthew 5:9 NIV).
- "Put your sword back where it belongs. All who use swords are destroyed by swords. Don't you realize that I am able right now to call to my Father, and twelve companies—

more, if I want them—of fighting angels would be here, battle-ready?" (Matthew 26:52–53 THE MESSAGE). Jesus is talking to Peter, who's trying to defend him from temple police who have come to arrest him for a secret trial.

On guard.
A British soldier in Iraq guards a checkpoint while others patrol the oil fields.

SHOULD WE KILL FOR JESUS?

We can die for Jesus, but we shouldn't kill for him.

That's how many Christians interpret the teachings of Jesus. *Pacifists*. That's what these folks are called. They're against fighting in war.

When a nation's leader issues a call to arms against "evildoers," pacifist Christians reply with Jesus' call to disarm:

- "But I say to you, Do not resist an evildoer" (Matthew 5:39 NRSV).
- "All who use swords will be killed with swords" (Matthew 26:52 NCV).

Uncomfortable as it is to hear this, Jesus may have meant exactly what he said. He lived and died by these very words. Kidnapped for a secret trial, he didn't resist. And when Peter drew a sword to fight off the kidnappers, Jesus gave Peter the sword speech.

Now obsolete are all the old Jewish laws about an eye for an eye, execution of criminals, and the fighting of wars to defend justice—that's what many Christians say.

Non-pacifist Christians, however, ask why God would give us a survival instinct if he didn't intend for us to use it. But a counterpoint might be: Why would God give single people a sex drive and tell them not to use it? The answer to both questions: God knows—and we trust God.

Non-pacifist Christians interpret the antiviolence teachings of Jesus in many ways. Here are a few. Jesus' teaching is:

- A snapshot of what heaven is like and what Christians should strive for on earth—an unreachable goal that we should try to reach anyhow.
- Advice for a special class of believers—super Christians such as apostles, preachers, and monks.
- Advice for Jesus' first-generation disciples only, to help jump-start the church with miracles and meekness.

Non-pacifist Christians also remind us that Paul told Christians to "submit to governing authorities" (Romans 13:1). And they say this might include going to war for the country. Pacifist Christians would argue that this doesn't mean we have to do everything our political leaders tell us to do—especially if the orders conflict with the laws of God.

While we struggle to figure out how to do what Jesus said we should do, perhaps the only practical solution is this: When in doubt, don't kill.

WISDOM

- "Have respect for me [God]. That will prove you are wise" (Job 28:28 NIrV).
- God gives out Wisdom free. . . plainspoken in Knowledge and Understanding. He's a rich mine of Common Sense for those who live well (Proverbs 2:6–7 THE MESSAGE).
- Thinking about your teachings gives me better understanding than my teachers, and obeying your laws makes me wiser than those who have lived a long time (Psalm 119:99–100 CEV).

WITNESSING

- "Go and make disciples of all the nations, baptizing them in the name of the Father and the Son and the Holy Spirit. Teach these new disciples to obey all the commands I have given you. And be sure of this: I am with you always, even to the end of the age" (Matthew 28:19–20). Known as the Great Commission, these are the last words of Jesus to his disciples.
- If someone asks about your Christian hope, always be ready to explain it. But you must do this in a gentle and respectful way (1 Peter 3:15–16).
- God has not given us a spirit of fear and timidity, but of power, love, and self-discipline. So never be ashamed to tell others about our Lord (2 Timothy 1:7–8).
- "The fields are already ripe for harvest. The harvesters are paid good wages, and the fruit they harvest is people brought to eternal life. What

joy awaits both the planter and the harvester alike! (John 4:35–36).
- When I am with those who are weak, I share their weakness, for I want to bring the weak to Christ. Yes, I try to find common ground with everyone, doing everything I can to save some (1 Corinthians 9:22).
- I, too, try to please everyone in everything I do. I don't just do what is best for me; I do what is best for others so that many may be saved (1 Corinthians 10:33).
- "I will watch what I do and not sin in what I say. I will hold my tongue when the ungodly are around me" (Psalm 39:1).

WORRY

- Don't fret or worry. Instead of worrying, pray. Let petitions and praises shape your worries into prayers, letting God know your concerns. Before you know it, a sense of God's wholeness, everything coming together for good, will come and settle you down. It's wonderful what happens when Christ displaces worry at the center of your life (Philippians 4:6–7 THE MESSAGE).
- "I tell you not to worry about everyday life—whether you have enough food to eat or enough clothes to wear. . . . Can all your worries add a single moment to your life? . . . Don't worry about such things. These things dominate the thoughts of unbelievers all over the world, but your Father already knows your needs. Seek the Kingdom of God above all else, and he will give you everything you need" (Luke 12:22–31). Even if we're cold and starving,

destined to die, God gives us what we need: life that never ends.

- **"The battle is not yours, but God's"** (2 Chronicles 20:15). These are God's words to a Jewish king about to face an invasion force. But these words are repeated throughout the Bible, and they apply to all of life's battles for those of us who serve God.

WORSHIP

Some people say they worship best when they're alone—perhaps during a walk outside or even while watching television. Though it's true that we can and should worship God when we're alone, the Bible teaches that it's important to worship with other believers, too. Healthy spiritual relationships help us grow. We need each other.

Call to worship

- **Let us not neglect our meeting together, as some people do** (Hebrews 10:25).
- **"Where two or three gather together as my followers, I am there among them"** (Matthew 18:20).
- **"You have six days each week for your ordinary work, but the seventh day is a Sabbath day of complete rest, an official day for holy assembly. It is the LORD's Sabbath day, and it must be observed wherever you live"** (Leviticus 23:3). Number four of the 10 Commandments. Jews worship from sunset Friday to sunset Saturday. In honor of Jesus' resurrection, Christians started worshipping on Sundays.
- **Worship the LORD with gladness. Come before him, singing with joy** (Psalm 100:2).

- **Because of your great mercy, I come to your house, LORD, and I am filled with wonder as I bow down to worship** (Psalm 5:7 CEV).
- **"What does the LORD your God require of you? . . . Live in a way that pleases him, and love him and serve him with all your heart and soul"** (Deuteronomy 10:12).
- **When he [Jesus] came to the village of Nazareth, his boyhood home, he went as usual to the synagogue on the Sabbath** (Luke 4:16).

Fake worship

- **Do you think all GOD wants are. . . empty rituals just for show? He wants you to listen to him! Plain listening is the thing, not staging a lavish religious production** (1 Samuel 15:22 THE MESSAGE).
- **"These people honor me with their lips, but their hearts are far from me. Their worship is a farce, for they teach man-made ideas as commands from God"** (Mark 7:6–7). Jesus criticizes Jewish leaders who create their own rules for living that are supposedly based on the Bible. But those man-made rules often clash with Bible principles—harming people instead of helping them.
- **"You must not have any other god but me"** (Exodus 20:3). That's the first and most important of the 10 Commandments.

See also *Music*

YOUTH

- Do not let anyone treat you as if you are unimportant because you are young. Instead, be an example to the believers with your words, your actions, your love, your faith, and your pure life (1 Timothy 4:12 NCV).
- Don't let the excitement of youth cause you to forget your Creator. Honor him in your youth (Ecclesiastes 12:1).

- You who are young, make the most of your youth. Relish your youthful vigor. Follow the impulses of your heart. If something looks good to you, pursue it. But know also that not just anything goes; you have to answer to God for every last bit of it. Live footloose and fancy free—you won't be young forever (Ecclesiastes 11:9–10 THE MESSAGE).

After the hurricane. New Jersey high school students wheel supplies they collected for victims of the Katrina hurricane. From the left, they are Courtney Higgins, Bobby Lodato, Tyler Crum, Dan Arabia (all age 14) and Juliet Carafello, age 16. They not only helped fill a 40-foot trailer with clothing and other supplies, they helped pay the cost of shipping it 1,200 miles to New Orleans.

SIXTY-SIX BOOKS—THE SHORT COURSE

old testament

Genesis

sum it up

God creates a sinless utopia. But Adam and Eve, humanity's first couple, break God's one and only rule—they eat fruit from a forbidden tree. Somehow this sin changes them and the rest of creation. Sin spreads like a plague until God decides to cleanse the world with a flood, saving the family of the world's only righteous man: Noah. Next, God begins working his plan to restore his perfect creation and save human beings from sin. He starts with one man, Abraham, who becomes the father of the Jewish nation—a people devoted to God and destined to point the world to him.

5 W'S

- *Who wrote it?* Unknown. Moses wrote the first five books in the Bible, according to Jewish tradition. But most scholars today say they doubt it and that the stories read like a beautifully edited compilation.
- *What's it about?* Beginnings: of the universe, humanity, sin, and the Jewish nation
- *When did it take place?* The date of creation is unknown. Abraham, father of the Jews, lived about 2100 BC.
- *Where?* Throughout the Middle East, including Iraq, Israel, and Egypt
- *Why was it written?* To show that God is the source of life and founder of the Jewish nation

most famous quote

"In the beginning God created the heavens and the earth" (GENESIS 1:1).

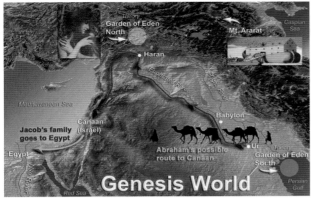

Genesis World

Mapping the beginning.

The Garden of Eden, according to one theory, may have been in the mountains that feed the Tigris and Euphrates rivers. Or, according to another theory, it may rest in the depths of the Persian Gulf—which is thought to have been a river before melting ice from the Ice Age raised the oceans and sent the Arabian Sea pouring into the river valley. Abraham grew up in Ur, in what is now southern Iraq, before moving to what is now Israel. His grandson Jacob later led the family into Egypt to escape a drought. There the Hebrews ended up as slaves. Moses led them home some 400 years later.

Biggest scene

"Let there be Light." Into the cosmic darkness of a starless void, God spoke those words. And there was light. "God called the light 'day' and the darkness 'night' " (Genesis 1:5).

Biggest ideas

God is the creator. Genesis isn't a science book about the how of creation. It's a religion book about the Who. Ancient stories said gods of Babylon created the world. But Genesis sets the record straight: the God of Israel is the Creator.

God punishes sin. From sin number one, it's clear in the Bible that God doesn't tolerate it. He will forgive us when we repent. But he won't let sin continue unchecked and unpunished.

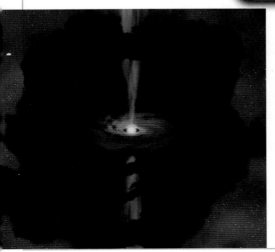

"Let there be light." With these words, the Bible says God began creation. Astronomers theorize that a star like our sun developed inside a dense cloud of gas and dust, as shown in this artist's interpretation. Gravity from the newborn star draws in the dust, which forms a swirling disc. Jets of some kind of material seem to spray out at both poles, based on evidence gathered from peering into these clouds with NASA's Spitzer Space Telescope. Genesis doesn't answer questions about how the universe was created. Instead, it answers the question of *who* created it.

Exodus

sum it up

A drought in what is now Israel drives Jacob's extended family to Egypt. For some reason they stay—430 years. Somewhere during that time their race grows so large that Egyptians fear they might take over. So the Egyptians enslave them. With God's help, Moses wins their freedom and leads them out of Egypt. On their way home, God organizes them into a nation—even giving them an elaborate set of laws that acts like a constitution, a legal code, and a church manual all rolled into one.

5 W's

- *Who wrote it?* Unknown. Jewish tradition says Moses.
- *What's it about?* The most famous event in 4,000 years of Jewish history: God freeing the Jews from Egyptian slavery.
- *When did it take place?* Either in the 1400s BC or the 1200s BC. Scholars don't agree.
- *Where?* Egypt
- *Why was it written?* To show that God himself took the Jews—his chosen people—and forged them into a nation uniquely devoted to him

most famous quote

"Let my people go" (EXODUS 5:1).

This is God's command to the king of Egypt.

Parting the water.

It's unclear what body of water Moses and the Hebrews crossed. The original Hebrew words call it *yam sup. Yam* means "sea." But *sup* can mean "reeds"—as in Sea of Reeds. Or it can mean "far away"—as in the Faraway Sea. Maybe the body of water was one of the large lakes in the area. Or maybe it was the northern tip of the Red Sea, at the narrow Gulf of Suez. Scientists have theorized that a wind blowing about 45 mph for 10 hours could push back the shallow northern shoreline for about a mile. If the Israelites crossed on a raised sandbar, there could have been water on both sides of them.

Biggest scene

Parting the Red Sea. Trapped between the advancing Egyptian chariot corps and a huge body of water, the fleeing Jewish refugees think they're doomed. But at God's command, Moses raises his walking stick and a wind blows all night, parting the water "so the people of Israel walked through the middle of the sea on dry ground" (Exodus 14:22). When the Egyptians follow, the water rushes in on them, killing them all.

Biggest idea

God shows his true colors. God reveals what he's like. His name is "I Am Who I Am" (Exodus 3:14). His nature is holy. His power is unlimited. And his plan is salvation—first for the Jews, but now for all who choose to serve him.

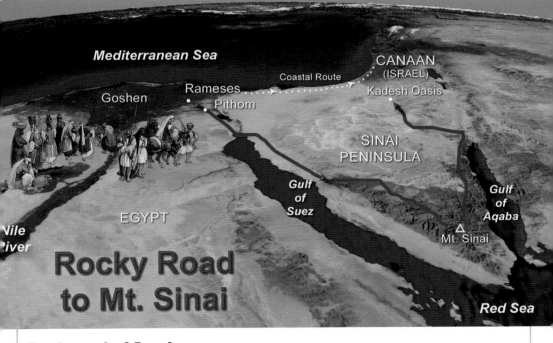

Mediterranean Sea

Coastal Route

CANAAN (ISRAEL)

Goshen   Rameses

Pithom

Kadesh Oasis

SINAI PENINSULA

Gulf of Suez

Gulf of Aqaba

EGYPT

Mt. Sinai

Nile River

Rocky Road to Mt. Sinai

Red Sea

Exodus out of Egypt. Freed from slavery in Egypt, the Hebrews didn't go home to Canaan—modern-day Israel—by the shortest route: along the coast. Egyptian forts guarded that road. So Moses turned the refugees south, to familiar land where he had once grazed his father-in-law's sheep. They spent about a year camped at Mount Sinai, getting organized as a nation. Then they moved up to an oasis at Kadesh-barnea where they stayed an entire generation—on God's order.

Leviticus

sum it up

After escaping the Egyptian army, Moses and the Jews camp for about a year at the foot of Mount Sinai. It's here they receive the 10 Commandments and hundreds of other laws that will guide them not only in worship, but also in running their nation. Also, here is where they build their first worship center, a tent called the tabernacle. This is a portable version of the temple that Jews will later build in Jerusalem.

5 W's

- *Who wrote it?* Unknown, though Jewish tradition says Moses wrote it.
- *What's it about?* Laws God gave Moses to govern the Jews
- *When did it take place?* Either in the 1400s BC or the 1200s BC
- *Where?* At the foot of Mount Sinai, probably in Egypt's Sinai Peninsula
- *Why was it written?* To preserve Jewish law and the story of their birth as a nation

MOST famous quote

"You must be holy because I am holy" (LEVITICUS 11:45 NCV).

Home of the 10 Commandments.

In a painting from the middle 1800s, a monastery marks the spot where Israelites camped at the foot of Mount Sinai while Moses climbed the mountain to receive the 10 Commandments.

Biggest scene

ordaining Israel's first priest. God selects Aaron, older brother of Moses, to become Israel's first high priest. Moses "poured some of the anointing oil on Aaron's head, anointing him and making him holy for his work" (Leviticus 8:12). Aaron and his sons lead the nation's worship.

Biggest idea

Holiness. This word shows up 152 times in Leviticus. There are two kinds of holiness: God's and ours. God's holiness is pure goodness off the scale. Human holiness is devotion to this holy God. When Jews wanted to use a utensil in the worship center, such as a candleholder, they had to perform rituals to devote the tool for use in God's service. That's when the utensil became holy. And when Jews wanted to worship God, they had to perform rituals to devote themselves to him—such as sacrificing an animal. Then they became holy.

It's the law.

Moses carries the stone tablets engraved with the 10 Commandments, the most basic rules on which all of Israel's laws were based.

Numbers

sum it up

After a year camped near Mount Sinai, the Jews take a census and continue their journey home. They arrive at the Promised Land's border but refuse to go farther—terrified by scouting reports of walled cities, armies, and giants. For their refusal and lack of faith, God sentences them to 40 years in the desert.

5 W's

- *Who wrote it?* Jewish tradition says Moses. That's partly because the book says, "Moses kept a written record of their progress" (Numbers 33:2).
- *What's it about?* Moses leading the Jewish refugees to the border of the Promised Land
- *When did it take place?* 1400s BC or 1200s BC
- *Where?* The Jews travel from what is now Egypt's Sinai Peninsula to an oasis near the southern border of Israel.

most famous quote

"*The LORD bless you and keep you; the LORD make His face shine upon you, and be gracious to you*" (NUMBERS 6:24–25 NKJV).

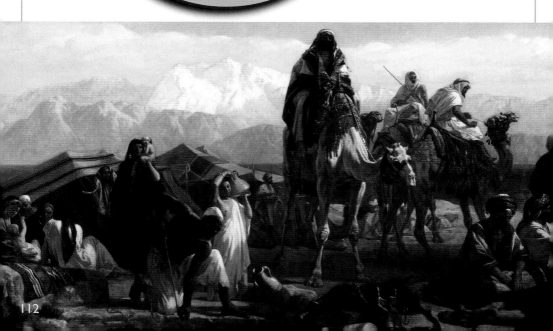

Biggest scene

sentenced to 40 years in the desert. With the Jews camped near the border of their homeland, Moses sends scouts ahead. Forty days later they come back with news: The land is fertile, but it's full of heavily fortified cities. "We even saw giants," the scouts said. "Next to them we felt like grasshoppers" (Numbers 13:33). Terrified, the Jews refuse to go farther. God sentences them to 40 years in the desert—one year for each day the scouts were in the land.

Biggest idea

Blatant sin gets stern punishment. After all the miracles the Jews had seen God perform—plagues in Egypt, parting the sea, providing manna—they still didn't have faith to believe he would defeat their enemies. When they refused to invade their homeland, God declared, "Not one of these people will ever enter that land" (Numbers 14:22).

Refugee census. Camped along the shores of the Red Sea, a Hebrew clan leader counts the people in his extended family. Moses ordered the census during the Exodus because the Hebrew refugees, recently freed from slavery in Egypt, would have to fight to take back their homeland of Canaan, now called Israel. Total count of fighting men age 20 and older: 603,550.

Deuteronomy

sum it up

A generation of Exodus Jews is dead. Their children, kids of the Exodus who are now grown, stand on the border of their ancestral homeland—eager to invade. Moses, near death, gathers them one more time to review the laws God gave them. He reminds them that their fathers made an agreement with God. If the nation obeys God, the people will be blessed. If they don't, they'll face hardship. Moses names Joshua his successor and then dies—never making it into the Promised Land.

5 W's

- *Who wrote it?* "Moses wrote this entire body of instruction in a book and gave it to the priests" (Deuteronomy 31:9).
- *What's it about?* Laws that Jews are to obey as their part of an agreement between God and the nation
- *When did it take place?* 1400s BC or 1200s BC
- *Where?* On Israel's eastern border, in what is now Jordan
- *Why was it written?* To preserve Jewish law

most famous quote

"Love the LORD your God with all your heart, all your soul, and all your strength" (DEUTERONOMY 6:5).

This was the most important Jewish law.

Biggest scene

choosing between Life and death. Near death himself, Moses tells the Jews they have to choose between life and death. If they honor their agreement with God and obey his laws, "God will set [them] high above all the nations of the world" (Deuteronomy 28:1). If they don't, "the LORD will scatter [them] among all the nations from one end of the earth to the other" (Deuteronomy 28:64).

Biggest idea

contract with God. *Deuteronomy* means "repeated law." For a second generation of Exodus Jews, Moses repeats the law God gave Generation One. This law is part of the covenant—or contract—between God and the Jews. And it's structured like ancient contracts and treaties, identifying the ruler, the history of the relationship, and the obligations of the ruler and the servant. As long as the Jews hold up their end of the agreement—obeying the law—God will protect and bless them.

Obey God's law or die.

Surrounded by members of his synagogue, a rabbi in 1878 holds a huge scroll containing Genesis through Deuteronomy—a section of the Bible that Jews call the Law. More than 3,000 years earlier, Moses warned the Jews that if they didn't obey the laws in these books, God would destroy their nation and drive the survivors out of the Promised Land. Invaders did, in fact, wipe the Jewish nation off the map in 586 BC. But God allowed the Jews to return 50 years later.

Joshua

sum it up

After 430 years in Egypt and 40 years in the desert badlands, the Jews finally come back to the land God promised them and their ancestor Abraham: Canaan, later called Israel. Joshua leads the Jewish invasion force, and they capture many walled cities in the highlands where foot soldiers have an advantage over chariots. Then Joshua divides the land among the 12 tribes of Israel and assigns each tribe the job of mopping up the last of the enemies in their own territory.

5 W's

- *Who wrote it?* Unknown. Joshua may have written it or at least supplied the information.
- *What's it about?* Jews taking back their homeland
- *When did it take place?* 1400s BC or 1200s BC
- *Where?* Canaan, in what is now Israel
- *Why was it written?* To preserve the story of how God helped the Jews regain their homeland

MOST famous quote

"Choose today whom you will serve. . . . But as for me and my family, we will serve the LORD" (JOSHUA 24:15).

From elderly Joshua's last speech to the Jews.

Biggest scene

Jericho walls come tumblin' down. The border town of Jericho, near the Jordan River, is the first to fall. And it falls literally. Jewish soldiers march around the city walls once a day for six days. Then on the seventh, they march around it seven times and blow ram's horn trumpets. The walls collapse—perhaps in a miracle of timing since the entire river valley sits on a massive, earthquake-producing rift in the earth's crust.

Biggest idea

The Land is God's gift. The Jewish invasion isn't a case of stealing land that belongs to people who have been living there for centuries. The land belongs to the Creator, and the Bible says he gave it to the Jews: "Wherever you set foot, you will be on land I have given you" (Joshua 1:3).

Taking the high ground.

Launching the invasion into what is now Israel, Joshua concentrates on the cities in the hills. There, his lightly armed militia has the advantage of mobility over heavily armed soldiers and their chariot corps.

Mt. Hermon

Mediterranean Sea

Hazor
Merom

Sea of Galilee

Achshaph

Shimron

Dor

3 DESTROY NORTHERN FORCES

2 DESTROY SOUTHERN FORCES

Bethel
Beth-Horon · · Ai   Gilgal
Gezer
Aijalon · Gibeon   Jericho
Jerusalem
Azekah · Jarmuth
Libnah
Lachish   Makkedah
Hebron   Dead Sea
Eglon
Debir

1 INVASION STARTS

· Army or city defeated
○ Battle

0 10 20 Miles
20 30 Kilometers

Jordan River

Judges

sum it up

Joshua dies and each tribe runs its own territory. But they don't finish the invasion by getting rid of all Canaanites living in the land. Instead, they treat Canaanites as neighbors and even begin worshipping their idols. God punishes the Jews, sending raiders to oppress them. The Jews call on God for help, and he sends a hero—known as a judge—who defeats the enemy. Judges like Samson, Gideon, and Deborah. The cycle of sin, punishment, repentance, and deliverance repeats a dozen times. By the book's end, anarchy reigns.

5 W's

- *Who wrote it?* Unknown. Jews in ancient times said the prophet Samuel compiled these stories.
- *What's it about?* Sins of the Jews making it impossible to find lasting peace in their homeland
- *When did it take place?* From the 1400s BC or the 1200s BC until about 1050 BC
- *Where?* Israel
- *Why was it written?* Perhaps to show how Israel's 12 tribes became alienated from God and from each other, to the point that they needed a king to reunite them politically and spiritually

most famous quote

"In those days Israel had no king; all the people did whatever seemed right in their own eyes" (JUDGES 21:25).

This one-sentence portrait of anarchy ends the sad book.

Biggest scene

Samson gets a haircut. Philistines hire Delilah to find the source of this muscleman's strength. "If my head were shaved, my strength would leave me," he confides, before laying his locks on her lap and taking a nap (Judges 16:17). He wakes up with a buzz.

Biggest idea

God's relentless love. There are 12 heroic judges in this stretch of Jewish history. A dozen times the Jews slip into idolatry, face punishing oppression, and then call on God for help. And God helps them—every time. The story feels like the parable of the prodigal son in a loop, with sinners leaving and then coming home to papa over and over. Papa is always waiting with open arms. Love is like that.

Bringing down the house.
Captured, blinded, and imprisoned by the Philistines, Israelite hero Samson gets his revenge. He pushes over the pillars supporting their crowded temple, killing more Philistines in that single moment than in all his years of fighting them. Samson dies, too.

Ruth

sum it up

A Jew from Bethlehem moves his family to Moab, in what is now Jordan, to escape a drought. His two sons marry Moabite women, but the sons and father die. His elderly wife, Naomi, decides to go home to Bethlehem. One daughter-in-law, Ruth, goes with her. There, Ruth marries Boaz and gives birth to a son: Obed, grandfather of King David.

5 W's

- *Who wrote it?* Unknown, but a masterful writer of one of the Bible's best-crafted stories
- *What's it about?* A non-Jewish widow who becomes mother of Israel's most famous family of kings
- *When did it take place?* 1100s BC
- *Where?* In Moab (now Jordan) and in Bethlehem
- *Why was it written?* To show that the royal family of David and Solomon began with a non-Jewish woman —perhaps to refute the argument that it was still wrong for Jews to marry non-Jews

most famous quote

"Wherever you go, I will go; wherever you live, I will live. Your people will be my people, and your God will be my God" (RUTH 1:16).

Ruth, speaking to her mother-in-law, Naomi.

Biggest scene

Ruth sneaks under the covers of a man. When a rich farmer makes his bed outside to protect his crops at harvest-time, Ruth bathes, puts on perfume and her best clothes, and then slips under his covers while he's asleep. It's not a setup. It's custom—a way for Ruth to ask a relative of her dead husband to marry her. The Jewish welfare system encouraged men to marry and care for widows of their dead relatives. The man, Boaz, agrees to Ruth's request: "I will redeem you myself!" (Ruth 3:13).

Biggest idea

God Loves outsiders. God repeatedly tells the Jews to take care of widows, the poor, and strangers in the land. He practices what he preaches. Ruth—who was all the above—becomes mother of Israel's greatest dynasty of kings.

Arab mother of Jewish kings. Ruth,

the mother of Israel's most revered family of kings, including David and Solomon, was no more Jewish than this Arab woman from Egypt. Ruth grew up in what is now Jordan, Israel's Arab neighbor to the east. But she married a Jewish man from Bethlehem. Their son became the grandfather of King David and a descendant of Jesus.

1 Samuel

sum it up

Last of Israel's heroic judges, the prophet Samuel leads the tribes of Israel until Jewish elders ask for a king. Samuel's feelings are hurt, but God says, "It is me they are rejecting, not you. They don't want me to be their king any longer" (1 Samuel 8:7). At God's command, Samuel warns the people that kings will demand a lot: money, land, servants. But the people persist, so Samuel anoints their first king: Saul. Years later, Saul breaks God's law by offering a sacrifice only a priest is allowed to offer. So God has Samuel anoint young David as the future king who will take over when Saul dies.

5 W's

- *Who wrote it?* Unknown. Samuel may have written part of it, since it seems he did write some history in a lost book called *The Record of Samuel the Seer* (1 Chronicles 29:29).
- *What's it about?* Israel's transition from a loose-knit coalition of 12 tribes to a nation under one king
- *When did it take place?* The stories begin with the birth of Samuel in about 1100 BC.
- *Where?* Israel
- *Why was it written?* To preserve the story of how Israel became a nation ruled by kings

most famous quote

"Obedience is better than sacrifice" (1 SAMUEL 15:22).

Biggest scene

Giant killer. Armed with just a slingshot, the shepherd boy David takes on the Philistine champion Goliath, a giant armed with the best weapons of his day—including newly invented iron hardware. With the Jewish army cowardly watching from a distance, David drops Goliath, takes the giant's sword, and cuts off the head of his victim (1 Samuel 17:51).

Biggest idea

It's the thought that counts. "People judge by outward appearance, but the Lord looks at the heart" (1 Samuel 16:7). That's what God tells Samuel when Samuel nearly chooses David's older, taller, and handsome brother as Israel's next king. With God, it's the spirit of the person that matters, not the looks.

Stone Age beats Iron Age.

Philistines entrust their secret weapon to their greatest warrior, Goliath, a giant towering nearly seven feet tall—10 feet according to some ancient manuscripts. Armed with weapons made of iron, a strong new metal that can slice through the soft, bronze weapons of the Israelites, Goliath faces a shepherd boy in mortal combat. Goliath must have thought it was a joke—until David's slingshot fired a rock missile into his forehead.

B. Gallegos

2 Samuel

sum it up

King Saul and most of his sons die in a battle with the Philistines. David becomes the new king of Israel, and he proves himself a gifted military and political leader—though a flawed family man. He secures Israel's border by defeating the Philistines and other threatening neighbors, and he sets up his capital in Jerusalem. But at home, his family is falling apart. In time, one of his sons, Absalom, kills his own half brother and then leads a coup against David. Absalom dies in the battle.

5 W's

- *Who wrote it?* Unknown
- *What's it about?* David's reign as king of Israel
- *When did it take place?* David became king in about 1000 BC.
- *Where?* Israel
- *Why was it written?* To preserve the story of King David's life and leadership

most famous quote

"How the mighty have fallen!" (2 SAMUEL 1:19 NKJV).

David's reaction to the death of Saul and sons.

King David's bathing beauty.

David already has at least seven wives and 16 sons when he happens to see Bathsheba taking a bath. She's the wife of a soldier who's fighting a war about a three-day march from home. David likes what he sees, invites Bathsheba to the palace, has sex with her, and gets her pregnant. In the tragedy that follows, her husband and newborn son both end up dead. But she marries David and later gives birth to Solomon, who will become Israel's king after David.

Biggest scene

David watches Bathsheba bathe. With at least seven wives of his own, King David—walking on the flat roof of his palace—sees the wife of a soldier bathing below. David likes what he sees, so he invites her to the palace and has sex with her. She gets pregnant. To cover up the adultery, David orders her husband to the front line of battle, where he gets killed. David marries Bathsheba (2 Samuel 11).

Biggest idea

God's a forgiver. No sin is too big for God to forgive—not even adultery and murder. At least not for people like David, who sincerely repent (2 Samuel 12:13). Consequences for bad decisions are inevitable, but the loss of God's love is not one of them.

1 Kings

sum it up

Elderly David dies, but not before turning the nation over to his son Solomon, who builds a glorious kingdom—but at a high price. When Solomon's son takes over and refuses to reduce taxes and forced labor, the nation splits. Ten northern tribes break away and take the name of Israel. The two southern tribes remain loyal and take the name of the largest tribe: Judah. If we could measure sin on a scale, the northern nation—with evil rulers like Ahab and Jezebel—would probably win the heavyweight bout.

most famous quote

"Cut the living child in two, and give half to one woman and half to the other!" (1 Kings 3:25).

See "Biggest scene" for the background.

5 W's

- *Who wrote it?* Unknown. Jews in ancient times said the prophet Jeremiah wrote 1 and 2 Kings, which were originally a single book.
- *What's it about?* The united nation of Israel, rich and prosperous during Solomon's reign, but splitting in two after he dies
- *When did it take place?* This history covers about 120 years, from the beginning of Solomon's reign in about 970 BC until about 850 BC.
- *Where?* Israel
- *Why was it written?* To preserve highlights and dark days of Jewish history in both nations, north and south

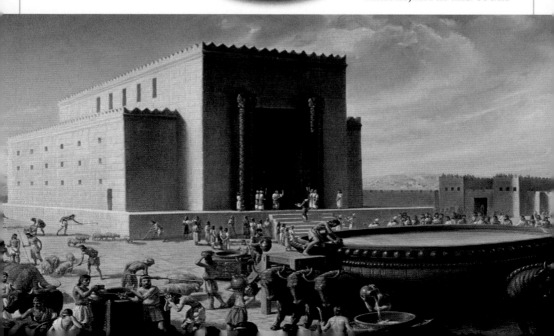

Biggest scene

A king, a sword, and a baby. In a court case, Solomon has to decide which of two women is actually the mother of a newborn son. Both women—who are prostitutes and roommates—delivered about the same time. But one accidentally rolled onto her son and suffocated him while they were sleeping together. Then she switched babies with her roommate. Solomon decides to slice the surviving baby in two, dividing it between the mothers. One agrees, but the other says, "Please do not kill him!" (1 Kings 3:26). Love link established as clearly as genetic links ever could be, Solomon returns the boy to his rightful mother.

Biggest idea

Getting what's coming to you. Focusing on kings at both ends of the character scale—godly and evil—the writer emphasizes that God rewards obedience and punishes sin.

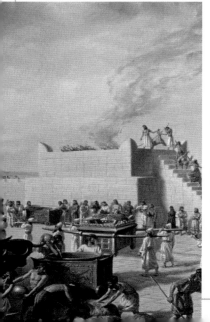

A place to worship. Solomon drafts nearly 200,000 men to work seven years building Israel's first permanent worship center: a temple in Jerusalem. Before that, Jews worshipped at a tent—a tradition started by Moses during the Exodus. Only priests are allowed inside the temple. All others stay out in the courtyard where they sacrifice animal offerings and burn them on top of a huge altar (right). The massive basin in the foreground holds water for the cleansing rituals, such as washing blood off the meat and the hands.

2 Kings

sum it up

Godly kings occasionally rule the two Jewish nations—but it's rare, especially in the north. Both nations are slipping into idolatry—distancing themselves from God. Patiently, God sends several generations of prophets to warn the Jews that they'll lose their homeland—as Moses had warned centuries earlier—if they continue to break their agreement with God. Sin plays on. So God sends invaders to carry out his punishment. Assyrians from what is now Iraq wipe the northern Jewish nation off the political map in 722 BC. And more than a century later, Babylonians, also from Iraq, do the same to the southern nation. Israel is gone.

5 W's

- *Who wrote it?* Unknown. Jews in ancient times said Jeremiah wrote 1 and 2 Kings.
- *What's it about?* Death of the Jewish nation
- *When did it take place?* Spanning almost 300 years, from about 850 BC until 586 BC, when invaders destroyed the last Jewish nation
- *Where?* The two Jewish nations: Israel in the north of modern-day Israel, and Judah in the south
- *Why was it written?* To show how sin brought the punishment Moses said would come if Jews broke their agreement with God: "The LORD will scatter you among all the nations" (Deuteronomy 28:64).

most famous quote

"He did what was evil in the LORD's sight" (2 KINGS 3:2).

This phrase is used more than two dozen times to describe the Jewish kings and people.

CASPIAN SEA
BLACK SEA
TURKEY
IRAN
Nineveh
SYRIA
IRAQ
LEBANON
KUWAIT
PERSIAN GULF
ISRAEL
WEST BANK
SAUDI ARABIA
MEDITERRANEAN SEA
GAZA STRIP
JORDAN
EGYPT
RED SEA
ASSYRIAN EMPIRE

Biggest scene

Jerusalem dies. The Babylonian king Nebuchadnezzar invades the last remaining Jewish nation for repeated rebellion. He levels one fortified city after another, saving Jerusalem for last. His army breaks through the walls, slaughters most of the people, levels the buildings, and takes survivors with him as prisoners. The Jewish nation survives only as a tragic memory.

Biggest idea

God punishes persistent sin. Both Jewish nations continued sinning, no matter what God did to warn them of the consequences. Eventually, God's patience gives way to punishment. But it's punishment with a purpose: to restore the Jewish nation as a godly people.

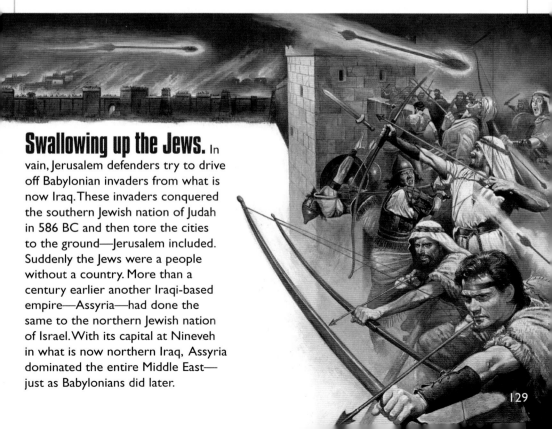

Swallowing up the Jews. In vain, Jerusalem defenders try to drive off Babylonian invaders from what is now Iraq. These invaders conquered the southern Jewish nation of Judah in 586 BC and then tore the cities to the ground—Jerusalem included. Suddenly the Jews were a people without a country. More than a century earlier another Iraqi-based empire—Assyria—had done the same to the northern Jewish nation of Israel. With its capital at Nineveh in what is now northern Iraq, Assyria dominated the entire Middle East— just as Babylonians did later.

1 Chronicles

sum it up

This book reads like a spin version of 1 Kings—accentuating the positive. But it's not spin. Both books cover much the same history: the time of Saul and David. But 1 Kings wants to show Jews exiled in what is now Iraq that it was sin that got them there. And 1 Chronicles wants to show Jews who have come back to Israel that it was God's forgiveness that brought them home. Each writer had a different purpose. One emphasizes sin. The other emphasizes God's mercy.

5 W's

- *Who wrote it?* Uncertain. Jews in ancient times said a priest named Ezra wrote both books of Chronicles, which were originally one book.
- *What's it about?* Jewish history, mostly during the reigns of kings Saul and David
- *When did it take place?* The story begins with a family tree starting at Adam. The book ends with the death of King David in about 970 BC.
- *Where?* Israel
- *Why was it written?* To convince Jews returned from exile that they are still God's chosen people and that Israel is still their promised land

most famous quote

"Give thanks to the LORD, for He is good! For His mercy endures forever" (1 CHRONICLES 16:34 NKJV).

Israel's treasure.

The gold-plated Ark of the Covenant was a chest that held the original 10 Commandments. Israel's most sacred object, the Ark was kept in the holiest room of the Temple.

Biggest scene

Jerusalem becomes a sacred city. After David makes Jerusalem the political capital of Israel, he makes it the spiritual capital, too. He accomplishes this by bringing to town the most sacred Jewish object: the ark of the covenant, a chest containing the 10 Commandments. And he does so, "skipping about and laughing with joy" (1 Chronicles 15:29).

Biggest idea

God has restored Israel. Jews are back in their homeland, rebuilding cities destroyed during an invasion several decades earlier. God's forgiveness and mercy are the reasons they are back. Once again, they have a future and a mission: "Sing to God, everyone. . . . Get out his salvation news. . . . Publish his glory among the godless nations" (1 Chronicles 16:23-24 THE MESSAGE).

David's Jerusalem.

Shaped a bit like Florida, David's Jerusalem covered just the bottom half of a ridge, below the white dots—about 15 acres. That's roughly the size of a shopping mall parking lot. His son Solomon later added the square section above, where he built the temple. Today, a 1,300-year-old, gold-domed Muslim shrine called the Dome of the Rock sits on the temple hilltop. And Jerusalem has spread out to cover about 47 square miles.

2 Chronicles

sum it up

Part two of this generally upbeat history of Israel starts with the reign of Solomon, who led the Jews during their most prosperous generation. The writer zeroes in on mainly the good kings who follow. But in the end, he admits that sin led to the nation's downfall. The Jewish nation splits into two countries. God sends invaders to crush both nations and to exile the survivors—first the northern country of Israel, then the southern country of Judah. But several decades after the fall of Judah, God also prompts the Persian king Cyrus to free the exiles—just as prophets had predicted.

5 W's

- *Who wrote it?* Uncertain. Jewish tradition says a priest named Ezra wrote it.
- *What's it about?* Jewish history from King Solomon to the Jewish return from exile
- *When did it take place?* Spanning almost 500 years, from about 970 BC to 500 BC
- *Where?* Israel, Iraq (then called Assyria and Babylon), Iran (Persia)
- *Why was it written?* To convince Jews back from exile that they are still God's chosen people and that Israel is still their promised land

most famous quote

"If my people who are called by my name will humble themselves and pray and seek my face and turn from their wicked ways, I will hear from heaven and will forgive their sins and restore their land" (2 CHRONICLES 7:14).

Biggest idea

Failure isn't final. Jews broke their agreement with God. Had they served him as they promised, he would have protected them—as he promised. But they failed him. Now, as they return to their decimated homeland, they want to know if they can have a fresh start—still the chosen people in the Promised Land. The writer's reply from history: "The LORD will stay with you as long as you stay with him!" (2 Chronicles 15:2).

Biggest scene

Emancipation proclamation for Jews. A people without a nation, Jews live as refugees in what is now Iraq and Iran for about 50 years—their homeland demolished by invaders. But a new empire rises to power. And its king, Cyrus of Persia, issues a decree freeing the Jews to go home (2 Chronicles 36:23).

Emperor Cyrus on the record.

After Persians from what is now Iran defeated the Babylonian Empire headquartered in modern-day Iraq, Persian emperor Cyrus freed the Jews from their exile. (Below) A nine-inch-long clay cylinder dating from that time—536 BC—confirms the Bible's report. The cylinder says Cyrus freed all Babylon's captives and told them to go back to their homelands, rebuild their temples, and pray for him every day.

Ezra

sum it up

After 50 years exiled in Iraq and Iran, the Jews are freed to return home and rebuild their nation. They start by rebuilding homes and later the Jerusalem temple. About 80 years after the first wave of Jews return, a priest named Ezra arrives with another group. To his horror, he discovers that many Jews are breaking some of God's most important laws. Knowing that this kind of sin led God to destroy the Jewish nation earlier, Ezra urgently begins teaching the laws to the people. Crowds repent of their sins and agree to serve God.

5 W'S

- *Who wrote it?* Unknown. Jews in ancient times said Ezra wrote it.
- *What's it about?* Jews returning from exile and rebuilding their nation
- *When did it take place?* After their exile from Israel in 586 BC, the first wave of Jews returns home about 50 years later, in about 538 BC. Ezra's group follows 80 years after the first wave, in about 458 BC.
- *Where?* The story begins in the empire of Babylon, in what is now Iraq. And it ends in Israel.
- *Why was it written?* To preserve the story of God graciously allowing the Jews to come back to the Promised Land, even though centuries of Jews had broken their agreement to serve God. This is the story of forgiveness and a second chance.

most famous quote

"He is good, for His mercy endures forever"

(Ezra 3:11 NKJV).

Caravaning home.

Pushing on to sundown, a camel caravan passes near Jerusalem. Ezra and other Jews followed a thousand-mile caravan route from what is now Iraq to Jerusalem—in a journey that took four months.

Biggest idea

God is no spectator in human history. He can even get godless rulers involved in his plan—just as he stirred the Persian king Cyrus to free the Jews (Ezra 1:1).

Biggest scene

A new temple. For 70 years, the Jews had no place to worship God. The only sacrifices they could offer were sacrifices of prayer and praise by reading their scriptures. Now home again, they rebuild the temple that invaders had leveled. As they laid the foundation, "all the people gave a great shout, praising the LORD" (Ezra 3:11).

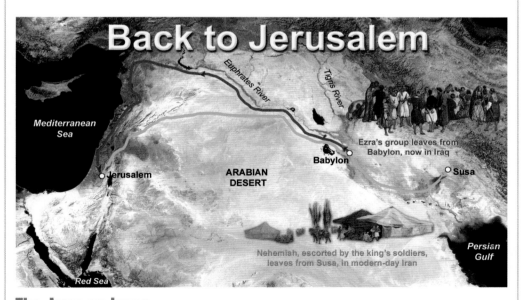

Back to Jerusalem

Mediterranean Sea

Euphrates River

Tigris River

Ezra's group leaves from Babylon, now in Iraq

Babylon

Susa

Jerusalem

ARABIAN DESERT

Nehemiah, escorted by the king's soldiers, leaves from Susa, in modern-day Iran

Persian Gulf

Red Sea

The Jews go home. Deported for 50 years into what are now Iraq and Iran, the first wave of Jews return home. Ezra and Nehemiah follow about a century later—Ezra from Babylon, in modern-day Iraq, and Nehemiah from Susa, in what is now Iran.

Nehemiah

sum it up

Nehemiah, a Jew who serves in the palace of the Persian king in what is now Iran, gets depressed when he hears that Jerusalem's walls are still busted—apparently by invaders who decimated the Jewish homeland some 140 years earlier. The king appoints Nehemiah temporary governor of the Jewish homeland and grants him a leave of absence to rebuild the walls. Nehemiah manages to accomplish the job in an astonishing 52 days, in spite of attempts by non-Jewish settlers in the region to assassinate him.

5 W's

- *Who wrote it?* Unknown. Jews in ancient times said a priest named Ezra wrote it along with the books of 1 and 2 Chronicles and Ezra.
- *What's it about?* A Jewish official in Persia—now called Iran—who returns to Jerusalem to rebuild the city walls
- *When did it take place?* Spanning a dozen years, between 445 and 433 BC
- *Where?* Nehemiah served the Persian king in Susa, a city now on Iran's border with Iraq. But he became temporary governor of Judah, in what is now southern Israel.
- *Why was it written?* To preserve the miraculous story of how Jerusalem's walls were rebuilt in only 52 days

Most famous quote

"The joy of the LORD is your strength!" (NEHEMIAH 8:10).

Fixing Jerusalem's walls.

Nehemiah leaves his palace job in what is now Iran to go back to his Jewish homeland and rebuild Jerusalem's walls. Bible experts debate how extensive Jerusalem's walls were at the time. One popular view, shown in this model, is that they rebuilt only around David's original settlement and the square temple area that Solomon added onto the city (top). That's about 1.5 miles of walls enclosing 50 acres.

Biggest idea

The can-do God. Restoring the walls of Jerusalem in less than two months was such a remarkable feat that even the non-Jews who had tried to stop the project "realized this work had been done with the help of our God" (Nehemiah 6:16).

Biggest scene

Armed builders. Non-Jews who settled in the land after the Jews were exiled aren't happy to see the Jews come back and start rebuilding Jerusalem. Nehemiah, fearing those settlers will attack, orders his builders to work with one hand and to hold a weapon with the other (Nehemiah 4:17).

Esther

sum it up

The number two official in Persia, a man named Haman, plots to kill all Jews in the empire—not realizing that Queen Esther is Jewish. Haman's motive is to get revenge on a Jew named Mordecai who refuses to bow to him. Without even identifying the target race, Haman convinces the king to sign an irrevocable order allowing citizens to slaughter the Jews on a certain day and take their property. Mordecai, Esther's cousin who raised her, convinces her to tell the king she's a Jew and to explain what's about to happen to her people. When the king finds out, he orders Haman hanged. Then he allows the Jews to protect themselves on the day set for the holocaust.

5 W'S

- *Who wrote it?* Unknown. But the writer seems to have been a Jew in Persia (modern-day Iran) well acquainted with customs of Persians and Jews.
- *What's it about?* A Jewish queen who stops a Persian-led holocaust of Jews
- *When did it take place?* Sometime during the 21-year reign of Xerxes, from 486 to 465 BC
- *Where?* The Persian city of Susa, in Iran near the border with Iraq
- *Why was it written?* To preserve the story of a near-holocaust and the history behind the Jewish springtime festival called Purim, which celebrates the holocaust missed

most famous quote

"Who knows, you may have been chosen queen for just such a time as this" (ESTHER 4:14 NCV).

From Jewish orphan to Arab queen.

Queen Esther enjoys a meal with her husband, the king of Persia. Esther was a young Jewish orphan raised by her cousin in what is now Iran. But as a young adult she got noticed during an empire-wide search for women beautiful enough to become the Persian king's wife. She won the beauty contest and became queen. Esther later used her influence to save the Jewish people from a Persian holocaust. One of the Persian officials hatched a plot to kill all Jews throughout the vast empire, which stretched 6,000 miles from what is now India to Libya.

Biggest idea

God at work behind the scenes. God's name doesn't even appear in this book. But many see him at work throughout the story in several events that seem more than a coincidence. One example, Esther—a Jewish orphan—becomes queen of an Arab empire just in time to protect her people from an empire-wide holocaust.

Biggest scene

A feast to die for. Queen Esther invites Haman to a royal banquet, which he thinks is to honor him. Instead, she reveals she's a Jew—a target of his plot. Haman falls on her, pleading for mercy, but the king thinks he's attacking and perhaps raping her (Esther 7:8). So the king orders Haman hanged immediately.

Daniel in the lions' den: a Jew in big trouble in Iran.

Persian palace guard

Queen Esther, a Jew, ruled with the king in Susa.

Job

sum it up

God lets Satan test the faith of a righteous man named Job. Raiders steal Job's livestock—more than 10,000 animals. A windstorm kills his 10 children. And then boils erupt all over his body. Friends plead with him to repent, since they're convinced God is punishing him for sin. But Job maintains his innocence and demands that God explain himself. Instead, God convinces Job to trust him no matter what. In time, God heals Job and gives him 10 more children and double the livestock he had before.

most famous quote

"Naked I came from my mother's womb, and naked shall I return" (JOB 1:21 NKJV).

5 W's

- *Who wrote it?* Unknown
- *What's it about?* A man who lost his children, health, and flocks—and who wants God to tell him why
- *When did it take place?* Clues in the story suggest it took place about the time of Israel's founding fathers—Abraham, Isaac, Jacob—roughly 2000 BC.
- *Where?* "In the land of Uz" (Job 1:1). It's unclear where Uz was.
- *Why was it written?* To show that suffering isn't always punishment from God. Sometimes it comes for reasons that only God knows.

Debating the Creator.

Job wasn't especially patient. After losing his health, herds, and children for no apparent reason, Job blamed God. In his misery, Job essentially asked, "Do you have any idea what you're doing to me?" God answered with questions like, "Can you shout to the clouds and make it rain?" (Job 38:34).

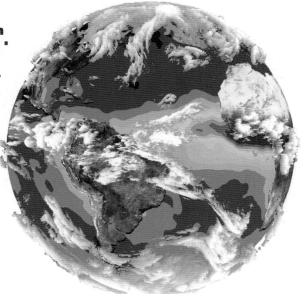

Biggest idea

Trusting God even when we can't understand him. Job asked God to explain why he would do something that seems so unjust—making a righteous man suffer for no apparent reason. God answers with questions such as this: "Where were you when I laid the foundations of the earth? Tell me, if you know so much" (Job 38:4). Job got the point: God knows what he's doing.

Biggest scene

Scraping boils. His livestock and children gone, Job now loses his health as well. His skin erupts into oozing, itching sores. And he sits in an ash pile, scratching his skin "with a piece of broken pottery" (Job 2:8). Sitting in ashes is a way to express grief. Job's wife advises him to curse God so God will kill him—putting Job out of his misery.

When life stinks. Job's wife pours cool water on him to ease the itching from boils that have erupted on his skin. His distressing story can be summed up in a single question he asks God: "Why?" Job wants God to tell him what he did to deserve losing his health, his children, and his vast herds. God's answer, essentially, is, "Trust me."

Psalms

sum it up

This is a Jewish songbook—lyrics without the musical notes. Most of the songs are complaints and requests, asking God for help. But many are praises and bold statements of faith. Jews sang them in their homes, while walking to Jerusalem, and in the temple courtyard when they gathered for a religious festival.

5 W'S

- *Who wrote it?* Seventy-three songs are attributed to David, but in a vague way that could mean "by David," "for David," or "in the style of David." Other songs are attributed to Solomon, Moses, and Asaph, one of David's musicians.
- *What's it about?* Complaints, praises, prayer requests, promises—just about anything a person would say to God
- *When did it take place?* The songs were probably written over many centuries, perhaps spanning nearly a thousand years from the time of Moses to the rebuilding of Jerusalem in the 500s BC.
- *Where?* The songs are set throughout the Middle East, from Persia (modern-day Iran) to Egypt.
- *Why was it written?* To express humanity's deepest feelings about spiritual matters—from anger and fear to faith

Most famous quote

"Though I walk through the valley of the shadow of death, I will fear no evil" (Psalm 23:4 NKJV).

Gentle shepherd. A shepherd smiles as he watches over his flock grazing in green pastures near Jericho. There's one particular psalm that people throughout the centuries have found comforting in times of crisis. It's a song that compares God to a loving shepherd. "The Lord is my shepherd; I have all that I need. He lets me rest in green meadows; he leads me beside peaceful streams" (Psalm 23:1–2).

Biggest idea

Be honest with God. No feeling we experience—high or low—needs censored from God. We can be completely honest with him, telling him about our anger, fears, problems, and dreams. He can take it. And sometimes we need him to take it, because we can't handle it on our own.

Biggest scene

A near-death experience. In the face of imminent death, one notable poet compares God to a shepherd. The poet vows, "I will not be afraid, for you are close beside me. Your rod and your staff protect and comfort me" (Psalm 23:4). This chapter is read at the bedside of the dying perhaps more than any other words ever written.

Psalms you can dance to. "Praise him with the tambourine and dancing," urges the poet of a song in Israel's ancient hymnbook, "praise him with strings and flutes" (Psalms 150:4). Many of the psalms were song lyrics set to music, though the tunes have been lost to history. Jewish families used to sing the psalms while working, playing, and worshipping.

Proverbs

sum it up

This book sounds like a collection of advice from a convention of grandfathers worried about their grandkids. King Solomon and other Jewish elders pass along lessons of life especially for young men—though most tips are just as relevant for men and women of any age. Short and snappy, most suggestions are two-liners—making them easy to remember. They cover the kind of practical topics we don't usually study in school but need to learn from someone. A sampling: when not to loan money, how to avoid sexual temptation, how to discipline kids, and the short course on a nagging spouse.

5 W'S

- *Who wrote it?* Solomon and other wise men
- *What's it about?* Conveying "knowledge and sense to the young" (Proverbs 1:4 NCV)
- *When did it take place?* Solomon lived and wrote in the 900s BC.
- *Where?* Israel
- *Why was it written?* As a "a manual for living, for learning what's right and just" (Proverbs 1:3 THE MESSAGE)

most famous quote

"Those who spare the rod hate their children" (PROVERBS 13:24 NRSV).

This verse that spawned the saying, "Spare the rod, spoil the child," isn't a command from God to beat kids. Shepherds used rods to gently nudge their straying sheep back to safety. This verse is a call from Jewish elders for parents to correct their kids when the kids do something wrong.

How to treat the lady of the house.

Wise old men behind all the good advice in Proverbs have a particular piece of advice for young married men: "Drink water from your own well—share your love only with your wife" (Proverbs 5:15). No women on the side. Men should treat their wives as a treasure more valuable than jewels. For "she is more precious than rubies" (Proverbs 31:10).

Biggest idea

Trust God. "Trust God from the bottom of your heart; don't try to figure out everything on your own. Listen for God's voice in everything you do, everywhere you go; he's the one who will keep you on track" (Proverbs 3:5-6 THE MESSAGE).

Biggest scene

Treasure your wife. Saving some of the best advice for last, sages close the book by telling each young man to cherish his wife. "A truly good wife is the most precious treasure a man can find!" And when found, she deserves to hear these words: "There are many good women, but you are the best!" (Proverbs 31:10, 29 CEV).

Good advice from wise old men. Jewish men study the Bible and compare their thoughts. Proverbs is a collection of practical advice about godly living—offered by elderly men for young men. These elders have high hopes that the young men of Generation Next won't have to learn life's lessons like they did—the hard way.

Ecclesiastes

sum it up

In what sounds like a wise man working through a midlife crisis—contemplating his inevitable death—Ecclesiastes starts off with a bleak observation about life: "Everything is meaningless" (Ecclesiastes 1:2). We get rich and die, and then someone else spends our money. We make no difference in the universe— the sun rises with or without us. Life is short, the writer concludes, so we should enjoy it while we can—as a gift from God.

5 w's

● *Who wrote it?* "These are the words of the Teacher, King David's son, who ruled in Jerusalem" (Ecclesiastes 1:1), presumably Solomon.

● *What's it about?* The meaning of life

● *When did it take place?* Solomon lived in the 900s BC.

● *Where?* Israel

● *Why was it written?* As a reflection of one man's attempt to discover what life is all about

most famous quote

"Eat, drink, and enjoy life" (ECCLESIASTES 8:15).

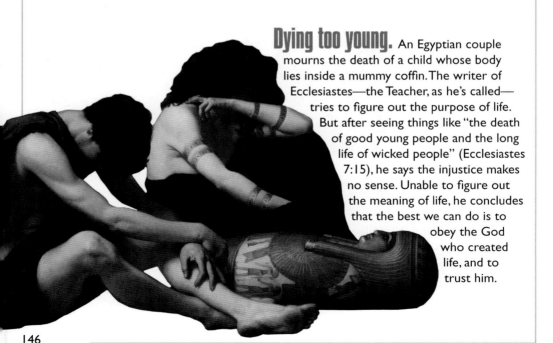

Dying too young. An Egyptian couple mourns the death of a child whose body lies inside a mummy coffin. The writer of Ecclesiastes—the Teacher, as he's called— tries to figure out the purpose of life. But after seeing things like "the death of good young people and the long life of wicked people" (Ecclesiastes 7:15), he says the injustice makes no sense. Unable to figure out the meaning of life, he concludes that the best we can do is to obey the God who created life, and to trust him.

Biggest idea

OBEY GOD. "Everything you were taught can be put into a few words: Respect and obey God! This is what life is all about" (Ecclesiastes 12:13 CEV).

Biggest scene

"To everything there is a season, a time for every purpose under heaven: a time to be born, and a time to die" (Ecclesiastes 3:1-2 NKJV).

A time to eat. A buffet delight fills the table as friends share a meal. The writer of Ecclesiastes encourages people to enjoy the blessings God gives them—and to share with others. "Someday you will be rewarded" (Ecclesiastes 11:1 CEV).

Song of Songs

sum it up

There's a reason we don't hear this book read in churches very often. It can be a bit embarrassing to read out loud because it's full of intimate sex talk. Without being crude or vulgar, a man and woman in love unapologetically express their desire for each other—including their desire to make love. Scholars in ancient times said this story is a metaphor about God's love for people. But most Bible experts today disagree. Imagine God telling humanity, "Your navel is perfectly formed like a goblet filled with mixed wine" (Song of Songs 7:2). Most scholars agree that this is a love song about a man and a woman, not a metaphor of God's love for us.

5 W's

- *Who wrote it?* "This is Solomon's song of songs" (Song of Songs 1:1), though it may have been written *for* him instead of *by* him.
- *What's it about?* A couple in love
- *When did it take place?* Solomon reigned from about 970 to 930 BC.
- *Where?* Israel
- *Why was it written?* As a love song, perhaps to entertain wedding guests

MOST famous quote

"Your love is sweeter than wine" (Song of Songs 1:2).

Armed and dangerous.

Helping romance along, Cupid—mythological son of Venus, goddess of love—loads a hormone-laced arrow for his next target. Presbyterians in the 1600s were among the first to say the Song of Songs was about physical love. Furious, most British church leaders argued that it was shameful to treat the sacred Song as "a hot carnal pamphlet formed by some loose Apollo or Cupid."

Biggest idea

sexuality is a gift of God. God gave us sexuality to express the intimate feelings we have for the person we've promised ourselves to for life.

Biggest scene

Anticipating the honeymoon. In sensually intimate love talk, the man tells the woman of his dreams: "You are slender like a palm tree, and your breasts are like its clusters of fruit. . . . I will climb the palm tree and take hold of its fruit" (Song of Songs 7:7-8).

Love song. Reading Solomon's Song of Songs is a bit like eavesdropping on a young couple in love, listening to their intimate love talk—including their desire to make love.

Isaiah

sum it up

The prophet Isaiah didn't have a prayer. When God told him to warn the Jews to stop sinning or to suffer the consequences, Isaiah asked how long he should do this. "Until their towns are empty," God said, "their houses are deserted" (Isaiah 6:11). Isaiah lived to see Assyrian invaders wipe the northern Jewish nation of Israel off the map in 722 BC, exiling the survivors. The Babylonians did the same to the southern nation of Judah in 586 BC.

5 W's

- *Who wrote it?* Isaiah. Some scholars say he wrote only chapters 1–39, since 40–66 deal with later centuries. Others say Isaiah predicted those events.
- *What's it about?* A choice: Repent or suffer an invasion that will destroy the Jewish nation.
- *When did it take place?* Isaiah ministered about 740–700 BC.
- *Where?* Israel, with exile in Babylon, in what is now Iraq
- *Why was it written?* To warn the Jews that if they didn't repent, their nation would die

most famous quote

"Unto us a Child is born, unto us a Son is given. . . . His name will be called Wonderful, Counselor, Mighty God, Everlasting Father, Prince of Peace" (ISAIAH 9:6 NKJV).

Biggest idea

punishment with a purpose. Even in punishing people for sin, God's goal is to restore the broken relationship. So though the Jews face exile for their sins, God promises to bring them home happy in the Lord (Isaiah 41:16).

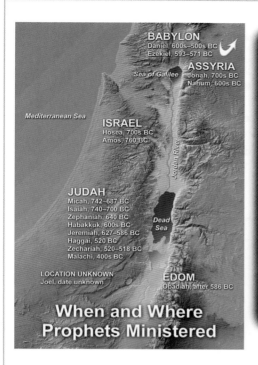

BABYLON
Daniel, 600s–500s BC
Ezekiel, 593–571 BC

ASSYRIA
Sea of Galilee
Jonah, 700s BC
Nahum, 600s BC

Mediterranean Sea

ISRAEL
Hosea, 700s BC
Amos, 760 BC

Jordan River

JUDAH
Micah, 742–687 BC
Isaiah, 740–700 BC
Zephaniah, 640 BC
Habakkuk, 600s BC
Jeremiah, 627–586 BC
Haggai, 520 BC
Zechariah, 520–518 BC
Malachi, 400s BC

Dead
Sea

LOCATION UNKNOWN
Joel, date unknown

EDOM
Obadiah, after 586 BC

When and Where Prophets Ministered

Biggest scene

God's suffering servant. Of the many prophecies in this book pointing to Jesus, the most dramatic one describes him as God's servant, suffering for others. "He was pierced for our rebellion, crushed for our sins. He was beaten so we could be whole. He was whipped so we could be healed. . . . He was struck down for the rebellion of my people. . . . He was put in a rich man's grave" (Isaiah 53:5–9).

Jesus, 700 BC. Roman

officials beat Jesus shortly before the Crucifixion. More than 700 years before Jesus, the prophet Isaiah described the beating, death, and burial of Jesus almost like an eyewitness would have done—identifying him only as a suffering servant. Isaiah explained the reason behind the suffering: "The LORD decided his servant would suffer as a sacrifice to take away the sin and guilt of others" (Isaiah 53:10 CEV). Isaiah's book has so many predictions about Jesus—more than any other book in the Old Testament—that Bible scholars have nicknamed it "the Fifth Gospel."

Jeremiah

sum it up

Jeremiah is the prophet who not only predicts the Jewish nation's death—he lives to see it. Jeremiah apparently helps start a revival in the early years of his ministry, with King Josiah tearing down pagan shrines. But when Josiah dies, sin is resurrected. Even the fall of the northern Jewish nation of Israel a century earlier didn't convince Jews in the southern nation of Judah that they might be headed for the same fate. But they were. Babylonian invaders pour into Judah and erase it from the world map.

5 W's

- *Who wrote it?* Jeremiah dictated it to a writer, Baruch.
- *What's it about.?* The last years of the Jewish nation of Judah
- *When did it take place?* Jeremiah prophesied about 40 years, from 627 to 586 BC.
- *Where?* Israel and Babylon (Iraq)
- *Why was it written?* To preserve the story of how sin caused the Jews to lose their homeland and how God's grace would restore it once they repented

most famous quote

"Can a leopard take away its spots?"
(JEREMIAH 13:23).

Biggest idea

The wages of sin is death. The Jewish national debt came due in 586 BC, after hundreds of years of persistent sin—with only an occasional righteous generation. "No amount of soap or lye can make you clean," God told them (Jeremiah 2:22). They were stained with guilt that could not be washed away. It didn't have to be like that. "No matter how deep the stain of your sins, I can remove it," God had said through a prophet a century earlier. "Though your sins are like scarlet, I will make them as white as snow" (Isaiah 1:18). But they didn't want a spiritual bath. So they ended up in a bloodbath.

Biggest scene

Good-bye, Jerusalem. After destroying walled cities throughout the Jewish nation, Babylonian invaders storm into the capital, Jerusalem. They slaughter many people, leveling the buildings—including the 400-year-old temple Solomon built. They even tear down "the walls of the city" (Jeremiah 39:8). Then they march survivors into exile.

When depression makes sense.

Beyond pensive, the prophet Jeremiah looks lost—with good reason. For years he has predicted God would punish the Jews for their sin by letting invaders destroy the Jewish nation. In his senior years, Jeremiah lives to see it.

Lamentations

sum it up

The saddest book in the Bible, this is a blues song—a bitter lament by a man who witnessed the massacre that turned Jerusalem into a ghost town. He tells of an invasion force from what is now Iraq wiping out the Jewish cities and then laying siege to Jerusalem for so long that starving people inside resorted to cannibalism. Jerusalem fell and survivors were taken prisoner to Babylon. There—remembering the promised land lost—this grieving writer cries "until the tears no longer come; my heart is broken. My spirit is poured out in agony as I see the desperate plight of my people" (Lamentations 2:11).

5 W's

- *Who wrote it?* Unknown, but it follows the book of Jeremiah because Jews in ancient times said Jeremiah wrote both books; the writing styles are similar.
- *What's it about?* Mourning over the loss of Jerusalem
- *When did it take place?* 500s BC
- *Where?* Perhaps written during exile in Babylon, in what is now Iraq
- *Why was it written?* As an expression of grief and a prayer for God's help

Most famous quote

"Great is thy faithfulness" (LAMENTATIONS 3:23 KJV).

Babylonian blues. "Beside the rivers of Babylon, we sat and wept as we thought of Jerusalem. We put away our harps, hanging them on the branches of poplar trees" (Psalm 137:1–2). Invaders from Babylon, now called Iraq, had overrun the Jewish nation and destroyed the capital city of Jerusalem. Then they took Jewish survivors back to Babylon as captives and asked them to sing songs about their former homeland. The Jews refused.

Biggest idea

GRIEF FROM A TO Z. Not only are the lyrics sad, but the book's format dramatically reinforces this message. Most chapters contain 22 verses—the length of the Hebrew alphabet. Each verse in each chapter starts with a different letter beginning with aleph—the Hebrew *a*—and working through the alphabet. The point: Jews have suffered grief from A to Z, many times over.

Biggest scene

CANNIBAL MOTHERS. Surrounded by an army for about two and a half years, starving people inside Jerusalem turn barbaric. "Mothers eat their own children, those they once bounced on their knees" (Lamentations 2:20).

Lamentations at a stone wall. A Jewish man prays at Jerusalem's Western Wall. Some read Lamentations here, too. It makes sense. This book laments the fall of Jerusalem and the temple. And the Western Wall—the holiest place in Judaism—is all that's left of the temple. This stone wall is part of a retaining wall that holds up the hillside where the temple once stood.

Ezekiel

sum it up

For five years, the young priest Ezekiel has been held hostage in what is now Iraq. He was taken there, into the heart of the Babylonian Empire, with about 10,000 other upper-class Jews. They were hostages, held to make sure the Jewish nation didn't rebel against the empire. In a dramatic vision there, God calls Ezekiel to become a prophet. Ezekiel warns that the Jewish nation will, in fact, rebel and will then be destroyed. Survivors will join him in a distant exile. But Ezekiel adds that in time God will "bring them home from the lands of their enemies" (Ezekiel 39:27).

5 W's

- *Who wrote it?* "Ezekiel son of Buzi, a priest" (Ezekiel 1:3)
- *What's it about?* The end of the Jewish nation, with the promise of a new beginning
- *When did it take place?* Ezekiel prophesied more than 20 years, from about 593 to 571 BC.
- *Where?* "In the land of the Babylonians" (Ezekiel 1:3), now Iraq
- *Why was it written?* To assure Jews—who will find themselves as refugees without a country—that God will eventually bring them home

Most famous quote

"Dry bones, hear the word of the LORD" (EZEKIEL 37:4 NCV).

Biggest idea

Sin doesn't stop God from loving us. God punishes us when we keep sinning—individually and sometimes on a national scale. But his punishment isn't vindictive. It's intended to correct us, because he never stops loving us.

Biggest scene

Dry bones come to Life. God gives Ezekiel a vision that takes place in a sprawling valley filled with human bones. It looks like the site of a long-ago massacre. Suddenly, detached bones start popping into place. Tendons, muscle, and skin erupt onto the skeletons. Then a wind blows life into newly formed lungs. The corpses stand, alive again. "These bones represent the people of Israel," God says. "I will open your graves of exile and cause you to rise again" (Ezekiel 37:11-12).

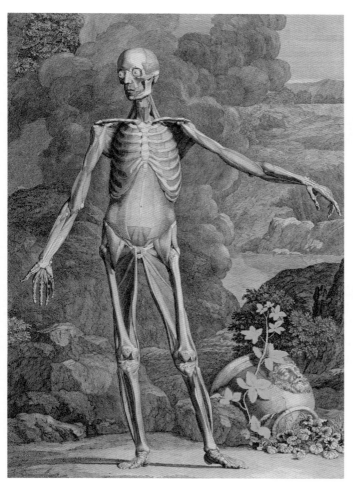

Alive again.

The human body, as envisioned by a medical artist in 1749. Ezekiel's most famous vision takes place in a valley full of human skeletons. Suddenly the bones snap together. Tissues start growing and cover the bones. Then, with lungs resuscitated by the wind, the bodies stand—alive. God says what he did for these bones, he'll do for Israel. The dead nation will live again.

Daniel

sum it up

Daniel and his friends—Shadrach, Meshach, and Abednego—are among thousands of upper-class Jews taken hostage to Babylon, now called Iraq, to keep the Jewish nation from rebelling. They are selected to serve in the palace. And they do so with distinction, though getting into trouble for refusing to worship other gods. Daniel survives the night in a lions' den, and his three friends survive a walk inside a furnace. The book ends with a collection of Daniel's visions that seem to point to end times.

5 W's

- *Who wrote it?* Unknown. Daniel may have written parts of it.
- *What's it about?* God's unstoppable power and his willingness to use it to help his people
- *When did it take place?* Daniel's story begins in about 605 BC and continues for some 60 years.
- *Where?* Babylon and Persia, now Iraq and Iran
- *Why was it written?* To preserve stories of Daniel in exile and his prophecies about the future

most famous quote

"God sent his angel to shut the lions' mouths" (DANIEL 6:22).

Biggest idea

God steps into human history. All creation belongs to God. He's not limited to some heavenly, parallel dimension. When circumstances demand it, he steps into the physical world—sometimes into a lions' den and sometimes into a furnace. "I see four men, unbound, walking around in the fire," the king declared after putting Daniel's three friends in a furnace. "Unharmed! And the fourth looks like a god!" (Daniel 3:25).

Biggest scene

Daniel in the Lions' den. Palace officials jealous of Daniel decide to get rid of him. They convince the king to sign an irrevocable law, ordering people to pray only to him—or become lion bait. For praying openly to God, Daniel spends the night in a lions' den and survives. The king, who is fond of Daniel and angry about being manipulated by the others, throws his conniving officials to the lions, which "tore them apart before they even hit the floor of the den" (Daniel 6:24).

Bow or die. Daniel's friends—Shadrach, Meshach, and Abednego—refuse to bow before the king's new golden idol. So they end up in a furnace. God, however, protects them. When the king sees they aren't burning, he orders them to come back out. "They didn't even smell of smoke!" (Daniel 3:27).

Hosea

sum it up

God asks a holy man—the prophet Hosea—to do the unthinkable in that ancient culture: marry a prostitute. Hosea's marriage would become an acted-out parable with an unforgettable message. The bride, Gomer, later gives birth to three kids—perhaps none of whom belongs to Hosea. Then she leaves her family, apparently becoming an enslaved prostitute. At God's order, Hosea buys her freedom and takes her back. The powerful message: People of Israel have committed spiritual adultery, but God is willing to forgive them and take them back.

5 W's

- *Who wrote it?* "Hosea the son of Beeri" (Hosea 1:1)
- *What's it about?* Israel's unfaithfulness by worshipping other gods
- *When did it take place?* Hosea ministered from about 750 to 722 BC, when invaders overran Israel.
- *Where?* The northern Jewish nation of Israel
- *Why was it written?* To show God's willingness to forgive

most famous quote

"Sow the wind, and reap the whirlwind" (HOSEA 8:7 NKJV).

Biggest idea

If we repent, God forgives–no matter how bad the sin.
For more than two centuries, Israel has been breaking the first and most important of the 10 Commandments: "You must not have any other god but me" (Exodus 20:3). Even then, God is still willing to forgive.

Biggest scene

DO you take this prostitute as your wedded wife? Essentially, that's the question God asked Hosea. "Go and marry a prostitute, so that some of her children will be conceived in prostitution. This will illustrate how Israel has acted like a prostitute by turning against the LORD and worshipping other gods" (Hosea 1:2). Hosea's reply: "I do."

Hosea and the hooker.

In God's most bizarre request of any prophet, he tells Hosea to marry a prostitute. Hosea's life becomes a living parable. It symbolizes how Israel has acted like a prostitute—committing spiritual adultery against God by worshipping other gods.

Joel

sum it up

Locusts by the millions swarm into Israel, devouring crops and even stripping bark off the trees. Without shade, the streams dry up, drought sets in, and people and their livestock begin to starve. The prophet Joel uses this disaster as an object lesson. He warns that an even worse invasion is coming—an army that will punish the Jewish people for their persistent sinning.

MOST famous quote

"Hammer your plowshares into swords and your pruning hooks into spears" (JOEL 3:10).

5 W's

- *Who wrote it?* "Joel son of Pethuel" (Joel 1:1)
- *What's it about?* A military invasion that will decimate the Jewish nation
- *When did it take place?* Unknown. Though Joel warns of an invasion, it's not clear which one: Assyrians in the 700s BC, Babylonians in the 500s BC, or perhaps Alexander the Great with his Greek army in the 300s BC.
- *Where?* Israel
- *Why was it written?* To urge the Jews to repent so God wouldn't send invaders to punish them

Desert locust. Photographed during a 1915 locust plague in what is now Israel, this short-legged cousin of a grasshopper eats its weight in food each day. A small one-ton swarm can out-eat 10 elephants. The bigger the swarm, the more agitated and aggressive the locusts become.

Biggest idea

when the Day of the Lord means trouble. The "Day of the Lord" used to mean good news for the Jews—God coming to Israel's rescue to punish their enemies. But Joel redefines that phrase. On this Day of the Lord, the Jews are the enemies. God is coming for them if they don't repent.

Biggest scene

Locust tsunamis. Four tidal waves of locusts crash onto Israel—one after another. "What the cutting locusts have left, the swarming locusts have eaten; what the swarming locusts have left, the hopping locusts have eaten; and what the hopping locusts have left, the destroying locusts have eaten" (Joel 1:4 NCV).

Locusts on vacation. Running from the beach, vacationers on the Canary Islands off the coast of North Africa fight their way through a swarm of locusts. Millions of these migratory grasshoppers devastated a third of the crops in North Africa during 2004. Locust infestations were even more common in Bible times, before pesticides. Joel uses an infestation as an object lesson to warn the Jews that something far more destructive is coming: a military invasion.

Amos

sum it up

Livid with anger, the prophet Amos warns several nations that God will punish them for their sins. But Amos is never more furious than when he's talking about the northern Jewish nation of Israel—a kingdom bustling with prosperity but spiritually dead, stuffed, and hanging on the wall trying to look pretty. "Sin all you want!" Amos says sarcastically. "Offer sacrifices the next morning" (Amos 4:4 CEV). The Jews are faking religion by sleepwalking through their worship rituals. But Amos assures them God won't fake their punishment. Even so, the Jews still have time to repent. "Come back to the LORD and live! Otherwise, he will roar through Israel like a fire, devouring you completely" (Amos 5:6).

5 w's

- *Who wrote it?* "Amos, a shepherd" (Amos 1:1)
- *What's it about?* Sin, especially injustice and exploitation of the poor
- *When did it take place?* Amos seems to have lived in the mid-700s BC, before Assyrian invaders decimated Israel in 722 BC.
- *Where?* Amos lived in Tekoa, in the southern Jewish nation of Judah. But he delivered his warning mainly to the northern Jewish nation of Israel.
- *Why was it written?* To warn the Jews to repent, or suffer the consequences: nationwide annihilation

most famous quote

"Prepare to meet your God" (AMOS 4:12).

biggest idea

A nation without justice. Rich Jews and their political leaders "trample helpless people in the dust and shove the oppressed out of the way" (Amos 2:7). Judges take bribes. And poor people are sold into slavery to pay off debts no higher than the price of a pair of sandals.

Biggest scene

Fat cows on the hook. "Listen to me, you fat cows living in Samaria, you women who oppress the poor and crush the needy, and who are always calling to your husbands, 'Bring us another drink!' . . . The time will come when you will be led away with hooks in your noses" (Amos 4:1-2).

"We're not beggars!" That's what these unemployed Palestinians and their families chant as they hold up pieces of bread and protest to their Palestinian leaders for the right to earn a living. Amos was a Jewish prophet who spoke out for the poor. He warned that God would soon punish the rich of Israel for exploiting the poor and for driving them deeper into poverty. Amos probably lived to see Assyrian invaders from what is now Iraq conquer Israel, confiscate the wealth, and take the rich people with them in chains.

Obadiah

sum it up

Invaders, probably from the Babylonian Empire in what is now Iraq, destroy cities throughout the Jewish nation. Jewish refugees run for their lives to the neighboring country of Edom, in what is now Jordan. Showing no pity, the people of Edom kill many of the frantic Jews. Then they arrest the others and hand them over to the invaders. Afterward, they loot the abandoned Jewish cities. What Edom did to Israel, God vows, Israel will one day do to Edom, "devouring everything. There will be no survivors in Edom" (Obadiah 18).

5 W's

- *Who wrote it?* A prophet named Obadiah
- *What's it about?* God's promise to destroy Edom
- *When did it take place?* Uncertain. Perhaps shortly after invaders from what is now Iraq destroyed Jerusalem in 586 BC.
- *Where?* Edom, in what is now Jordan
- *Why was it written?* To assure Jews that God would punish Edom for killing so many of them and for looting Jewish cities

most famous quote

"As you have done, it will be done to you" (OBADIAH 15 NIV).

166

Biggest idea

Payback. Though the Jews are powerless to avenge themselves and to give the people of Edom the punishment they deserve, God is not powerless. Edom's chief city, Petra, is now a ghost town visited by tourists.

Biggest scene

Refugee killers. Jews run for their lives from invaders, escaping to the rock hills of neighboring Edom. But instead of helping the Jews, people of Edom killed many and arrested others, "and handed them over in their terrible time of trouble" (Obadiah 14).

Rock City. A narrow passage through rock mountains (left) opens into Petra—hidden capital of ancient Edom. This natural barrier made it easy to defend the city. But Obadiah warned that Edom's rock fortress wouldn't stop God from punishing them.

Jonah

sum it up

God tells the prophet Jonah to take a nearly thousand-mile walk to the capital of Israel's most feared enemy: Nineveh, in the Assyrian Empire. Jonah's assignment: "Announce my judgment against it" (Jonah 1:2). Nineveh lies to the east. But Jonah books passage on a west-bound ship. When a gale-force storm threatens to sink the ship, Jonah tells the sailors that he's running from God and that the storm will calm if they throw him overboard. A large fish—not necessarily a whale—swallows him and spits him ashore. Jonah finally goes to Nineveh. Surprisingly, the people repent and God spares them.

5 W's

- *Who wrote it?* Bible experts can't tell if Jonah wrote it or if someone wrote it about him.
- *What's it about?* God sending a prophet to warn Assyrians they are about to be destroyed
- *When did it take place?* Uncertain. A prophet with the same name, "Jonah son of Amittai," lived during Assyrian times in the 700s BC (2 Kings 14:25).
- *Where?* Nineveh, near what is now Mosul, Iraq, along the northern border with Turkey
- *Why was it written?* To show that God loves everyone—even non-Jews

Most famous quote

"The LORD had arranged for a great fish to swallow Jonah" (JONAH 1:17).

Biggest idea

Mercy enough for everyone. Jonah was one of the Bible's few successful prophets. He actually convinced an Assyrian emperor and the entire capital city to repent. But Jonah got upset that God didn't destroy Nineveh. Jonah actually pouted about it and asked God to kill him. God replied with a question. "Nineveh has more than 120,000 people living in spiritual darkness," God said. "Shouldn't I feel sorry for such a great city?" (Jonah 4:11). This abrupt, unusual ending is one reason some Bible experts say the story is a parable, like those Jesus later told. Others say it's a true story.

Biggest scene

Fish bait. Sailors throw Jonah into the sea to calm a fierce storm that he caused by running from God. A big fish swallows him, and Jonah remains inside for "three days and three nights" (Jonah 1:17).

SPAIN
Tartessus

ITALY

Sardinia

GREECE

TURKEY

Nineveh

Carthage

Black Sea

Mediterranean Sea

ISRAEL
Joppa

EGYPT

Jonah's destination: unknown site called Tarshish. Possibly Tartessus, Sardinia, or Carthage.

Jonah's Scenic Route to Nineveh

Wrong-way Jonah. God orders the Israelite prophet Jonah east, to preach against Nineveh—capital of Israel's most feared enemy: the Assyrian Empire. It would have been like God ordering a rabbi to Germany during World War II to preach against Hitler. Survival instinct alive and well, Jonah books passage on a ship headed in the opposite direction. God does not approve. A gale-force storm lands Jonah in the water. And a large, unidentified fish gulps him down and three days later spits him up. Ashore again, Jonah starts his nearly thousand-mile walk to Nineveh.

Micah

sum it up

Saturated with corruption—that's how prophets described both Jewish nations in Micah's day: Israel in the north and Judah in the south. So God sends this small-town prophet to condemn the people. Rich princes feed off the poor: "You chop them up like meat for the cooking pot" (Micah 3:3). Prophets tell the future for a profit. Judges sell justice to the highest bidder. Bankers become loan sharks, circling the needy and then feeding in frenzies. Nearly everyone worships idols. For sins like these, Micah warns, God will wipe out both nations. Micah lives to see the northern nation fall in 722 BC.

5 W's

- *Who wrote it?* Micah
- *What's it about?* Sins of the two Jewish nations
- *When did it take place?* Micah lived during the time of three kings reigning from 750 to 686 BC
- *Where?* Micah lived in the hill-country village of Moresheth, about a day's walk from Jerusalem.
- *Why was it written?* To warn that God would destroy both Jewish nations

most famous quote

"*They will hammer their swords into plowshares and their spears into pruning hooks*" (MICAH 4:3).

This is Micah's portrait of a future era of peace.

Biggest idea

There's hope on the other side of doom. Micah and other prophets are famous for preaching doom. But they also promised that after God punished the nations for sin, he would restore the survivors and give them a fresh start: "Those who were exiles will become a strong nation" (Micah 4:7).

Biggest scene

Bethlehem's prince of peace. Micah predicts that when Israel is dominated by its enemies, a Jewish ruler will be born in Bethlehem. He will be one "whose origins are from the distant past. . . . And he will be the source of peace" (Micah 5:2, 5). Based on this verse, Jews expected that the Messiah would come from this village—where Jesus was born.

O little town. In a photo from a century ago, a Bethlehem woman draws water from a well on the outskirts of her hilltop hometown. Seven centuries before Jesus was born here, the prophet Micah predicted that this tiny village, former hometown of King David, would one day produce another great ruler.

Nahum

sum it up

The prophet Nahum has a promise for one of the vilest empires ever to rise like scum out of sewer water: God will flush them down. "I will send you to the grave. . . . You will never again make victims of others" (Nahum 1:14; 2:13 CEV). That promise is directed at the Assyrians—invaders from what is now Iraq who in 722 BC had erased the northern Jewish nation of Israel from the world map.

5 W's

- *Who wrote it?* Nahum
- *What's it about?* The end of the Assyrian Empire
- *When did it take place?* The Assyrian capital fell to Babylonians in 612 BC.
- *Where?* Elkosh, a village probably somewhere in the southern Jewish nation of Judah
- *Why was it written?* To assure Jews that God will punish the Assyrian Empire, known throughout the Middle East for its cruelty

most famous quote

"The LORD is good, a refuge in times of trouble" (NAHUM 1:7 NIV).

172

Biggest idea

God is the man. There is no greater power. Period. "Billowing clouds are the dust beneath his feet. . . . In his presence the mountains quake" (Nahum 1:3, 5).

Biggest scene

Nineveh exposed. Assyria's revered capital, Nineveh, is dishonored, exposed, and trashed. "I will pull your dress up over your face and show the nations your nakedness and the kingdoms your shame. I will throw filthy garbage on you" (Nahum 3:5-6 NCV).

Blood sport. Backed up by bodyguards, an Assyrian king kills lions for sport. The "hunt" takes place in the arena at his capital city of Nineveh in what is now northern Iraq. Assyrians used terror and violence to build their empire, invading countries throughout the Middle East and forcing them to pay annual taxes. Nahum predicted that God would send this city to the grave. Babylonian invaders from southern Iraq did just that, demolishing Nineveh in 612 BC. The once-great capital now lies in ruins, still buried under a mound of dirt.

Habakkuk

sum it up

The prophet Habakkuk isn't shy about complaining to God. Complaint number one: The Jewish nation is crazy with sin—violence, bribery, and injustice. So God promises to send Babylonian invaders to punish the Jews. Complaint number two: Habakkuk can't believe God is serious. "Don't sit by in silence while they gobble down people who are better than they are" (Habakkuk 1:13 CEV). But God assures Habakkuk that the invaders will eventually face their own judgment day, too.

5 W's

- *Who wrote it?* Habakkuk
- *What's it about?* An invasion force God is sending to punish the Jews
- *When did it take place?* Probably in the 600s BC, shortly before Babylonian invaders from what is now Iraq conquered the Jews in 586 BC
- *Where?* The southern Jewish nation of Judah
- *Why was it written?* As an expression of absolute faith in God no matter what happens

most famous quote

"The righteous will live by their faithfulness to God" (HABAKKUK 2:4).

This verse helped start the Protestant movement by convincing a German priest named Martin Luther that people are saved by faith in God, not through church rituals.

Biggest idea

In God we trust. Habakkuk trembles when he hears that invaders are coming. But he believes God knows what's best. "Counting on God's Rule to prevail, I take heart and gain strength. . . . I feel like I'm king of the mountain!" (Habakkuk 3:19 THE MESSAGE).

Biggest scene

Faith alive and well when everything else is dead. Invaders have decimated the land. But Habakkuk vows, "Even though the fig trees have no blossoms, and there are no grapes on the vines; even though the olive crop fails, and the fields lie empty and barren; even though the flocks die in the fields, and the cattle barns are empty, yet I will rejoice in the Lord!" (Habakkuk 3:17–18).

The first Protestant. Locked in a bitter debate with Roman Catholic leaders, a young monk named Martin Luther defends his belief that people are saved by faith—as taught first by the prophet Habakkuk and later by the apostle Paul. Catholic leaders, however, insist that people are saved by obeying the church officials and by observing church rituals. The clash splits the church, producing the Protestant movement and non-Catholic denominations such as Lutherans, Presbyterians, Baptists, and Methodists.

Zephaniah

sum it up

Already wiped off the world map by invaders, the northern Jewish nation of Israel is just a century-old memory. Zephaniah warns that the southern Jewish nation of Judah, with its revered capital in Jerusalem, is about to face the same doom. "I [God] will crush Judah and Jerusalem with my fist and destroy every last trace of their Baal worship. I will put an end to all the idolatrous priests, so that even the memory of them will disappear" (Zephaniah 1:4). Survivors will be scattered abroad as exiles and refugees. But God promises them a second chance: "I will gather you together and bring you home again. I will give you a good name, a name of distinction, among all the nations of the earth" (Zephaniah 3:20).

5 W's

- *Who wrote it?* Zephaniah, great-great grandson of Hezekiah—perhaps King Hezekiah
- *What's it about?* God punishing the Jews for continued sin and then giving them a fresh start
- *When did it take place?* Sometime during the 30-year reign of King Josiah (640–609 BC), who was the great-grandson of Hezekiah
- *Where?* The southern Jewish nation of Judah
- *Why was it written?* To warn the Jews that these were their nation's last days

most famous quote

"I'm going to make a clean sweep of the earth" (ZEPHANIAH 1:2 THE MESSAGE).

Biggest idea

Judgment day. Rampant sin calls for dramatic judgment, as in the days of Noah and the flood and the fire at Sodom and Gomorrah. Sin was purged. The Jewish nation will experience a similar annihilation. "My Judgment Day is near" (Zephaniah 1:7 THE MESSAGE).

Biggest scene

creation rewind. God's destruction of Judah will be so terrible that it's described as a reversal of Creation. God created fish, birds, land animals, and humans—reported in that order in Genesis. Zephaniah's order of destruction is exactly the opposite: "I will sweep away people and animals alike. I will sweep away the birds of the sky and the fish in the sea" (Zephaniah 1:3).

Planet killer. A meteor the size of Texas crashes into the earth in this artist's conception of an extinction-level disaster. The prophet Zephaniah predicts that God will destroy all life on the planet. Yet he also says God will bring the Jews back to their homeland. For this reason, many Bible experts say Zephaniah wasn't talking about end times. Instead, he was using symbolism to describe the Babylonian invasion and destruction of the Jewish nation. Survivors were exiled into what is now Iraq but were allowed to go home and rebuild their nation about 50 years later.

Haggai

sum it up

After a terrible harvest in the Jewish homeland, the prophet Haggai tells the people that God is punishing them. The Jews were exiled into what is now Iraq, but they've been allowed to come home and rebuild their nation, which was devastated by Babylonian invaders in 586 BC. Though the Jews have been home almost 20 years, they haven't taken the time to rebuild their worship center—the Jerusalem temple. Until they do, Haggai warns, farmers in this agricultural-based society—who have just experienced a year of poor harvest—will continue to reap more of little and plenty of nothing. So the Jews start working on the temple right away, in September. They finish laying the foundation by December.

5 W's

- *Who wrote it?* Haggai
- *What's it about?* Rebuilding the Jewish temple
- *When did it take place?* August through December 520 BC
- *Where?* Jerusalem
- *Why was it written?* To urge the Jews to stop putting off the job of rebuilding the temple ruins

most famous quote

"Is it right for you to be living in fancy houses while the Temple is still in ruins? (HAGGAI 1:4 NCV).

biggest idea

BLessings on hoLd. God sometimes withholds happy events—like a huge harvest—to get people's attention. That's because many folks don't give him much thought until they're in trouble. So he sends a little trouble their way. In Haggai's day, this gave him opportunity to tell the Jews what was wrong. Once they start rebuilding the temple, God promised, "You can count on a blessing" (Haggai 2:19 THE MESSAGE).

Biggest scene

A pitiful harvest, caused by God. "I have called for a drought on your fields and hills—a drought to wither the grain and grapes and olive trees and all your other crops, a drought to starve you and your livestock and to ruin everything you have worked so hard to get. . . . Why? Because my house lies in ruins, says the LORD of Heaven's Armies" (Haggai 1:11, 9).

Mount of Olives ridge

Temple Hilltop

Western Wall

Holy hill. About 2,500 years ago, Haggai pointed to this Jerusalem hilltop and convinced the Jews to rebuild their temple, which invaders destroyed. A gold-domed shrine now sits on the spot; Muslims built the shrine 1,300 years ago. All that remains of the temple is the Western Wall—now the holiest Jewish site on earth. It's just a wall that held up the temple hillside. But crowds of Jews go there to pray.

Zechariah

sum it up

A month or two after the prophet Haggai convinces the Jews to start rebuilding the Jerusalem temple—which had been destroyed by Babylonian invaders from what is now Iraq—the prophet Zechariah begins cheering the people on. He urges them to keep serving God, and he assures them that God will help them rebuild not only the temple, but the entire city and nation. "The towns of Israel will again overflow with prosperity" (Zechariah 1:17). Chapters 1–8 deal mostly with the rebuilding. Chapters 9–14 close the book with prophecies about the coming Messiah's reign, when the wicked are punished and the righteous are saved.

5 W's

- *Who wrote it?* Zechariah, a prophet who may also have been a priest
- *What's it about?* Rebuilding Israel
- *When did it take place?* At least from the autumn of 520 through December 518, and perhaps later
- *Where?* Jerusalem
- *Why was it written?* To assure the Jews that God would help them rebuild their nation and then send a special ruler—the Messiah—to lead them

most famous quote

"Strike down the shepherd, and the sheep will be scattered" (ZECHARIAH 13:7).

Jesus quoted this to predict what his disciples would do after he was arrested. "All of you will desert me" (Mark 14:27).

Biggest idea

A savior is coming. Zechariah is bursting with predictions about a coming savior, or messiah. New Testament writers quote them and then declare the predictions fulfilled by Jesus. A few examples:

- The Savior is betrayed for 30 pieces of silver (Zechariah 11:12; Matthew 26:15).
- This money is used to a buy potter's field (Zechariah 11:13; Matthew 27:7).
- The Savior is stabbed (Zechariah 12:10; John 19:34).

Biggest scene

A Jewish king rides into Jerusalem on a donkey. "Shout for joy, people of Jerusalem! Your king is coming to you. He does what is right, and he saves. He is gentle and riding on a donkey" (Zechariah 9:9 NCV). Two Gospel writers said Jesus fulfilled this prophecy on Palm Sunday (Matthew 21:5; John 12:15).

Lifting up Jesus. Christians in Burgos, Spain celebrate Palm Sunday by carrying a statue of Jesus riding a donkey—which is the way Jesus entered Jerusalem on Sunday before his crucifixion. Five hundred years before Jesus, the prophet Zechariah predicted this ride: "Your Lord is coming. . .humble, riding on a donkey."

Malachi

sum it up

Babylonian invaders from what is now Iraq erased the Jewish nation from the world map in 586 BC—God's punishment for Israel's sin. Though God later let the Jews rebuild their nation, they headed down the sin path again: lying in court, cheating in marriage, ignoring the poor, and being stingy with their offerings. So Malachi warns that "the day of judgment is coming" when God will "tread upon the wicked as if they were dust" and when the righteous will start "leaping with joy like calves let out to pasture" (Malachi 4:1–3).

5 W'S

- *Who wrote it?* A prophet named Malachi or a writer who described himself as *malachi*, a Hebrew word meaning "messenger"
- *What's it about?* Jews ignoring God's laws
- *When did it take place?* 400s BC
- *Where?* Israel
- *Why was it written?* To remind the Jews that God still punishes disobedience

most famous quote

"I am sending my messenger, and he will prepare the way before me" (MALACHI 3:1).

New Testament writers said this refers to John the Baptist preparing the way for Jesus (Matthew 11:10).

Biggest idea

Obey God's Law. Malachi makes a list of the nation's sins. Then he gives a stern warning from God: "Remember to obey the Law of Moses, my servant—all the decrees and regulations that I gave him on Mount Sinai for all Israel. . . . Otherwise I will come and strike the land with a curse" (Malachi 4:4, 6).

Biggest scene

Diseased gifts for God. By law, sacrificial animals were supposed to have "no defects" (Leviticus 1:3). But the Jews started bringing defective livestock. Malachi scolds them. "Isn't it wrong to offer animals that are crippled and diseased? Try giving gifts like that to your govenor, and see how pleased he is!" (Malachi 1:8).

Goat killers. A livestock official prepares to bury slaughtered goats infected with brucellosis, a bacteria that can spread through the herd and to humans. The prophet Malachi complained that Jews were bringing diseased livestock to the temple as sacrifices to God—though Jewish law prohibited defective offerings.

new testament

Matthew

sum it up

Matthew, the first of four Gospels (a word meaning "good news"), introduces Jesus as the Messiah. This is the person the prophets said would come from David's family and save Israel. Jesus is born to a virgin and grows up in a carpenter's family. At about age 30 he begins around three years of ministry, preaching and healing. So many people rally around him that Jewish leaders fear he'll lead a doomed revolt against Rome's occupying army. They have him crucified, not realizing that the salvation he offers is spiritual instead of political. Jesus rises from the dead and gives his followers an assignment called the Great Commission: "Go and make disciples of all the nations" (Matthew 28:19).

5 W's

- *Who wrote it?* Unknown. Church leaders in the AD 100s said it was written by Matthew, a tax collector who became one of Jesus' 12 disciples.
- *What's it about?* Jesus' ministry and teachings
- *When did it take place?* During Jesus' ministry, from about AD 27 to 30
- *Where?* Israel (called Palestine by the Romans)
- *Why was it written?* To prove that Jesus was the Messiah the prophets had said would set up God's kingdom

most famous quote

"Do to others whatever you would like them to do to you" (MATTHEW 7:12).

Biggest idea

Kingdom of heaven. Jews were expecting a warrior messiah like King David—someone who would restore Israel to its former glory, free of Romans. Instead, they got a pacifist Jesus announcing the arrival of God's kingdom and teaching that citizens of this spiritual kingdom should love their neighbors as they love themselves. This isn't just a kingdom for the future in heaven; it's a kingdom that begins here as people live the kind of lives Jesus spoke about in his teachings and parables.

Biggest scene

Sermon on the Mount. In his most famous sermon, Jesus sums up his main teachings, many of which seem radical—like love your enemy and don't worry about anything (Matthew 5-7).

Bumpy ride to Bethlehem. For Mary, nine months pregnant, the easiest route from Nazareth to Bethlehem would have been the longest route: 90 miles, traveling about five days through the Jordan River valley. The direct route—about 60 miles—ran south through the rugged hills of central Israel.

Mark

sum it up

A Gospel for the busiest students of all, Mark is the shortest and the most action-packed. Skipping childhood stories of Jesus, Mark fast-forwards to the start of Jesus' fiery ministry—jumping from miracle to miracle and argument to argument. Jesus is exorcising demons, calming storms, healing the sick, and humiliating Jewish scholars by outdebating them. These scholars get even by orchestrating his crucifixion. But Jesus doesn't stay dead. And his disciples start spreading the word.

5 W's

- *Who wrote it?* Unknown. Church leaders in the early AD 100s said the writer was John Mark, who drew from the insights of Peter, the leader of Jesus' disciples.
- *What's it about?* Jesus' ministry
- *When did it take place?* During Jesus' ministry, from about AD 27 to AD 30
- *Where?* Israel
- *Why was it written?* Christians were being fed to the lions and persecuted in other ways by Romans and Jews. John Mark reminded Christians that Jesus suffered, too.

most famous quote

"Follow Me, and I will make you become fishers of men" (MARK 1:17 NKJV).

Biggest idea

Jesus suffering. Don't expect to read much about the power and divinity of Jesus. Expect to learn about his suffering, which takes up nearly half of this short book. First, Jesus is suffering through persistent debates with Jewish scholars furious with him for breaking their religious rules and for claiming to be God's Son. Then comes his last week—the suffering and Crucifixion, which take up the last six chapters of this 16-chapter book.

Biggest scene

Dead Jesus. The Messiah many believed would save Israel hangs dead on a Roman cross, executed at the insistence of Jewish leaders. They wanted to prevent what they feared would be a doomed rebellion against Rome. So they charged Jesus with insurrection and claiming to be King of the Jews.

The king is dead.

Lifeless beneath a sign that calls him "King of the Jews," Jesus seems incapable of saving anyone—until his resurrection. Mark's story of Jesus emphasizes his suffering and death, which take up nearly half the book.

Luke

sum it up

The virgin Mary gives birth to "the Son of God" (Luke 1:35). The story that follows is the Bible's most detailed account of Jesus' life and ministry. At about age 30, Jesus starts his ministry of healing and teaching—with dynamic results. About three or four years later, he goes to Jerusalem, where crowds welcome him on Sunday like a king. But Jewish leaders secretly arrange for his execution. He rises from the dead, spends several weeks with his disciples, and ascends into the sky as they watch in amazement.

5 W's

- *Who wrote it?* Early church leaders said a non-Jewish physician named Luke wrote this Gospel and its sequel about the beginning of the church: Acts.
- *What's it about?* The life and ministry of Jesus
- *When did it take place?* During Jesus' ministry, from about AD 27 to 30
- *Where?* Israel
- *Why was it written?* For "most honorable Theophilus, so you can be certain of the truth of everything you were taught" (Luke 1:3–4). Theophilus may have been a Roman official.

most famous quote

"Our Father which art in heaven, hallowed be thy name. Thy kingdom come. Thy will be done" (LUKE 11:2 KJV).

Biggest idea

Good news for the entire world—not just Jews. In dedicating the newborn Jesus, the priest Simeon prays, "I have seen your salvation, which you have prepared for all people. He is a light to reveal God to the nations, and he is the glory of your people Israel!" (Luke 2:30-32). The Gospel writer repeats this idea throughout the book—which makes sense if the writer was a non-Jew.

Biggest scene

God's newborn Son on a bed of hay. In Bethlehem, Mary gave birth to Jesus. "She wrapped him snugly in strips of cloth and laid him in a manger, because there was no lodging available for them" (Luke 2:7).

Shepherds visit the Lamb of God.

From a makeshift crib—a feeding trough—Baby Jesus gazes up at his first visitors: shepherds. They represent a humble class of people. Placing them at the Nativity is one reason Luke's story about the life and ministry of Jesus earned the nickname "Gospel of the Outcasts."

John

sum it up

If the four Gospels were a series of courses, this is the last one we'd take: Gospel 401. Written by a deep thinker, it's the hardest to understand. There are no parable stories and only seven miracles. But if we want to know what Jesus said—more than what others had to say about him—this is the Gospel to read, since it's more about his teachings than his life.

5 W's

- *Who wrote it?* Scholars guess Jesus' close disciple, John, the only disciple not mentioned by name in the book.
- *What's it about?* The teachings of Jesus
- *When did it take place?* During Jesus' ministry, from about AD 27 to 30
- *Where?* Israel
- *Why was it written?* "So that you may continue to believe that Jesus is the Messiah, the Son of God" (John 20:31).

most famous quote

"For God loved the world so much that he gave his one and only Son, so that everyone who believes in him will not perish but have eternal life" (JOHN 3:16).

Biggest ideas

Jesus is divine. Jesus created everything, the writer says—calling him "the Word." Greek philosophers taught that the Word was the supreme force that created and manages the universe—a power through which "all things happen." To Jews, the Word meant God's message to people. The writer's point: Jesus has God's power and God's message.

Jesus, the great "I AM." When Moses asked God's name, God answered, "I AM" (Exodus 3:14). Jesus said much the same in seven "I Am" statements: "I am the bread of life" (6:35), "the light of the world" (8:12), "the gate for the sheep" (10:7), "the good shepherd" (10:14), "the resurrection and the life" (11:25), "the way, the truth, and the life" (14:6), "the true grapevine" (15:1).

Biggest scene

Resurrection Sunday. On the first Easter Sunday morning, a resurrected Jesus meets Mary Magdalene. She's crying near his empty tomb because she thinks someone stole his body (John 20).

Back from the dead.
Jesus rises from the grave the third day after his execution and burial. Roman soldiers are on guard to make sure his disciples don't steal the body and claim he rose from the dead—since that's what Jesus promised to do. With the soldiers on duty, Jesus keeps his promise. From that day on, his disciples no longer fear death because they know that they, too, will live again. Jesus promised.

Acts

sum it up

A sequel to the Gospel of Luke, Acts picks up the story with Jesus ascending into the sky. Then the Holy Spirit arrives to give Christ's disciples the ability to speak in other languages. It's the ideal gift for preaching to Jewish pilgrims who have come from throughout the Roman Empire to celebrate a religious holiday. The apostles preach about Jesus, backing up their words with miracles. Some 3,000 people believe what they see and hear about Jesus. In time, even a hard-line Jew named Paul converts. He becomes the first career missionary, planting churches all over the Roman Empire.

5 w's

- *Who wrote it?* Early church leaders said a non-Jewish physician named Luke wrote it as a sequel to the Gospel of Luke.
- *What's it about?* How the church got started
- *When did it take place?* From about AD 30 to the mid-60s. That's from Jesus' ascension to the end of Paul's ministry.
- *Where?* The Roman Empire, including what is now Egypt, Israel, Syria, Turkey, Greece, and Italy
- *Why was it written?* To preserve the story of the church's early years and perhaps to defend Christianity as a legitimate religion

most famous quote

"But you will receive power when the Holy Spirit comes upon you. And you will will be my witnesses, telling people about me everywhere—in Jerusalem, throughout Judea, in Samaria, and to the ends of the earth" (ACTS 1:8).

These are Jesus' last words to his disciples.

Biggest ideas

The Holy Spirit is the church's engine. After four accounts of Jesus' ministry, we come to Acts: the book about the work of the Holy Spirit. God's Spirit is portrayed as the spiritual power behind the apostles.

Non-Jews are kosher. When the church started, all believers were Jews. But the Holy Spirit convinced the apostles that non-Jews who believed in Jesus were just as much God's people as the Jews ever were (Acts 10).

Biggest scene

Jesus appears to Paul. On his way to arrest Jews in Damascus who believe Jesus rose from the dead, Paul is blinded by a light from heaven. There, he meets Jesus for himself (Acts 9).

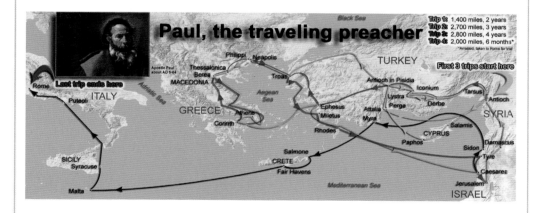

Paul, the traveling preacher

Trip 1: 1,400 miles, 2 years
Trip 2: 2,700 miles, 3 years
Trip 3: 2,800 miles, 4 years
Trip 4: 2,000 miles, 6 months*

*Arrested, taken to Rome for trial

First 3 trips start here

Good News to go. Paul covered nearly 10,000 miles in 20 years as a traveling missionary. And he may have spent nearly half that time in jail for disturbing the peace. As a Jew, he'd go to a synagogue and tell other Jews about Jesus. But most considered it blasphemy to teach that God had a son. So they'd chase Paul out of town. His preaching and the angry Jewish response drove him to cities all over the Roman Empire. He started churches wherever he went.

Romans

sum it up

Christian beliefs 101. That's the book of Romans. The apostle Paul wrote this letter to Christians in Rome, introducing himself and his beliefs. But in the process, he crafted a masterful essay that describes the Christian faith with more systematic style and completeness than any other book in the New Testament. For people who want to know what Christians believe and why, the answers are here.

5 W'S

- *Who wrote it?* The apostle Paul
- *What's it about?* Basic Christian beliefs
- *When did it take place?* In about AD 57, near the end of Paul's last missionary trip
- *Where?* Paul wrote to Christians in Rome, probably from Corinth, Greece.
- *Why was it written?* Paul was preparing the way for his visit to Rome.

most famous quote

"All have sinned and fall short of the glory of God" (ROMANS 3:23 NIV).

biggest ideas

HOW to get saved. Often called the Roman Road to Salvation, Paul's outline for salvation includes recognizing that we have all sinned, that sin is a capital offense in the eyes of a holy God, that God sent Jesus to take the punishment for humanity's sin, and that by accepting this gift we are cleared of guilt and "made right with God" (Romans 10:10).

IT's believing–not doing–that saves us. Paul makes it clear that we can't earn salvation by doing good deeds. Salvation is God's gift to everyone. All we have to do is accept the gift. "This is accomplished from start to finish by faith. As the Scriptures say, 'It is through faith that a righteous person has life'" (Romans 1:17).

Biggest scene

Jesus dying for us. On the cross, Jesus took the punishment for the sins we committed. "People are made right with God when they believe that Jesus sacrificed his life, shedding his blood" (Romans 3:25).

Downtown Rome.

Dominating a model of Rome in the first century, the circular Coliseum was a sports arena where gladiators fought each other and slaughtered Christians. Paul wrote the letter of Romans to Christians he hoped to visit in Rome. The Bible doesn't say where Paul died, but church leaders a few decades after him said the Romans tried him there and beheaded him.

1 Corinthians

sum it up

After spending two years in Corinth, Greece—getting a church started there—Paul moves on to start other churches. A traveling missionary, he normally spends just a few days or weeks in a town. Yet this church that got his special attention erupts into arguments after he leaves. They bicker over who should lead them, which spiritual gifts are most important, how to observe communion, and a long list of other worries.

most famous quote

"Don't you realize that your body is the temple of the Holy Spirit?" (1 CORINTHIANS 6:19).

5 W's

- *Who wrote it?* Paul
- *What's it about?* Problems in the new church at Corinth
- *When did it take place?* Paul started the church in about AD 50. He wrote the letter in about AD 55, a few years after leaving Corinth.
- *Where?* Corinth, Greece, was on a four-mile-wide isthmus south of Athens. It had ports in two oceans, on both sides of the isthmus. That made Corinth a busy crossroads town.
- *Why was it written?* Since Paul started the church, he felt compelled to help it even though he was long gone.

Biggest ideas

The greatest spiritual gift: Love. To a congregation squabbling over who had the greatest spiritual gift—such as preaching or speaking in heavenly languages—Paul pointed to one gift that would end all squabbling. "If I could speak all the languages of earth and of angels, but didn't love others, I would only be a noisy gong or a clanging cymbal" (1 Corinthians 13:1).

church unity. "Live in harmony with each other. Let there be no divisions in the church. Rather, be of one mind, united in thought and purpose" (1 Corinthians 1:10).

Biggest scene

incest in the church. A member of the church was sleeping with his father's wife, presumably a stepmother. Paul bluntly says, "You should remove this man from your fellowship" (1 Corinthians 5:2).

Adriatic Sea

Corinthian Gulf

Canal, 1906

Port at Lechaeum
Modern Corinth

CORINTH

Port at Cenchrea

Aegean Sea

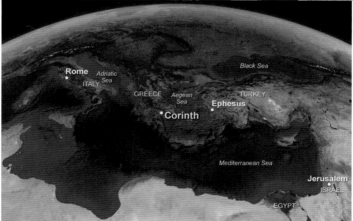

Rome   Adriatic
ITALY   Sea

Black Sea

GREECE   Aegean
                Sea

TURKEY

Ephesus

Corinth

Mediterranean Sea

Jerusalem
ISRAEL

EGYPT

International shortcut. With ports in two oceans separated by only a four-mile wedge of land, Corinth was a busy shipping center when Paul arrived. Cargo ships sailing east or west could stop here to cut 200 miles off their voyage—and avoid the dangerous surf and unpredictable weather along the southern tip of Greece. Crews unloaded their cargo onto wagons that hauled it to ships waiting in the opposite sea. Smaller ships didn't have to bother. Dock workers pulled the entire, loaded ships out of the water and up onto a wheeled platform that hauled the ship across the isthmus. Ships today have it even easier. They sail through a 75-foot-wide canal finished in 1893.

2 Corinthians

sum it up

In a letter of self-defense, Paul tries to fight off a hostile takeover of the Corinthian church by intruders attacking his character. Based on Paul's reply, the intruders called him:

- *A self-appointed apostle.* "When I was with you, I certainly gave you proof that I am an apostle. For I patiently did many signs and wonders and miracles among you" (2 Corinthians 12:12).

- *Money-hungry.* "We do not sell the word of God for a profit as many other people do" (2 Corinthians 2:17 NCV). In fact, Paul paid his own way by making tents (Acts 18:3).

5 W'S

- *Who wrote it?* "This letter is from Paul" (2 Corinthians 1:1).
- *What's it about?* Paul defending himself against critics who said he was a fake apostle
- *When did it take place?* Paul probably wrote this letter a few months after he wrote 1 Corinthians in AD 55.
- *Where?* Corinth, Greece
- *Why was it written?* To keep traveling preachers from taking control of the church in Corinth

most famous quote

"God loves a cheerful giver" (2 CORINTHIANS 9:7 NKJV).

Biggest ideas

Helping the poor. Even criticism of pocketing church donations doesn't stop Paul from collecting an offering for the poor. Thinking positively, he wrote, "I know how eager you are to help" (2 Corinthians 9:2).

God's message entrusted to frail humans. "We have this treasure from God, but we are like clay jars that hold the treasure. This shows that the great power is from God, not from us" (2 Corinthians 4:7 NCV).

Biggest scene

Bragging rights. Reluctantly, Paul defends himself by bragging about what he has suffered during his three missionary expeditions. "Five different times the Jewish leaders gave me thirty-nine lashes. Three times I was beaten with rods. Once I was stoned. Three times I was shipwrecked" (2 Corinthians 11:24-25).

Snakebit apostle.

Gathering firewood after a shipwreck on the island of Malta, near Italy, the apostle Paul finds a fanged surprise among the brush. He survives its poisonous bite. Accused of being in the ministry for money, Paul assures the Corinthians that it would take more than money to keep him doing such dangerous work. He had already been severely beaten eight times, stoned once and left for dead, and shipwrecked three times. Yet to come was this shipwreck on Malta followed by his execution, probably in Rome.

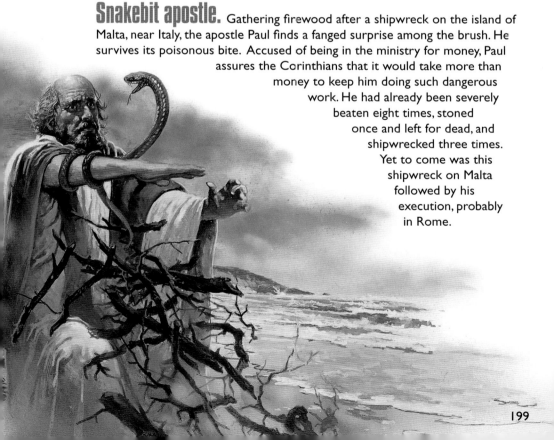

Galatians
sum it up

Paul is vein-popping livid when he writes this letter. When he started churches throughout Galatia, in what is now Turkey, he told the people they could be saved by believing in Jesus. But a group of Jewish Christians arrive later and convince many people that faith in Jesus isn't enough. Believers also have to convert to the Jewish religion and observe all Jewish traditions, including circumcision. To that Paul wrote, "Why don't these agitators, obsessive as they are about circumcision, go all the way and castrate themselves!" (Galatians 5:12 THE MESSAGE). Yep, he was angry.

5 W'S

- *Who wrote it?* Paul
- *What's it about?* Salvation through faith in Jesus, not through following Jewish laws
- *When did it take place?* Paul probably wrote this letter in the mid AD 50s, after two missionary expeditions into Galatia.
- *Where?* Galatia, a territory in what is now Turkey
- *Why was it written?* To counter a heresy that tried to turn Christianity into just another branch of the Jewish religion

most famous quote

"You reap whatever you sow" (GALATIANS 6:7 NRSV).

Biggest idea

Jewish religion is obsolete. Laws written on scrolls have been replaced by laws written on the heart. "Christ has set us free! . . . Now hold on to your freedom and don't ever become slaves of the Law again." On the other hand, Paul adds, "Don't use your freedom as an excuse to do anything you want. Use it as an opportunity to serve each other with love" (Galatians 5:1, 13 CEV).

Biggest scene

Hypocrite Peter. Paul publicly calls Peter a hypocrite for refusing to eat with non-Jewish Christians. Peter stopped eating with them only after a delegation of Jews arrived from Jerusalem and convinced him to follow Jewish law that said it was wrong to mix with non-Jews. "If keeping the law could make us right with God," Paul argues, "then there was no need for Christ to die" (Galatians 2:21).

Frolic in the flowers.
Frolic is what it takes to worship Bacchus, Roman god of wine and parties. People had to check their morals at the temple door. Sexual acts disgraced the rituals of this religion, which was popular in Galatia (modern-day Turkey) and throughout the Roman Empire. Many of these acts appeared on Paul's not-to-do list: sexual immorality, impurity, lustful pleasures, idolatry, drunkenness, and wild parties (Galatians 5:19–21).

Ephesians

sum it up

Paul spent three years starting a church in the megacity of Ephesus—more time than in any other church. This letter reads like it—as loving and gentle advice from a pastor to his people. Much of the letter talks about how to get along with one another: Put others first, try to stay united in goals for the church, and let the Holy Spirit help you grow.

5 W'S

- *Who wrote it?* Paul
- *What's it about?* How to live like a Christian
- *When did it take place?* Paul wrote from jail perhaps during his two-year arrest in Rome during the early AD 60s.
- *Where?* Ephesus, a city on Turkey's west coast
- *Why was it written?* To encourage the church in Ephesus to "live a life filled with love, following the example of Christ" (Ephesians 5:2)

most famous quote

"Don't let the sun go down while you are still angry" (EPHESIANS 4:26).

Biggest idea

practical tips for Living Like a christian. Paul gives a long list of practical advice for Christian living. Here's a sampling:

- "Be patient with each other, making allowance for each other's faults because of your love" (Ephesians 4:2).
- "Let everything you say be good and helpful, so that your words will be an encouragement" (Ephesians 4:29).
- "Obscene stories, foolish talk, and coarse jokes—these are not for you" (Ephesians 5:4).
- Husbands and wives, "submit to one another out of reverence for Christ" (Ephesians 5:21).

Biggest scene

suit up for spiritual battle. Paul said Christians fight spiritual battles against "authorities of the unseen world, against mighty powers in this dark world, and against evil spirits in the heavenly places" (Ephesians 6:12). Using the metaphor of battle gear, Paul tells believers to suit up: belt (truth); body armor (righteousness); shoes (peace); shield (faith); helmet (salvation); sword (Word of God).

PUT ON GOD'S ARMOR

Physical armor*	Spiritual equal	Jewish Bible background
Belt	Truth	"He will wear a belt of what is right and good and faithful" (Isaiah 11:5 NLV).
Body armor	God's righteousness	"He put on righteousness as his body armor" (Isaiah 59:17).
Shoes	Peace from the good news	"How beautiful on the mountains are the feet of the messenger who brings good news, the good news of peace" (Isaiah 52:7).
Shield	Faith	"My God is my rock, in whom I find protection. He is my shield, the power that saves me" (2 Samuel 22:3).
Helmet	Salvation	"He...placed the helmet of salvation on his head" (Isaiah 59:17).
Sword	Word of God	"The LORD...made my words of judgment as sharp as a sword" (Isaiah 49:1–2).

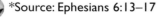

*Source: Ephesians 6:13–17

Philippians

sum it up

While Paul is in prison, Christians at the church he started in Philippi send him gifts. Philippians is Paul's letter of thanks. Paul also warns the people that there are tough times ahead. They may have to suffer—just as he is suffering and as Jesus suffered. But he says that whatever they endure will be worth the price, given the reward: eternity with Christ. "If I live, it will be for Christ, and if I die, I will gain even more" (Philippians 1:21 CEV).

5 W's

- *Who wrote it?* Paul and his colleague Timothy
- *What's it about?* Holding on to the Christian faith in hard times
- *When did it take place?* Paul and Timothy were in prison, perhaps during their two-year arrest at Rome in the early AD 60s.
- *Where?* Philippi, Greece—hometown of the first known church in Europe
- *Why was it written?* As a thank-you note for a gift to Paul and Timothy in prison—perhaps gifts of food, clothing, and money

Most famous quote

"At the name of Jesus every knee should bow" (Philippians 2:10).

Biggest ideas

suffering ahead. After three decades of suffering at the hands of Jews and Romans, Paul sees more of the same for Christians. Jesus suffered, too, he says. Paul adds that God puts our suffering to good use. "Because of my imprisonment, most of the believers here have gained confidence and boldly speak God's message without fear" (Philippians 1:14).

joy even in tough situations. This letter from prison is one of Paul's most joyful. "Always be full of joy in the Lord. I say it again—rejoice!" (Philippians 4:4).

Biggest scene

Run the race. Using a word picture from Greek Olympic games, Paul cheers on Christians at Philippi, urging them to follow him to God's finish line. "I press on to reach the end of the race and receive the heavenly prize for which God, through Christ Jesus, is calling us" (Philippians 3:14).

X-rated entertainment.
Gladiators fight to the death, entertaining packed arenas throughout the Roman Empire. A few years after Paul wrote to Christians at Philippi, warning them to prepare for suffering, the empire started targeting them. Many Christians died in the arenas—target practice for gladiators and fresh meat for wild animals. The slaughter continued off and on for three centuries, until Roman Emperor Constantine endorsed Christianity.

Colossians

sum it up

Fake Christian teachers slip into the church at Colosse and lure believers away from authentic Christian teachings. Apparently there's just enough truth in the false teachings to fool many believers. Paul feels compelled to warn the people about what's going on.

5 W'S

- *Who wrote it?* Paul
- *What's it about?* Warped religious teachings in the church at Colosse
- *When did it take place?* Paul may have written this about the same time he wrote Ephesians, perhaps in the early AD 60s while in prison at Rome.
- *Where?* Colosse was a city in what is now Turkey.
- *Why was it written?* To steer Christians in Colosse away from a new religious movement full of distorted teachings

most famous quote

"Whatever you do in word or deed, do all in the name of the Lord Jesus" (Colossians 3:17 nkjv).

Biggest ideas

It's heresy to think we can earn salvation. Paul doesn't say which false teachings threatened the church. But here are a few possibilities, based on his warnings which follow. The heretics taught that true Christians:

- follow strict rules. "Don't let anyone condemn you for what you eat or drink, or for not celebrating certain holy days" (Colossians 2:16).
- deprive themselves, to prove their spirit is stronger than their body. " 'Don't handle! Don't taste! Don't touch!' Such rules are mere human teachings. . . . They provide no help in conquering a person's evil desires" (Colossians 2:21-23).
- discover secret knowledge. Christians already know "God's secret, that is, Christ himself" (Colossians 2:2 ncv).

Biggest scene

Jesus dying for our sins. Paul said we're saved not because of anything we do, but because God's Son "became a human and died. So God made peace with you, and now he lets you stand in his presence as people who are holy and faultless and innocent" (Colossians 1:22 cev).

Mercury　Venus　Earth　Mars　Jupiter　Saturn　Uranus　Neptune

GREAT
BEAR

LEO

Spirits in the sky.
Like an arrow shot from a divine bow, a spray of stars courses through the northern sky. It soars above the constellation Leo, piercing the Great Bear. Many Romans in Paul's day believe that celestial spirits, planetary gods, and the movement of the constellations affect their day-to-day life. But Paul reminds Christians that Jesus created everything and "he disarmed the spiritual rulers and authorities. . . . He has set you free from the spiritual powers of this world" (Colossians 2:15, 20).

Astrology and hambone folk theology may have been part of the problem at the church in Colosse, some scholars say.

A church leader from Paul's century—Elchasai—may have given us a taste of this celestial hambone. His main teachings are preserved in a history written in the AD 200s by the church leader Hippolytus of Rome.

Here are three excerpts—bite-sized morsels that Paul would have found tough to swallow:

- "There are some wicked stars up there. . . . Don't do anything important when they're at their most powerful—especially on the days when the moon passes through them. That includes baptizing people."
- "Honor the Sabbath. That's one of the days when the wicked stars are strongest."
- "Don't start a big project the third day before the Sabbath. That's because. . . all the wicked kingdoms of the world are in a state of confusion."

1 Thessalonians

sum it up

On his second missionary trip, Paul arrives in the Greek town of Thessalonica. He spends only about three weeks there, preaching in the synagogue. Then Jews run him out of town for teaching heresy. But in that short time, Paul manages to start a church. He later sends his associate Timothy to check on the converts. Timothy returns with news that they are being persecuted, and they have questions—especially about the return of Jesus. Paul responds with this letter.

5 W's

- *Who wrote it?* Paul, with associates Silas and Timothy
- *What's it about?* Holy living during persecution
- *When did it take place?* Written in about AD 51, just 20 years after the crucifixion—making it perhaps the oldest piece of writing in the New Testament
- *Where?* Thessalonica, a busy seaside town in northern Greece
- *Why was it written?* To encourage new converts to keep living for God and to assure them that those who die before Jesus returns will be raised from the dead

most famous quote

"The Lord's return will come unexpectedly, like a thief in the night" (1 THESSALONIANS 5:2).

biggest idea

HOW to Live the holy Life. "Live a quiet life, minding your own business," Paul writes. "Then people who are not Christians will respect the way you live" (1 Thessalonians 4:11-12).

Biggest scene

second coming. "The Lord himself will come down from heaven with a commanding shout, with the voice of the archangel, and with the trumpet call of God. First, the Christians who have died will rise from their graves. Then, together with them, we who are still alive and remain on the earth will be caught up in the clouds to meet the Lord in the air. Then we will be with the Lord forever" (1 Thessalonians 4:16-17).

Living a holy life. Saint Francis of Assisi prays near a crucifix of Jesus in the AD 1200s. A Christian holy man who founded the Franciscan Order of monks in the Roman Catholic Church, Francis sought prayer and solitude in an attempt to live a holy life. The apostle Paul told Christians at Thessalonica to live holy lives. Yet he stopped short of urging them to live in seclusion.

2 Thessalonians

sum it up

Persecuted Christians in Thessalonica can't stop thinking about the return of Jesus. Paul writes this second letter to encourage them during their persecution and to tell them to get over the Second Coming—get on with life. We're not in a wait mode, Paul says. We're in a work mode—spreading the good news of salvation. "You ought to imitate us," Paul says. "We worked hard day and night" (2 Thessalonians 3:7–8).

5 W's

- *Who wrote it?* Paul, with associates Timothy and Silas
- *What's it about?* How to live like a Christian
- *When did it take place?* Paul probably wrote this follow-up letter to 1 Thessalonians in AD 51 or 52.
- *Where?* The port city of Thessalonica, Greece
- *Why was it written?* To encourage new converts who were being persecuted and to correct misunderstandings about the Second Coming of Jesus

most famous quote

"Those unwilling to work will not get to eat" (2 Thessalonians 3:10).

That's Paul's advice about Christians who quit their jobs to wait on Jesus to come back.

Biggest idea

End-time fever. To help the Christians get over their obsession with the Second Coming and to get busy spreading the good news about Jesus, Paul tells them about events that need to happen before the end time. "That day will not come until there is a great rebellion against God and the man of lawlessness is revealed—the one who brings destruction" (2 Thessalonians 2:3). Bible scholars have many theories about this rebel: He's the Antichrist, or an evil religious leader, or a symbol for the Roman Empire that leveled Jerusalem and the temple in AD 70.

Biggest scene

Waiting for Jesus. Some Christians are so sure that Jesus will return any day that they stop working and depend on charity. Paul has a message for them: "Settle down and work to earn [your] own living" (2 Thessalonians 3:12).

Expecting Jesus any moment. Escorted by angels, Christians begin their ascent into heaven. In Paul's time, many new converts in Thessalonica became Second Coming fanatics, expecting Jesus to return right away and take them to heaven. Some believers even quit their jobs and depended on charity. But Paul told the Christians to keep living and working as usual. Healthy people who don't work, he added, shouldn't eat.

1 Timothy

sum it up

After starting the church in Ephesus, Paul moves on—assigning Timothy to stay behind as pastor. On the road somewhere, Paul writes Timothy as an elder pastor to a young pastor. Paul gives him advice about how to run the church and what kind of people to select as church leaders. This letter along with 2 Timothy and Titus are called the Pastoral Epistles (Writings) because they offer advice on how to pastor a church.

5 W's

- *Who wrote it?* Paul
- *What's it about?* How to lead a church
- *When did it take place?* Paul probably wrote this letter in the AD 60s, shortly before his execution
- *Where?* Ephesus, on Turkey's west coast
- *Why was it written?* To advise Timothy on how to run the church

Most famous quote

"The love of money is a root of all kinds of evil" (1 TIMOTHY 6:10 NKJV).

Biggest ideas

Qualifications of a church leader. Paul, in chapter 3, tells Timothy that a church leader should:

- Have a good reputation
- Be faithful to his wife
- Enjoy having guests in his home
- Be gentle
- Not love money
- Be respected by his children

Warped teachings. "Stop those whose teaching is contrary to the truth. Don't let them waste their time in endless discussion. . . . These things only lead to meaningless speculations, which don't help people live a life of faith in God" (1 Timothy 1:3-4).

Biggest scene

women silent in church. Paul advises Timothy to have women "learn quietly and submissively. I do not let women teach men or have authority over them" (1 Timothy 2:11-12). Scholars debate why Paul said this, since in other churches women served as leaders and since Paul said men and women are equal in God's eyes (Galatians 3:28). Some say Paul's advice shows that men and women have different roles to fill. Others say Paul's advice was limited to churches where women were causing trouble—in Ephesus and Corinth.

Young pastor Timothy.

Paul names his associate, Timothy, pastor of the church Paul started in Ephesus. Young Timothy, who was like a son to Paul, may have been about the age of this man from a portrait painted in Roman times. Ephesus was a big assignment for someone so young. It was the third largest city in the Roman Empire, after Rome and Alexandria, Egypt.

2 Timothy

sum it up

This is the letter of a dead man writing—Paul's last known words. He's writing to his dearest friend, Timothy. "The time of my death is near" (2 Timothy 4:6). Chained in prison and sitting on death row, Paul pleads for Timothy to come—even though it's a thousand-mile sea voyage from Timothy's church in Ephesus to Paul's prison in Rome. In case Timothy doesn't make it in time, Paul offers last words of advice—perhaps best summed up in a sentence: "Never be ashamed to tell others about our Lord" (2 Timothy 1:8).

5 W's

- *Who wrote it?* Paul
- *What's it about?* How to keep the church healthy in tough times
- *When did it take place?* Perhaps in the mid AD 60s, when the Roman emperor Nero started killing Christians
- *Where?* Paul wrote from prison in Rome. He was writing to Timothy, pastor of a church in Ephesus, a city on Turkey's west coast.
- *Why was it written?* To give Timothy advice on pastoring a church and to ask him to come and be with Paul at his execution

most famous quote

"I have fought the good fight, I have finished the race, and I have remained faithful" (2 TIMOTHY 4:7).

biggest idea

TRUST THE BIBLE. Paul warns that in the last days there will be an overdose of bizarre teachings. "But you should continue following the teachings you learned. You know they are true, because you trust those who taught you. Since you were a child you have known the Holy Scriptures which are able to make you wise. And that wisdom leads to salvation through faith in Christ Jesus" (2 Timothy 3:14-15 NCV).

Biggest scene

Paul on death row. "I am locked up in jail and treated like a criminal" (2 Timothy 2:9 CEV). Yet Paul remains joyful: "If we die with him, we will also live with him" (2 Timothy 2:11).

Paul's last words. A Roman official beheads the apostle Paul. The Bible doesn't say how Paul died. But letters from church leaders a generation later said he was executed by beheading in Rome. It was probably in his final weeks that Paul wrote a tender letter to Timothy, asking him to come quickly. "The time has come for me to leave this life. I have fought the good fight, I have finished the race, I have kept the faith. Now, a crown is being held for me" (2 Timothy 4:6–8 NCV).

Titus

sum it up

After starting churches on the island of Crete, Paul assigns Titus to organize the churches there. Later, Paul writes this letter giving Titus advice. It's much like the letters he wrote to Timothy, pastor of the church in Ephesus. Paul tells Titus what to look for in church leaders, how to minister to different groups in the church, and how to deal with warped teachings that try to worm their way into the church.

5 W's

- *Who wrote it?* Paul
- *What's it about?* How to lead churches
- *When did it take place?* Uncertain. Acts, which reports Paul's travels, never puts him in Crete. Paul may have gone there later, in the AD 60s, during an unreported fourth missionary trip.
- *Where?* Crete, an island south of Greece
- *Why was it written?* To give advice on how to build healthy congregations

most famous quote

"The people of Crete are all liars, cruel animals, and lazy gluttons" (TITUS 1:12).

Politically incorrect today, Paul quotes a Cretan poet who had said this. Then Paul agrees. Perhaps his point is to acknowledge that Titus has a tough job ahead.

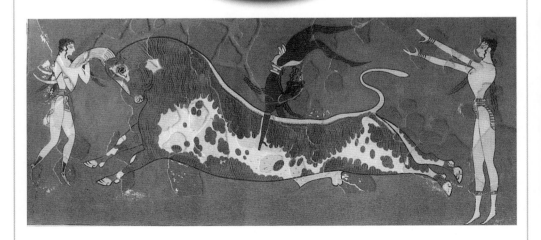

216

Biggest idea

Be a do-gooder. "Remind the people to be. . .ready to do whatever is good, to slander no one, to be peaceable and considerate, and to show true humility toward all men" (Titus 3:1-2 NIV).

Biggest scene

Qualifications for pastors. Paul tells Titus that each pastor "must live a blameless life. . .be faithful to his wife, and his children must be believers who don't have a reputation for being wild or rebellious. . . . He must not be arrogant or quick-tempered. . .a heavy drinker, violent, or dishonest with money" (Titus 1:6-8).

Before cretans came to Crete.

Paintings of bull jumping, (left) majestic architecture, and ornate pottery (right) reveal that 1,500 years before Paul a lively and cultured society of Minoans ruled the island of Crete. Something wiped them out—a tidal wave may have started their demise, according to some historians. Mercenaries and pirates moved in. By Paul's day, the island had a terrible reputation. No longer famous for jumping the bull, the people were famed for slinging the bull: "Liars all," as one of their own writers described them.

Philemon

sum it up

Philemon is a Christian slave owner. The church at Colosse actually meets in his home. This letter is about one of Philemon's runaway slaves—a man named Onesimus, converted under Paul's ministry. Paul sends Onesimus home with this short, 25-verse letter, asking Philemon to welcome him not as a slave, but "as a brother in the Lord" (Philemon 16).

5 W's

- *Who wrote it?* Paul
- *What's it about?* How to treat a Christian who's at the bottom of the social barrel
- *When did it take place?* Unknown. Paul was in prison, perhaps in Rome in the AD 60s.
- *Where?* Colosse, a city in Turkey
- *Why was it written?* To protect Onesimus from execution, the punishment for runaway slaves

most famous quote

"He is no longer like a slave to you. . . . He is a beloved brother, especially to me" (PHILEMON 16).

STORAX · SERVORVM MANGO

218

Biggest idea

Mercy. Paul asked for something no runaway slave could ever expect—beyond forgiveness and freedom: mercy that made the slave an equal. "I became his father in the faith. . . . So if you consider me your partner, welcome him as you would welcome me" (Philemon 10, 17).

Biggest scene

A runaway slave comes home. Onesimus delivers Paul's letter, which contains not-so-subtle hints that Paul wants Onesimus freed. "I wanted to keep him here with me. . . . But I didn't want to do anything without your consent" (Philemon 13-14). Freedom may have come. Fifty years later, Ephesus had a bishop named Onesimus.

Slaves for sale. Called "living tools" by philosopher Aristotle, slaves were treated as property bought and sold even by Christians. People often entered slavery as prisoners from defeated cities. Some were kidnap victims or poor folks unable to pay their bills. Paul wrote a Christian slave-owner named Philemon this short letter. Paul asked Philemon to welcome "as a brother" the man delivering the letter: one of Philemon's runaway slaves whom Paul had converted.

Hebrews

sum it up

Persecution drives some Jewish Christians back to the Jewish religion. But the writer warns there's nothing to go back to. The Jewish faith is obsolete. God has replaced the old covenant—a contract spelled out in the laws of the Old Testament—with a new agreement. Instead of prophets, priests, and sacrifices, we have Jesus. And instead of laws written on scrolls, we have the Holy Spirit teaching us right from wrong.

5 W's

- *Who wrote it?* Unknown. Probably not Paul, since the writer implies he never met Jesus (Hebrews 2:3).
- *What's it about?* Christianity, as the next step in God's plan to save humanity
- *When did it take place?* Probably before AD 70, when Romans destroyed the Jerusalem temple. This news—not reported in Hebrews—would have fit nicely into the message that Jesus' sacrifice made the Jewish sacrificial system obsolete. That's because Jews stopped sacrificing animals after Romans destroyed the temple—which was the only place where sacrifices could take place.
- *Where?* Perhaps a general letter circulated among the churches
- *Why was it written?* To stop Jewish Christians from returning to synagogues

most famous quote

"Faith is the substance of things hoped for, the evidence of things not seen" (Hebrews 11:1 nkjv).

Biggest idea

God writes a new contract. Jewish laws about sacrifices, kosher food, and circumcision are outdated. That's because God made a new covenant with humanity—as he said he would (Jeremiah 31:31-32). "God called this a new agreement, so he has made the first agreement old. And anything that is old and worn out is ready to disappear" (Hebrews 8:13 ncv).

Biggest scene

Jesus dead–sacrificed for everyone's sins. Death is God's punishment for sin. But God set up a system of animal sacrifice to allow people to get forgiveness. "The life of the body is in the blood, and I have given you rules for pouring that blood on the altar to remove your sins" (Leviticus 17:11 NCV). God later sent his Son as a blood sacrifice. "By his one sacrifice he has forever set free from sin the people he brings to God" (Hebrews 10:14 CEV).

Having Christians for dinner.
Fresh meat for wild animals and entertainment for Roman crowds, a small group of Christians huddles together for one last prayer. Surrounding them are human torches—a technique Emperor Nero is said to have used once to light the evening entertainment. Nero started persecuting Christians in AD 64, apparently after accusing them of setting fire to Rome. Because of this, many Jewish Christians abandoned the faith and returned to their old-time religion at their local synagogues.

James

sum it up

This letter reads a bit like a collection of wise sayings from Christian fortune cookies. In fact, James sounds so much like the Old Testament book of Proverbs—nuggets of wise sayings from Jewish elders to young men—that Bible experts call it the wisdom book of the New Testament. The advice James gives is practical—dealing with how to live like a Christian. Advice like: watch your mouth, help the poor, and pray for the sick.

5 W's

- *Who wrote it?* James, a servant of God. Christian writers a century later said he was the brother of Jesus. This James led the Jerusalem church until Jews stoned him to death in the late AD 60s.
- *What's it about?* Putting faith into action
- *When did it take place?* Perhaps in the AD 50s or 60s, just two or three decades after the crucifixion
- *Where?* "To Jewish believers scattered abroad" (James 1:1)
- *Why was it written?* To encourage believers to act like Christians

most famous quote

"Faith by itself isn't enough. Unless it produces good deeds, it is dead and useless" (James 2:17).

Biggest ideas

practice what you preach. There's no such thing as private religion when it comes to Christianity—no keeping it to ourselves. "God-talk without God-acts is outrageous nonsense" (James 2:17 THE MESSAGE).

Don't play favorites with rich folks. From James's perspective, it's wrong to treat rich people like VIPs just because they're rich. "Doesn't this discrimination show that your judgments are guided by evil motives?" (James 2:4).

Biggest scene

Running off at the mouth. Like a small rudder that controls a massive ship, or a six-inch steel bit that can steer a one-ton horse, a tiny tongue can change the course of a life—for better or worse (James 3:3-5).

Wealth on display. A slave repositions a new sculpture onto its pedestal—adding it to the gallery of a rich Roman household. The advice James had for wealthy people sounds more like stern warnings. "This treasure you have accumulated will stand as evidence against you on the day of judgment. For listen! Hear the cries of the field workers whom you have cheated of their pay" (James 5:3–4).

1 Peter

sum it up

Christians in Turkey are facing organized persecution—perhaps the Roman terror that began in AD 64 when Emperor Nero blamed Christians for setting the fire that destroyed two-thirds of Rome. Peter urges Christians to hold on to their faith, keep living holy lives, and obey their political leaders.

5 W'S

- *Who wrote it?* Peter with Silas's help
- *What's it about?* Living as Christians even if it means arrest and execution
- *When did it take place?* Uncertain. Perhaps during Nero's empire-wide persecution of Christians in AD 64, or during Jewish persecution earlier.
- *Where?* Peter wrote from "Babylon," a code name for Rome. He wrote to Christians throughout what is now Turkey.
- *Why was it written?* "My purpose in writing is to encourage you and assure you that what you are experiencing is truly part of God's grace for you" (1 Peter 5:12).

most famous quote

"Give all your worries and cares to God, for he cares about you" (1 PETER 5:7).

Biggest ideas

suffer in silence. "If you suffer for doing what is right, God will reward you for it. . . . Christ suffered for our sins. . .but he was raised to life in the Spirit" (1 Peter 3:14, 18).

submit to your nation's Leaders. "Make the Master proud of you by being good citizens. Respect the authorities, whatever their level" (1 Peter 2:13 THE MESSAGE).

Be holy. "As obedient children, let yourselves be pulled into a way of life shaped by God's life, a life energetic and blazing with holiness" (1 Peter 1:15 THE MESSAGE).

Biggest scene

christians fed to Lions. Peter doesn't identify exactly what kind of "fiery trials" (1 Peter 4:12) Christians are facing. But he lived long enough to see Romans execute Christians in many creative ways—including as entertainment in arenas: fed to lions or forced to fight gladiators.

Dressing for success.

Roman high society loved the elegant look. And common folks loved to copy aristocratic fashion. But Peter advised Christian women not to worry about fancy clothes and sculpted hairstyles. "You should clothe yourselves instead with the beauty that comes from within" (1 Peter 3:3–4).

2 Peter

sum it up

Believing he's about to die soon, Peter writes one last letter. He warns believers that heretics will infiltrate the church. They'll swindle Christians out of money and salvation, convincing many that we are free to live any way we want—that rules of morality don't matter in the spiritual world. "They will bring sudden destruction on themselves" (2 Peter 2:1).

5 W's

- *Who wrote it?* "Simon Peter. . .apostle of Jesus Christ" (2 Peter 1:1).
- *What's it about?* Heretics at work in the church
- *When did it take place?* Uncertain. But Peter said, "I must soon leave this earthly life" (2 Peter 1:14), and church leaders in the AD 100s said Romans crucified him in the 60s.
- *Where?* Peter said this was his second letter, possibly following 1 Peter, which was written from Rome to Christians in Turkey.
- *Why was it written?* To tell Christians how to deal with false teachers and how to grow spiritually

most famous quote

"A day is like a thousand years to the Lord, and a thousand years is like a day" (2 PETER 3:8).

Peter said this to Christians wondering why Jesus hadn't come back yet.

Biggest idea

prescription for spiritual Growth. "To your faith, add goodness; and to your goodness, add knowledge; and to your knowledge, add self-control; and to your self-control, add patience; and to your patience, add service for God; and to your service for God, add kindness for your brothers and sisters in Christ; and to this kindness, add love" (2 Peter 1:5-7 NCV).

Biggest scene

Heretics on the Loose in the church. The brand of heretic that Peter warns about separates spirituality from behavior. "They think it is fun to have wild parties. . . . All they think about is having sex with someone else's husband or wife" (2 Peter 2:13-14 CEV).

Crucified feet up.

Nailed to a cross, Peter is hoisted feet up instead of in the typical position of head up. Early church leaders said Peter died a martyr in Rome. One historian, Eusebius, said Emperor Nero ordered him crucified. *Acts of Peter*, a book written in the AD 100s, adds that Peter felt unworthy to be crucified like Jesus—so he asked to hang upside down.

1 John

sum it up

There's a split in the church. A group of people John calls "antichrists" have started a breakaway movement. They're teaching strange things about Jesus—that he wasn't really human and he didn't really suffer because he was only a spiritual being who looked human. It's not Jesus who saves us, these people teach. They say we're saved by secret knowledge and by rituals—such as punishing the physical body, which they consider evil. To them, anything physical is evil. John writes to assure Christians that the teachings they heard from the beginning are the right ones. Jesus saves.

5 W's

- *Who wrote it?* Probably Jesus' disciple John, because the style and message so closely match those of John's Gospel, along with 2 and 3 John
- *What's it about?* A warped brand of Christianity
- *When did it take place?* Church leaders in the AD 100s said John wrote this letter in the 90s.
- *Where?* John is said to have moved to Turkey's west coast, in the city of Ephesus.
- *Why was it written?* To expose false teachers "who want to lead you astray" (1 John 2:26).

most famous quote

"If we confess our sins to him, he is faithful and just to forgive us and to cleanse us from all wickedness" (1 JOHN 1:9).

Biggest idea

Antichrist. You have heard that the Antichrist is coming, and already many such antichrists have appeared. . . . These people left our churches, but they never really belonged with us" (1 John 2:18-19). For John, an antichrist is anyone opposed to Christ.

Biggest scene

spotting a heretic. "Don't believe everyone who claims to have the Spirit of God. Test them all to find out if they really do come from God. . . . His Spirit says that Jesus Christ had a truly human body. But when someone doesn't say this about Jesus, you know that person has a spirit that doesn't come from God" (1 John 4:1-3 CEV).

Hell's tag team. Satan whispers instructions to the Antichrist, a mysterious figure whose title shows up in only a few passing references in the Bible—and only in the letters of John. According to John, anyone opposed to Christ is an antichrist. But for more than a thousand years, some Christians have speculated that this mysterious person is the beast of Revelation. The beast gains world domination with the devil's help, and performs miracles that fool many into believing he's a god.

2 John

sum it up

In a tiny letter that reads like a P.S. to 1 John, Christians are urged to love one another and to show heretics the road. The heretics John is talking about "deny that Jesus Christ came in a real body" (2 John 7). If that teaching is true, Jesus didn't really suffer and die for us—he only pretended to, using a spiritual body that felt no pain. John says anyone teaching this is a deceiver and an antichrist.

5 W's

- *Who wrote it?* The writer identifies himself only as a church leader, but many experts agree it was Jesus' disciple John.
- *What's it about?* Heretics in the church
- *When did it take place?* The letter was probably written in the AD 90s.
- *Where?* John is said to have lived in Ephesus, a city on Turkey's west coast.
- *Why was it written?* To advise Christians to shoo away people teaching warped ideas about Jesus and Christianity

MOST famous quote

"Love one another" (2 JOHN 5).

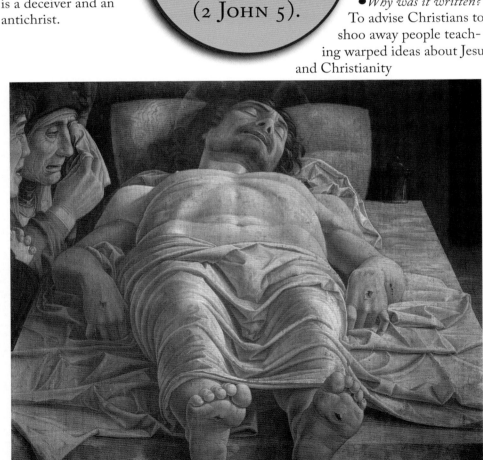

Biggest ideas

Love others and obey God. "I ask you that we all love each other. And love means living the way God commanded us to live. As you have heard from the beginning, his command is this: Live a life of love" (2 John 5-6 ncv).

Don't encourage people who teach distorted Christianity. "Anyone who encourages such people becomes a partner in their evil work" (2 John 11).

Biggest scene

Heretic at the front door. Though it was customary for Christians to welcome traveling missionaries as guests in their homes—providing free room and lodging—John advises against treating heretics with the same hospitality. "Don't invite that person into your home or give any kind of encouragement" (2 John 10).

He's just pretending. That's what some Christians were starting to say about Jesus.
Trying to mix and match Greek philosophy with Christianity, they argued that the spiritual world is holy and the physical world is evil—so God's Son couldn't possibly have taken human form. He only pretended to be human, to die, and to rise from the dead. John wrote this letter to insist that Jesus did have a human body—and that anyone who says otherwise is clueless.

3 John

sum it up

This is a private letter from the apostle John to a Christian named Gaius. John praises Gaius for showing hospitality to traveling ministers—apparently risky business because Gaius's pastor, Diotrephes, doesn't approve. Diotrephes relishes his power and refuses to tolerate any competition, so he excommunicates believers who welcome traveling ministers. John promises to come for a visit and to bring charges against the control-freak pastor.

5 W'S

- *Who wrote it?* The writer says only that he's a church leader, but many experts say he was Jesus' disciple John.
- *What's it about?* Welcoming traveling ministers
- *When did it take place?* John probably wrote this letter near the end of his life, in the AD 90s.
- *Where?* John is said to have lived his final years in Ephesus, a city on Turkey's west coast.
- *Why was it written?* To encourage a Christian named Gaius to keep showing hospitality to traveling ministers

most famous quote

"Those who do good prove that they are God's children, and those who do evil prove that they do not know God" (3 JOHN 11).

232

Biggest idea

support christian ministers. "We ourselves should support them so that we can be their partners as they teach the truth" (3 John 8).

Biggest scene

A pastor brought up on charges. Protecting his power is job one for a dictatorial pastor named Diotrephes. So when traveling ministers come to town, Diotrephes refuses to welcome them—and he boots out of his church any Christians who do otherwise. In the early church there was no earthly authority higher than an apostle—a disciple of Jesus who had learned from Jesus himself. So the apostle John vows to play his trump card. He says he's coming to town to "report some of the things he [Diotrephes] is doing and the evil accusations he is making against us" (3 John 10).

On the road again. In Bible times, there weren't many rest stops. That's why it was the custom to invite strangers in for food and shelter. But one pastor didn't want his church members to host traveling preachers—he considered them the competition. John urged the church members to ignore this pastor and do the right thing.

Jude

sum it up

Jude is worried. "I've dropped everything to write you," he says, addressing Christians everywhere. "Some people have infiltrated our ranks" (Jude 3–4 THE MESSAGE). These people claim to have had dreams that reveal it's okay to live as immorally as we want because God will forgive us. Jude quickly refutes this warped idea, essentially saying, "Tell it to Sodom and Gomorrah." God punishes sin.

5 W's

- *Who wrote it?* Jude, a nickname for Judas. He also identifies himself as a brother of James. Jude may have been a brother of Jesus because two of Jesus' brothers were James and Judas (Matthew 13:55).
- *What's it about?* A new heresy threatening the Christian faith
- *When did it take place?* Unknown. Paul wrote about the same problem in the AD 60s.
- *Where?* This was an open letter to all Christians.
- *Why was it written?* As a warning. "Some ungodly people have wormed their way into your churches, saying that God's marvelous grace allows us to live immoral lives" (Jude 4).

most famous quote

"Now to Him who is able to keep you from stumbling, and to present you faultless before the presence of His glory with exceeding joy, to God our Savior, who alone is wise, be glory and majesty, dominion and power, both now and forever. Amen."
(JUDE 24–25 NKJV).

Biggest idea

Trust the authentic Christian message. There's no such thing as a new and improved Christianity. "Build each other up in your most holy faith" (Jude 20).

Biggest scene

Sodom and Gomorrah on fire. To counter the argument that God's forgiving nature allows us to sin as much as we like, Jude reminds Christians that the twin sin cities of Sodom and Gomorrah "were destroyed by fire and serve as a warning of the eternal fire of God's judgment" (Jude 7).

Sin City. An angel lingers behind after rushing Lot and his family out of Sodom, a city so sinful that God burns it off the planet. Jude wrote to Christians who were getting an earful of heresy. The heretics taught that it's okay to sin because God has already forgiven us. Jude offers a short history lesson: Remember Sodom. And Cain who murdered his brother. And Balaam who sold prophecy for profit. And Korah who led a revolt against Moses. God punished sinners in the past, and he'll do it in the future.

Revelation

sum it up

John has a series of visions—horrifying images of war, famine, and disease. He sees martyred Christians and cataclysmic natural disasters. Then in a celestial battle, God's forces defeat Satan's army. Satan and his followers are thrown into a lake of fire. But followers of Jesus are rewarded with eternal life in heaven.

5 W's

- *Who wrote it?* Someone named John. Later church leaders said it was Jesus' disciple.
- *What's it about?* The end of human history and the beginning of eternity with God
- *When did it take place?* Most Bible experts say this prophecy was written in the AD 90s.
- *Where?* Patmos, a prison island—a bit like Alcatraz—off the west coast of Turkey
- *Why was it written?* Jesus told John to write down everything he saw.

most famous quote

"I am the Alpha and the Omega—the beginning and the end" (REVELATION 1:8).

Biggest ideas

God wins, satan Loses. "The devil. . .was thrown into the fiery lake of burning sulfur, joining the beast and the false prophet. There they will be tormented day and night forever and ever" (Revelation 20:10).

God's people enjoy heaven forever. "I heard a voice thunder from the Throne: 'Look! Look! God has moved into the neighborhood, making his home with men and women! They're his people, he's their God. He'll wipe every tear from their eyes. Death is gone for good—tears gone, crying gone, pain gone" (Revelation 21:3-4 THE MESSAGE).

Biggest scene

A glimpse of heaven. John sees a heavenly city. He tries to describe what may be indescribable to physics-bound humans. Drawing from the most precious objects on earth, John talks about jasper walls, golden streets, and pearl gates. The entire city shimmers with light, "for the glory of God illuminates the city, and the Lamb is its light" (Revelation 21:23).

Good guys win.

Bloodied robe, a rider on a white horse leads a heavenly army as they defeat Satan and his allies in the famous end-time battle of Armageddon. Code words in this highly symbolic book suggest the rider is Jesus. His robe "dipped in blood" is perhaps a reference to his earlier death on the cross.

FIFTY BIBLE HEROES AND JERKS

We're all jerks from time to time. But some Bible characters seemed to adopt it as a lifestyle.

Others are remembered as heroes of the faith, even though they occasionally did some jerk-like things to other people.

There are nearly 3,500 people mentioned in the Bible. Here are 50 of the most famous—or in some cases, infamous.

Abraham
(A bruh ham)
HERO
2100s BC
First mention: Genesis 17:5 (Genesis 11:26 for Abram)
Founding father of the Jewish race, Abram moved from what is now Iraq to Israel. There, God promised to give him all this land—and enough descendants to fill it. God renamed him *Abraham* to seal the promise. Abraham was 100 years old when his son Isaac was born.

Hundred-year-old daddy. With his 90-year-old eavesdropping wife Sarah laughing from inside the tent, 99-year-old Abraham listens to a bizarre predic-

Adam
(ADD um)
JERK
Before 4000 BC
First mention: Genesis 2:19
"God formed the man from the dust of the ground. He breathed the breath of life into the man's nostrils, and the man became a living person" (Genesis 2:7). That man was Adam, the first human being. For bringing sin into the world, Adam and his wife, Eve, got kicked out of the Garden of Eden.

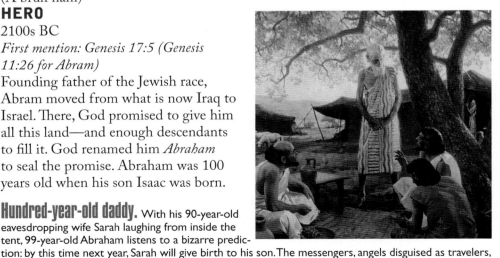

tion: by this time next year, Sarah will give birth to his son. The messengers, angels disguised as travelers, say that this son will produce descendants as countless as the stars in the sky, and that they will inherit the land today called Israel. Isaac is born within the year. And Isaac's son, Jacob, produces 12 sons whose extended families grow into what become the 12 tribes of Israel.

Amos
(A muhs)
HERO
About 760 BC

First mention: Amos 1:1
Though Amos was a herder and a fig orchard farmer, God chose him to deliver an important prophecy to Israel's leaders. The message: God was going to send invaders to overrun the nation because the Jews had broken their promise to serve God. Among their sins, the rich people exploited the poor.

Barnabas
(BARN uh bus)
HERO
First century AD
First mention: Acts 4:36
After leading the first known church that included non-Jews, Barnabas recruited Paul to help as an associate minister. This church later sent the pair on what became history's first reported missionary trip. Barnabas and Paul started congregations throughout the island of Cyprus and in Turkey.

Daniel
(DAN yull)
HERO
600s–500s BC
First mention: Daniel 1:6
Famous for spending a night in a lions' den—punishment for praying to God instead of the king—Daniel was a Jewish noble taken hostage to Babylon. Babylonians, in modern-day Iraq, mistakenly hoped that taking leaders like Daniel would discourage the Jews from revolting. Daniel's gift of interpreting dreams raised him to the position of palace advisor for the Babylonians as well as for their conquerors, the Persians.

David
(DAY vid)
HERO
Reigned about 1010–970 BC
First mention: Ruth 4:17
A jerk of a family man who cheated on his wives and alienated some of his children, David became Israel's most revered king. A brilliant warrior and political leader, he set up Jerusalem as the capital and then defeated his neighboring enemies, securing Israel's borders. This paved the way for Israel's golden age of prosperity, which continued through the reign of his son Solomon.

Delilah
(dee LIE lah)
JERK
About 1075 BC
First mention: Judges 16:4
This Philistine woman did what the entire Philistine army couldn't do: She captured the Israelite strong man Samson. Delilah was Samson's lover. But she loved money more than him and accepted a bribe from Philistine leaders to learn the secret of his strength. Essentially, she nagged him to death. Samson gave in, telling her he vowed to God never to cut his hair. So while Samson slept, Delilah gave him a haircut and then called in the soldiers.

Elijah
(ee LIE jah)
HERO
Prophesied from about 865–850 BC
First mention: 1 Kings 17:1
Before getting carried off to heaven in a whirlwind accompanied by chariots of

fire, the prophet Elijah called fire down from heaven to consume a sacrifice. This miracle was part of a battle of the gods, pitting Elijah's God against the gods of Queen Jezebel—winner take all. After calling down the fire—something Jezebel's 850 prophets couldn't do—Elijah ordered the false prophets executed.

Chariots of fire. Lifted by a whirlwind into a chariot of fire, the prophet Elijah is carried into the heavens while his student, Elisha, watches in dismay. Jews later taught that Elijah would return to prepare the way for the Messiah. The New Testament suggests this happened literally and figuratively. Jesus said John the Baptist fulfilled Elijah's role by introducing Jesus to the people. And later, just before Jesus' arrest and crucifixion, Elijah and Moses both met with Jesus on a mountain.

Esau
(E saw)
JERK
1900s BC
First mention: Genesis 25:25
Twin brother of Jacob, Esau is most famous for making a stupid gut decision. Hungry after returning home from hunting, he agreed to trade his inheritance for a bowl of stew. As the oldest twin son of wealthy Isaac, Esau would have gotten a double share of the family estate. It's unclear if he traded away just the extra share or everything. Either way, he paid an idiot's price for a bowl of stew.

Esther
(ESS tur)
HERO
400s BC
First mention: Esther 2:7
Some 2,400 years before Hitler fired up European furnaces for the Holocaust, a Jewish queen living in Iran stopped a holocaust that would have spanned the Persian Empire, from India to Egypt. Esther became queen of the Persians after an empire-wide search for a woman beautiful enough to satisfy the king.

Eve
JERK
Before 4000 BC
First mention: Genesis 3:20
Created as Adam's partner, Eve—the mother of humanity—got both of them kicked out of the Garden of Eden. A snake, identified later in the Bible as Satan, tricked her into eating forbidden fruit. She convinced Adam to eat some, too.

Ezekiel
(e ZEEK e ul)
HERO
Prophesied from 593–571 BC
First Mention: Ezekiel 1:3
Ezekiel was a prophet who lived through the worst catastrophe in ancient Jewish history. In 586 BC, Babylon, wiped the Jewish nation off the map because the people rebelled. Then the Babylonians escorted the survivors into exile, to what is now Iraq. Ezekiel saw it coming. He told the Jews, but assured them that in time God would bring them home to rebuild their nation. The return began in 538 BC.

Gabriel

(GAY bree uhl)

HERO

First mention: Daniel 8:16

"I stand in the very presence of God" (Luke 1:19). That's how the angel Gabriel described himself to young Mary when he told her she would give birth to Jesus, the Son of God. Gabriel also announced the miraculous birth of John the Baptist to an elderly couple. Several hundred years earlier, Gabriel explained to Daniel the meaning of visions the prophet experienced.

God's messenger. The Bible reveals the names of only two angels: Gabriel and Michael. Both archangels—top angels who stood in God's presence—they were sent by God on missions to earth, often to deliver messages. But other ancient Jewish and Christian writings said there were two more archangels: Raphael and Uriel.

God the Father

HERO

First mention: Genesis 1:1

"God is love" (1 John 4:8). He is also Creator of "the heavens and the earth" (Genesis 1:1). Since Adam and Eve introduced sin into the world, somehow contaminating and distorting creation, God has been working his plan to save people from the harm that sin causes. He started with one man, Abraham, and then expanded to a nation, the Jews— providing guidance for holy living. Born of a Jewish virgin, God's Son, Jesus, took it to the next level. Jesus preached repentance and forgiveness for all people, not just the Jews. At the end of human history, God promises to defeat sin and to live among his people forever. "There will be no more death or sorrow or crying or pain. All these things are gone forever" (Revelation 21:4).

Goliath

(go LIE uhth)

JERK

1000s BC

First mention: 1 Samuel 17:4

Champion warrior of the Philistine nation, Goliath stood nearly seven feet tall by some accounts—nearly 10 feet according to other ancient copies of the Bible. Armed with state-of-the-art weaponry, including the new metal of iron, he taunted the Jewish army to send out their champion to meet him in mortal combat. The Jews sent a shepherd boy named David, armed with only a slingshot. A stone to the forehead brought the giant down.

Herod the Great

(HAIR uhd)
JERK
Ruled 4 BC–AD 37
First mention: Matthew 2:1
Appointed king of the Jews by the Roman Empire, Herod ruled with vicious authority. By the time Jesus was born and declared by visiting wise men as the next king of the Jews, Herod had already killed others who threatened his power: including two of his own sons and his wife. Herod tried to kill Jesus, too, ordering the slaughter of every boy in Bethlehem who was age two or younger. Herod died a short time later, eaten up by a gangrene infection that attracted maggots.

Not quite the family man. Herod orders his wife, Miriamne, executed because he mistakenly thinks she's plotting to overthrow him. He orders two of his sons executed, too, fearing they threaten his hold on power. Later, he orders boys age two and under executed in Bethlehem after hearing that a new king of the Jews has been born there. Baby Jesus escapes the slaughter because his family flees to Egypt.

Hezekiah

(hez uh KIH uh)
HERO
Ruled 715–687 BC
First mention: 2 Kings 16:20
Hezekiah was one of the godliest kings Israel ever had. Unfortunately, his son and successor, Manasseh, was probably the worst—even sacrificing one of his sons to an idol. But Hezekiah saw to it that his own generation worshipped God. When Assyrian invaders surrounded Jerusalem, Hezekiah trusted the prophet Isaiah, who told him that God would drive the invaders out. The next day, they were gone—with 185,000 of their soldiers mysteriously killed.

Holy Spirit

HERO
First mention: Genesis 1:2
Third person of the Trinity, the Holy Spirit is the toughest of the three to visualize. Artists generally paint him as a bird. That's in keeping with the story about the Spirit descending on Jesus like a dove at Jesus' baptism. In Old Testament times, the Spirit took a low profile, and he is mentioned most often as giving special power to leaders such as King David. In the New Testament, this power gave boldness to Jesus' disciples after Jesus ascended to heaven. And then the Spirit's power became available to all believers, as prophesied: "I will pour out my Spirit upon all people" (Joel 2:28). This Counselor, as Jesus called him, "is the Holy Spirit, who leads into all truth" (John 14:17).

Isaac

(EYE zack)
HERO
2000s BC
First mention: Genesis 17:19
Son of Abraham, Isaac became one of the founding fathers of Israel. He is best known for almost getting sacrificed by his father—a test of faith in which an angel stopped Abraham at the last moment. Isaac and his wife, Rebekah, had twin sons, Esau and Jacob. It was through Jacob—father of 12 sons—that the Jewish race grew to become the 12 tribes of Israel.

In the nick of time. An angel stops Abraham from sacrificing his son Isaac. Bible experts aren't sure why God asked Abraham to sacrifice the boy, and then stopped him at the last moment. An all-knowing God doesn't need to test people to see if they will obey. Perhaps this was a foreshadowing of Jesus' death some 2,000 years later. What Abraham was willing to do—sacrifice his beloved son—God actually did.

Isaiah
(eye ZAY uh)
HERO
About 740–700 BC
First mention: 2 Kings 19:2
More than any other prophet in the Old Testament, Isaiah pointed to Jesus— seven centuries in the future. So many of Isaiah's prophecies were fulfilled by Jesus that Bible experts call his book the "Fifth Gospel." Isaiah predicted the Messiah would come from David's family, be born to a virgin, and would become known as *Immanuel*, meaning "God with us." But Isaiah's most famous prophecy talks about a Suffering Servant "pierced. . .crushed for our

sins," "whipped, so we could be healed," "led like a lamb to the slaughter," and "buried like a criminal. . .in a rich man's grave" (Isaiah 53).

Jacob
(JAY cub)
HERO
1900s BC
First mention: Genesis 25:26
Abraham's grandson started off as a jerk, cheating his brother Esau out of the family inheritance and even tricking his elderly father, Isaac, out of his last request. Before Isaac died, he wanted to give a blessing to Esau, perhaps putting him in charge of the family. But Jacob tricked blind Isaac into giving him the blessing. Jacob then ran off to his mother's family north of Israel, so Esau wouldn't kill him. There, Jacob raised a family. Wealthy, he returned home and made peace with his brother. Jacob's 12 sons produced families that grew to become the 12 tribes of Israel.

James
HERO
Executed about AD 44
First mention: Matthew 4:21
James was among Jesus' three closest disciples, who went where others weren't invited. When Jesus raised a girl from the dead, Jesus "wouldn't let anyone go with him except Peter, James, and John" (Mark 5:37). "Sons of thunder" is what James and John were nicknamed, perhaps for their bold temperament. Actually, they were sons of Zebedee, a fisherman. During an early period of Christian persecution, Herod Agrippa ordered James "killed with a sword" (Acts 12:2).

Jeremiah

(jair uh MY uh)
HERO
Born 640 BC
First mention: 2 Chronicles 35:25
Jeremiah was only about 13 years old when God called him to start delivering the worst news in Israel's 400-year history: The end is near. What Assyrian invaders had done to the northern Jewish nation of Israel in 722 BC—decimate the cities and exile the survivors—Babylonians would do to the last remaining Jewish nation: Judah in the southland. Jeremiah lived to see the capital city of Jerusalem crumble in 586 BC. Babylonians spared him for urging the Jews to surrender. But a group of Jewish survivors forced him to go with them to Egypt, where he was never heard from again.

Jesus Christ

(GEES us)
HERO
About 6 BC–AD 30
First mention: Matthew 1:1
Jesus is the divine Son of God. Along with God the Father and the Holy Spirit, Jesus is part of the Trinity that is some-how mysteriously made up of three enti-ties, yet a single essence. "The Father and I are one" (John 10:30). Though Jesus shows up in the Bible first as the newborn son of a virgin, Mary, he was alive "in the begin-ning with God. God created everything through him, and nothing was created except through him" (John 1:2–3). Jesus came to earth, taught people about how to live for God, died as an innocent sacrifice for humanity's sin, and then rose from the dead—proving that death isn't the end of life. The Bible says Jesus will come again to take his followers to heaven where they will live with him forever. In the mean-time, Christians who die are with Jesus now and will one day return with him: "When Jesus returns, God will bring back with him the believers who have died" (1 Thessalonians 4:14).

Jezebel

(JEZZ uh bell)
JERK
Ruled with Ahab
875–854 BC
First mention: 1 Kings 16:31
The Jewish queen of mean was no Jew. Her husband was, however—King Ahab. Jezebel had been a Baal-worshipping princess from what is now Lebanon. After she became queen, she persecuted Jewish leaders, slaughtering as many of their prophets as she could—all the while hosting 850 of her own prophets in the palace. She outlived her husband, but was assassinated in a coup while her son was king. Palace servants pushed her from an upper window, and dogs ate her corpse.

Job

(JOHB)
HERO
Perhaps about 2000 BC
First mention: Job 1:1
In what appeared to be a test of wealthy Job's faith, God allowed Job to lose nearly everything important to him. Raiders stole his vast herds. A windstorm destroyed a house, killing all 10 of his children. And oozing boils erupted on his body. Angry with God, Job demanded an explanation. Instead, God asked questions such as, "Have you ever commanded the morn-ing to appear?" (Job 38:12) Job got the message: there's a limit to what humans can understand. So Job vowed to trust God. Job got well and fathered 10 more children.

John
HERO
First century AD
First mention: Matthew 4:21
The brothers James and John were two of Jesus' closest disciples. Fishermen, they were among the first he invited to follow him. As Jesus hung on the cross, he apparently entrusted to John the care of his mother, Mary. Church leaders say that John and Mary moved to Turkey's west coast and that John wrote the Gospel and three letters named after him, as well as the book of Revelation.

John the Baptist
HERO
About 6 BC–AD 28
First mention: Matthew 3:1
Related to Jesus in some way, perhaps as a cousin, John was born into a family of priests who served in the Jerusalem temple. But he became a monklike prophet who lived off the land and preached that people should repent of their sins. He became famous for baptizing those who repented. He also baptized Jesus when Jesus began his ministry. John was beheaded for publicly condemning a ruler, Herod Antipas, who married his own brother's ex-wife. Jewish law called that marriage incest.

Getting a head. Sword and platter ready, Salome waits for the head of John the Baptist. It's her reward for dancing so beautifully for her stepfather, Herod Antipas, ruler of Galilee.

Jonah
(JOE nuh)
JERK
700s BC
First mention: 2 Kings 14:25
God ordered this Jewish prophet to go to the Assyrian capital of Nineveh, in what is now northern Iraq, and tell them the city would be destroyed. Afraid of this vicious empire, Jonah caught a boat headed the opposite direction—and ended up swallowed by a big fish. Spit ashore, he went to Nineveh and delivered the message. Surprisingly, the people repented and God spared them. The story ends with Jonah pouting because the destruction he predicted didn't come true. God simply told Jonah that he had a right to show mercy to the people.

Joseph
(JOE suhf)
HEROES
Joseph #1: About 1800s BC
Joseph #2: Died first century AD
First mention:
Joseph #1: Genesis 30:24
Joseph #2: Matthew 1:16
1. Jacob's son. A jerk who became a hero, Joseph was the pampered favorite son who wore a beautiful robe his father gave him and who bragged about dreams that his family would someday bow to him. Furious, his older brothers sold him to slave-traders. Joseph ended up in Egypt, where his ability to interpret dreams elevated him to the number two position—answering only to the king. During a seven-year drought, Joseph convinced his extended family to move down to Egypt, where there was plenty of water near the Nile River.
2. Mary's husband. Kind and gracious, Joseph didn't make a scene when he found

out his fiancée, Mary, was pregnant. He planned to quietly end the engagement, until a dream convinced him that the child was God's Son. He raised his family in Nazareth, working as a carpenter. He's not mentioned after the story about 12-year-old Jesus talking with scholars at the temple. So it's presumed that he died before Jesus started his ministry.

Joseph's workshop. Pausing from his carpentry work, Joseph reaches to greet young Jesus as the boy kisses Mary, his mother.

Joshua
(JOSH oo wuh)
HERO
1400s BC (some say 1200s BC)
First mention: Exodus 17:9
Leader of Moses' militia during the Exodus, Joshua became Moses' successor when it came time to conquer the promised land—modern-day Israel. Joshua led the invasion, first destroying the border town of Jericho and then overrunning cities throughout the highlands in the south and then in the north. Afterward, he divided the land among the 12 tribes and told each tribe to finish the mopping-up action in its own territory.

Judas Iscariot
(JEW dus is CARE e uht)
JERK
Died about AD 30
First mention: Matthew 10:4
"I chose the twelve of you," Jesus once told his disciples, "but one is a devil" (John 6:70). He was talking about Judas. The Bible says nothing good about Judas. Gospel writers said he served as the group's treasurer—stealing money for himself. He's most famous for using a kiss to point out Jesus to arresting officers. For that betrayal, Judas was paid 30 silver coins. But he returned the money when he learned that Jewish officials decided to crucify Jesus. Perhaps Judas had hoped the arrest would force Jesus to declare himself the Messiah and to launch a revolt against Rome.

Mary
HEROES
First century AD
First mention:
Mary #1: Matthew 1:16
Mary #2: Matthew 27:56
1. Mother of Jesus. The Bible says surprisingly little about the young virgin who became the mother of God's Son, Jesus. When shepherds arrived in Bethlehem to see Mary's newborn, she "kept all these things in her heart" (Luke 2:19). She married Joseph, a carpenter, and raised a family in Nazareth. The Bible says Jesus had some sisters and four brothers. As Jesus hung on the cross, he entrusted Mary to one of his disciples, probably John. Church leaders said Mary and John moved to Turkey's west coast, where she died.
2. Mary Magdalene. Mary was apparently part of a group of women from Galilee, in northern Israel, who contributed money to Jesus' ministry and followed him. Jesus

had exorcized Mary of seven demons. Though she's often identified as the un-named "immoral woman" who washed Jesus' feet with her tears and hair, many scholars say that's unlikely. Mary was the first one to see Jesus after his resurrection.

No prostitute. Some students of the Bible speculate that Mary Magadalene was the unidentified "immoral woman" (Luke 7:37) who wept as she poured expensive oil on Jesus' feet and wiped it with her hair. But most Bible experts say that's unlikely, since that would have been the perfect opportunity to introduce her. Instead, Luke introduced Mary in the very next story as a woman whom Jesus healed of demon possession, and who financially supported his ministry in gratitude.

Matthew
(MATH you)
HERO
First century AD
First mention: Matthew 9:9
"Why does your teacher eat with such scum?" (Matthew 9:11). That's what Jew-ish leaders asked some of Jesus' disciples. The "scum" included Matthew, host of a meal for his fellow tax collector friends—in honor of Jesus. Matthew worked a toll booth near Capernaum, until Jesus

invited him to join his band of disciples. Church leaders say Matthew wrote the Gospel eventually named after him.

Moses
(MOW zuhs)
HERO
About 1520–1400 BC (some say 1200s BC)
First mention: Exodus 2:10
Probably the most famous man in Jewish history, Moses managed to win the freedom of his fellow Israelites. For many generations the Egyptians had used Israelites as a race of slave labor, to build cities. Moses led these thousands of refugees on an exodus back to their homeland, in what is now Israel. He also delivered the 10 Commandments, along with hundreds of other religious, civil, and criminal laws that helped organize the people into a nation.

Noah
(NO uh)
HERO
Before 2500 BC
First mention: Genesis 5:29
Sin was so widespread that God decided to wash the earth clean and start over with Noah, "the only blameless person living on earth at the time" (Genesis 6:9). Noah and his family built a huge houseboat longer than a football field. It looked like a floating warehouse. They brought pairs of animals on board, and everyone stayed in the boat for a year—until the floodwater subsided.

Paul
HERO
About AD 5–64
First mention: Acts 13:8 (Acts 7:58 for Saul)
A formerly intolerant Jewish scholar who converted to Christianity, Paul seemed more responsible for the spread

of Christian teachings than anyone else but Jesus—disciples included. He wrote nearly half the books in the New Testament. And he traveled some 10,000 miles throughout the Roman Empire as a missionary, starting scores of churches. Church leaders from a later generation said he was beheaded in Rome, as punishment for teaching a banned religion.

Peter
HERO
Died about AD 64

First mention: Matthew 4:18

One of Jesus' three closest disciples—with James and John—Peter became leader of the disciples, and their spokesman. He is named first in every Bible list of the disciples. He walked on water with Jesus—at least for a moment—and he performed many miracles. But he's best known for protecting himself on the night of Jesus' arrest by denying he knew Jesus—and denying it three times. After Jesus rose from the dead, he asked his disciples to spread the news about his teachings, and then he ascended to heaven. Peter led the mission, preaching the first sermon which led some 3,000 Jews to convert. Church leaders said Peter was crucified upside down in Rome after more than 30 years of ministry.

Pilate
(PIE luht)
JERK
Governed about AD 26–37

First mention: Matthew 27:2

Roman governor of Judea in what is now southern Israel, Pilate had to give his approval before Jews could execute anyone. Reluctantly, he ordered Jesus crucified though he said Jesus didn't deserve it. He gave in probably because the Jews said, "If you release this man, you are no 'friend of Caesar.' Anyone who declares himself a king is a rebel against Caesar" (John 19:12). Several years later, in fact, the Jews got Pilate removed from office for ordering an attack on unarmed citizens.

Ruth
HERO
1100s BC

First mention: Ruth 1:4

The mother of Israel's most revered dynasty of kings—including David and Solomon—was no Jew. Ruth came from what is now Jordan. It was there she married a Jew who died young. Ruth and her mother-in-law, Naomi, both became destitute widows. So they moved back to Naomi's hometown of Bethlehem, hoping someone in Naomi's family would take them in. Ruth married a rich farmer, Boaz, and had a son: Obed, grandfather of David.

Samson
(SAM son)
JERK
About 1100–1050 BC

First mention: Judges 13:24

Strongest man in the Bible, Samson was also one of the dumbest. He was one of the most selfish, too, driven by lust and revenge. He killed a lion with his bare hands, and he wiped out a Philistine army with nothing but a donkey's jawbone. But he was putty in the hands of beautiful women. His entire story spins around his relationships with three unsavory women and the trouble they got him into. He foolishly told his fatal attraction, Delilah, that his strength depended on keeping a vow never to cut his hair. So, promised a Philistine reward, Delilah cut his hair while he was napping. Philistines captured and blinded Samson. But when his hair grew back he pushed down two support pillars in a temple, killing himself and a crowd of Philistines.

Samuel
(SAM you uhl)
HERO
About 1100–1010 BC
First mention: 1 Samuel 1:20
Samuel's mother was infertile. In a desperate prayer she promised that if God gave her a son, she would give the boy back as a worker in the worship center. Samuel was born, and after he was old enough to eat solid food, his mother took him to Israel's worship center. Priest Eli raised the boy as a priest. Samuel also became a respected prophet as well as a judge, traveling to key cities and settling disputes. Samuel anointed Saul as Israel's first king. Later, he anointed young David, promising that David would become Israel's future king.

Sarah
(SAIR uh)
HERO
2100s BC
First mention: Genesis 17:15 (Genesis 11:29 for Sarai)
Abraham's wife, Sarai, became mother of the Jewish nation by delivering her one and only child—Isaac—when she was 91 years old. To seal God's promise that Sarai would have a son, God changed her name to *Sarah*—just as he had changed her husband's name from Abram when making a similar promise to him. Sarah died at age 127, and she was buried in what became a family tomb at Hebron.

Satan
(SAY ton)
JERK
First mention: 1 Chronicles 21:1
His name means "Enemy" in Hebrew. *Devil* comes from the Greek translation: *diabolos*. He first shows up as a snake, tempting Eve to eat forbidden fruit. He also tried tempting Jesus at the beginning of Jesus' ministry, but without success. Revelation portrays him as a fallen angel—"thrown down to the earth with all his angels" (Revelation 12:9). On earth, he fights spiritual battles against God's people. A Christian defense: "Resist the devil, and he will flee from you" (James 4:7). Someday in the future, God will throw Satan and his kindred spirits "into the fiery lake. . . . [where] they will be tormented day and night forever" (Revelation 20:10).

Fallen angel. After losing a rebel war in heaven, Satan gets the celestial boot. God orders him "thrown down to the earth with all his angels" (Revelation 12:9).

Saul
JERK
About 1065–1010 BC
First mention: 1 Samuel 9:2
Israel's first king, Saul didn't want the job. He preferred herding donkeys for his father. But after he accepted the job, he grew jealous of the rising popularity of a shepherd boy, David, who killed

Goliath in a battle of champions—Israelite against Philistine. Eventually Saul decided to kill David and spent much of his time and resources hunting him, without success. Saul died in a battle against the Philistines, along with most of his sons. Fatally wounded, Saul fell on his sword to finish himself off so he couldn't be tortured.

Solomon
(SAH luh muhn)
HERO
Ruled about 970–930 BC
First mention: 2 Samuel 5:14
Wisest ruler who ever lived or ever would live—that's how the Bible describes him. Solomon gained fame by settling a court case between two women who each claimed a newborn son. Solomon offered to sword-split the baby between the two of them, and then he concluded that the one woman opposed to the idea was the rightful mother. Solomon ruled Israel during its most prosperous time in history. It was Solomon who built Israel's first temple, in Jerusalem. Married to a thousand wives, Solomon began worshipping some of their idols. Sadly, that's how his story ends.

Stephen
(STEVE un)
HERO
First century AD
First mention: Acts 6:5
When the disciples started organizing the church, after Jesus' ascension, they assigned Stephen and several other respected men to handle the food distribution program to the poor. But Stephen became a gifted speaker, debating the merits of the Christian faith with Jewish scholars. In one blistering defense, before the Jewish council, he so upset the opposition that they stoned him to death—turning him into the first known Christian martyr.

The first Christian martyr. In a bitter debate with Jerusalem Jews, Stephen, a Jewish convert to Christianity, accuses his fellow Jews of having a long and violent history of killing messengers sent from God. True to form, they kill *him*. Stoned to death, Stephen becomes the first in a long line of Christians murdered because of their religious beliefs. Most of Jesus' dozen disciples were martyred, as well.

Timothy
(TIM uh thee)
HERO
Started working with Paul about AD 50
First mention: Acts 16:1
When Paul sat in a Roman prison, waiting to be executed, he wrote his last known letter to Timothy—a colleague he loved like a son. That letter is 2 Timothy. Paul and Timothy traveled thousands of miles together, starting churches throughout Turkey and Greece. Paul then assigned Timothy to pastor the church at Ephesus—third largest city in the empire and located on Turkey's west coast. As Paul faced death, he asked Timothy to come and be with him in those last moments.

SEARCH ENGINE INDEX

ART RESOURCES

KEY TO ABBREVIATIONS:

AA: Art Archive
AKG: AKG-Images
ALB: Albatross
AN: Anonymous
AR: Art Resource, NY
BAL: Bridgeman Art Library
BM: Bradley M. Miller
GS: Greg Schneider
HIP: Heritage Image Partnership
IS: i-Stockphoto
LC: Library of Congress
DR: David Roberts
NG: National Geographic
RC/GSI/SM: Rani Calvo/Geological Survey of Israel/rendered by Stephen M. Miller
RF: Royalty Free
SM: Stephen M. Miller
TF: Topfoto
TYN: Tyndale House Publishers
UNLM: US National Library of Medicine
WM: Wikimedia
WW: William Whitaker
ZR: Zev Radovan

10. (globe) NASA; (Noah's ark) Edward Hicks/MHM-com/WM; (Moses) Gustave Dore/AKG; (David) Scala/AR; (pyramids) David Roberts/LC; (pharaoh) Conscious/WM; (Troy horse) AKG; (discus thrower) Matthias Kabel/WM; (Buddha) SM; (Assyrian Archer) AN; 11. (birth of Jesus) BM; (Cleopatra) BM; (Jesus on cross) Diego Velázquez/Luestling/WM; (Paul crucified) Michelangelo Merisi da Caravaggio/Panairjdde/WM; (Roman soldier) AN; (Mount Vesuvius) Reunion des Musees Nationaux/AR; 12. Corbis RF; 13. Corbis RF; 14. Corbis RF; 16. Corbis RF; 18. Corbis RF; 20. (Road) Corbis RF; (baby) Skip O'Donnell/IS; 21. Erich Lessing/AR; 25. Wassilij Dimitriewitsch Polenow/Alex Bakharev/WM; 26. Pietro Cavallini/The Yorck Project/WM; 28. Quadell/WM; 29. Gemma Longman/WM; 30. NASA; 33. GS; 35. Wally McNamee/Corbis; 37. James L. Stanfield/NG; 38. Linda Miller; 41. Asbestos/WM; 45. Janet Jarman/Corbis; 47. Andrew Lichtenstein/Corbis; 49. Petronas/WM; 50. Tate, London/AR; 53. Rainer Zenz/WM; 56. Abimelec Olan/IS; 59. Gary Salter/Zefa/Corbis; 61. NASA/ESA/ESO/Wolfram Freudling et al. (STECF); 62. William-Adolphe Bouguereau/Thebrid/WM; 65. Yorck Project/WM; 66. Roger Ressmeer/Corbis; 71. Alinari/AR; 74. Tate, London/AR; 75. Jelani Memory/IS; 76. HIP/AR; 78. Cristian Ardelean/IS; 80. Grace/Zefa/Corbis; 83. Yanik Chauvin/IS; 85. Heide Benser/Zefa/Corbis; 87. BM; 90. Carl Pendle/Getty; 96. Betsy Dupuis/IS; 99. eva serrabassa/IS; 102. Toby Melville/Pool/POOL/epa/Corbis; 105. Jerry McCrea/Star Ledger/Corbis; 106. Corbis RF; 107. (map art Eve) Lucien Levy-Dhurmer/WM; (map art Noah's ark) Edward Hicks/MHM-com/WM; (map)RC/GSI/SM; (star) NASA/JPL-Caltech/R. Hurt (SSC); 108. TYN; 109. (map art of travelers) David Roberts/LC; NASA/WorldWind/rendered by SM; 110. Roberts, David/Stapleton Collection, UK/BAL; 111. Scala/AR; 112–113. HIP/AR; 115. Maurycy Gottlieb/Grendelkhan/WM; 116. Tom Lovell/NG; 117.

RC/GSI/SM; 119. TYN; 121. John Van Hasselt/Corbis SYGMA; 122. TYN; 125. WW; 126. Tom Lovell/NG; 128. (archer) AN; NASA/WorldWind/rendered by SM; (statue) BM; 129. TYN; 130. Vassil/WM; 131. ZR; 133. (Persian) BM; (cylinder of Cyrus) HIP/AR; 134. G. Eric and Edith Matson Photograph Collection/LC; 135. (map art of travelers) David Roberts/LC; NASA/LC rendered by SM; 137. Leen Ritmeyer; 138. Peter V. Bianchi/NG; 139. (map) Tom Patterson, US National Park Service/rendered by SM; (archer) BM; (Daniel, lions), Peter Paul Rubens/WM; (queen) William Adolph Bouguereau/Thebrid/WM; 140. NASA; 141. Albrecht Dürer/The Yorck Project/WM; 142. GS; 143. William-Adolphe Bouguereau/WM; 144. WW; 145. Bill Aron; 146. Charles Sprague Pearce/William Avery/WM; 147. The Art Archive/Musée du Louvre Paris/Alfredo Dagli Orti; 148. William-Adolphe Bouguereau/Thebrid/WM; 149. Frederick Leighton/Irish Pearl/WM; 151. (Jesus) William-Adolphe Bouguereau/Thebrid/WM; (map) RC/GSI/SM; 153. Art Media/HIP/The Image Works; 154. Herbert Gustave Schmalz/Private Collection, Photo © Christie's Images/BAL; 155. SM; 157. USNLM/Artist, Jan Wandelaar/Anatomist, Bernhard Siegfried Albinus; 159. AN; 161. Benjamin Constant/Grendelkhan/WM; 162. G. Eric and Edith Matson Photograph Collection/LC; 163. Juan Medina/Reuters/Corbis; 165. Reuters/Corbis; 166. GS; 167. Jodi Cobb/NG; 168. Rama/WM; 169. NASA/rendered by SM; (whale) SM; (boat) Zev Radovan; 171. G. Eric and Edith Matson Photograph Collection/LC; 172. Frederick Arthur Bridgman/AR; 175. Bildarchiv Preussischer Kulturbesitz/AR; 177. Topham/The Image Works; 179. ALB; 181. Corbis RF; 183. Rungroj Yongrit/epa/Corbis; 185. Thomas Nebbia/NG; 187. Francisco de Zurbaran/Erik Möller/WM; 189. BM; 191. Erich Lessing/AR; 193. Tom Patterson, US National Park Service/rendered by SM; (Paul) Diego Velazquez/SM; 195. Araldo de Luca/Corbis; 197. (top map) Christoph Hormann/rendered by SM; (man) LC; (bottom map) NASA/WorldWind; 199. TYN; 201. Lawrence Alma-Tadema/Shawnlipowski/WM; 203. Peter Connolly/AKG; 205. AN; 207. (top) The International Astronomical Union/Martin Kommesser; (bottom) NASA/JPL-Caltech/T.Pyle (SSC); 209. BM; 210. WM; 213. Erik Möller/WM; 215. Cameraphoto Arte, Venice/AR; 216–217. Harrieta171/WM; 218. Bettmann/Corbis Bettmann/Corbis; 221. Jean-Léon Gérôme/Matthias Sebulke/WM; 223. Lawrence Alma Tadema/WM; 225. Frederic Leighton/Grendelkhan/WM; 227. Michelangelo Merisi da Caravaggio/Panairjdde/WM; 229. Sandro Vannini/Corbis; 230. Scala/AR; 232–234. Wassilij Dimitriewitsch Polenow/Alex Bakharev/WM; 235. The Art Archive/Corbis; 237. AN; 238. Tom Lovell/NG; 239. Peter Paul Rubens/David Monniaux/WM; 240. Peter Paul Rubens/Burstein Collection/Corbis; 241. Franz von Stuck/The Yorck Project/WM; 242. Massimo Listri/Corbis; 243. Scala/AR; 245. Michelangelo Merisi da Caravaggio/Erik Möller/WM; 246. Sir John Everett Millais/Erik Möller/WM; 247. Anthony Frederick Augustus Sandys/TAnthony/WM; 249. Franz von Stuck/AKG; 250. Erich Lessing/AR.